WILLIAM DWIGHT WHITNEY
LINGUISTIC SERIES

EDITED BY
FRANKLIN EDGERTON   EDWARD SAPIR
EDUARD PROKOSCH   EDGAR H. STURTEVANT
of the Department of Linguistics in Yale University

A HITTITE GLOSSARY

BY
EDGAR H. STURTEVANT

Second Edition

A HITTITE GLOSSARY

Words of Known or Conjectured Meaning with Sumerian
and Akkadian Words Occurring in Hittite Texts

BY

EDGAR H. STURTEVANT

Professor of Linguistics in Yale University

SECOND EDITION

*WILLIAM DWIGHT WHITNEY
LINGUISTIC SERIES*

WIPF & STOCK · Eugene, Oregon

Wipf and Stock Publishers
199 W 8th Ave, Suite 3
Eugene, OR 97401

A Hittite Glossary
Words of Known or Conjectured Meaning with Sumerian and
Akkadian Words Occurring in Hittite Texts
By Sturtevant, Edward H.
ISBN 13: 978-1-60608-291-1
Publication date 11/25/2008
Previously published by University of Pennsylvania, 1936

PREFACE

The first edition of my Hittite Glossary (Baltimore, 1931) is already antiquated. Many Hittite words have been interpreted or re-interpreted during these five years and our understanding of morphology and etymology has been improved at many points. Furthermore a number of errors and omissions have been discovered, especially in the Akkadian and Sumerian material. While the time has not yet arrived for a thoroughgoing lexicographical treatment of the language, one may hope that a new edition of the Glossary will be of service for considerably more than five years.

Consequently the treatment has been amplified to some extent. More forms are cited to illustrate orthography and morphology. More references are given, particularly to the pioneer works on Hittite grammar and the interpretation of the texts. There are many more cross references.

The book is still primarily an index to the literature about Hittite words. The lexicographical conclusions drawn from the literature are stated with the utmost brevity. Inevitably these conclusions are my own; it must not be assumed that the authors referred to have stated their results precisely as I have. In fact, there is often more or less disagreement between two or more authors cited under a single word. In case of considerable disagreement between my opinion and that of an author cited, I have inserted 'Cf.' before the citation.

I am under obligations to all the authors cited in the book. In addition the manuscript has been read and criticized by Dr. George Bechtel and Dr. Arnold Walther of the University of Chicago, and Prof. Albrecht Goetze of Yale University. The last named scholar has discussed many problems with me and has generously put at my disposal his wide knowledge of the Hittite and Akkadian texts. Suggestions that I owe to these men, but which do not appear in their published works, are indicated by initials in parentheses. Professor E. Adelaide Hahn of Hunter College has read part of the manuscript and all of the proof.

TABLE OF CONTENTS

	PAGE
Abbreviations	9
Introduction	15
Word List	18
Numerals	189
Additions and Corrections	192

ABBREVIATIONS

1. BOOKS AND PERIODICALS

All references are to pages or columns unless otherwise indicated, except that cuneiform texts are referred to by number.

AJP = The American Journal of Philology, founded by B. L. Gildersleeve. Baltimore.
AJSL = The American Journal of Semitic Languages and Literatures. Chicago.
Altorient. Stud. = Altorientalistische Studien Bruno Meissner zum Sechzigsten Geburtstag Gewidmet von Freunden, Kollegen, und Schülern. Erster Band. Leipzig. 1928.
AO = Der Alte Orient, Gemeinverständliche Darstellungen, herausgegeben von der Vorderasiatisch-Aegyptischen Gesellschaft. Leipzig.
AOF = Archiv für Orientforschung, internationale Zeitschrift für die Wissenschaft vom Vorderen Orient. Berlin. (The first two volumes are entitled: Archiv für Keilschriftforschung.)
AOr. = Archiv Orientální, Journal of the Czechoslovak Oriental Institute. Prague.
Berl. Mus. Ber. = Berliner Museen, Berichte aus den Preussischen Kunstsammlungen.
Boissier, Mantique = Alfred Boissier, Mantique Babylonienne et Mantique Hittite. Paris. 1935.
BoSt. = Boghazköi-Studien, herausgegeben von Otto Weber. 10 parts. Leipzig. 1917–24.
BoTU = Die Boghazköi-Texte in Umschrift, von Emil Forrer. 2 vols. = 41 and 42 Wissenschaftliche Veröffentlichung der Deutschen Orient-Gesellschaft. Leipzig. 1922–6.
BSL = Bulletin de la Société de Linguistique de Paris. Paris.
Chrest. = Edgar H. Sturtevant and George Bechtel, A Hittite Chrestomathy. Philadelphia. 1935.
Congr. 1 = Actes du Premier Congrès International de Linguistes. The Hague. 1928.
Congr. 2 = Actes du Second Congrès International de Linguistes. Geneva. 1931.

Couvreur, Hett. h = Walter Couvreur, De Hettitische ḫ = Philologische Studiën, Teksten- en Verhandelingenreeks, Nummer 12. Leuven. 1935.
Deimel = P. Anton Deimel, Šumerisches Lexikon. Rome. 1928–
Delaporte, Voc. = Louis Delaporte, Vocabulaire = Textes Hittites en Écriture Cunéiforme et Vocabulaire, second part. Paris. 1933.
Encyc. Brit. = The Encyclopaedia Britannica, 14th Ed. Vol. 11. London and New York. 1929.
Forrer, Forsch. = Emil Forrer, Forschungen. Berlin. 1926–.
Friedrich, Vert. = Johannes Friedrich, Staatsverträge des Ḫatti-Reiches in Hethitischer Sprache. 2 parts = Hethitische Texte in Umschrift mit Uebersetzung und Erläuterungen. Heft II, IV. = MVAG 31.1, 34.1. Leipzig. 1926–30.
Glotta = Glotta, Zeitschrift für griechische und lateinische Sprache. Göttingen.
Götze, AM = Albrecht Götze, Die Annalen des Muršiliš = Hethitische Texte in Umschrift. Heft VI = MVAG 38. Leipzig. 1933.
Götze, Hatt. = A. Götze, Ḫattušiliš, der Bericht über seine Thronbesteigung nebst den Paralleltexten = Hethitische Texte in Umschrift. Heft I = MVAG 29.3. Leipzig. 1925.
Götze, KlH = A. Götze, Kleinasien zur Hethiterzeit, eine geographische Untersuchung = Orient und Antike 1. Heidelberg. 1924.
Götze, Kulturg. = Kulturgeschichte des alten Orients 3.1. A. Götze, Kleinasien = W. Otto, Handbuch der Altertumswissenschaft. Dritte Abteilung. Erster Teil. Dritter Band. Dritter Abschnitt. Erste Lieferung. Munich. 1933.
Götze, Madd. = A. Götze, Madduwattaš = Hethitische Texte in Umschrift. Heft III. = MVAG 32.1. Leipzig. 1928.
Götze, NBr. = A. Götze, Neue Bruchstücke zum Grossen Texte des Ḫattušiliš und den Paralleltexten = Hethitische Texte in Umschrift. Heft V = MVAG 34.5. Leipzig. 1930.
Götze-Pedersen, MS = Albrecht Götze and Holger Pedersen, Muršilis Sprachlähmung, ein hethitischer Text mit philologischen und linguistischen Erörterungen = Det Kgl. Danske Videnskabernes Selskab, Historisk-filologiske Meddelelser 21.2. Copenhagen. 1934.
HG = Edgar H. Sturtevant. A Comparative Grammar of the Hittite Language. Philadelphia. 1933.
Hrozný, CH = Frédéric Hrozný, Code Hittite Provenant de l'Asie Mineure. Première Partie = Hethitica, collection de travaux

relatifs à la philologie, l'histoire, et l'archéologie hittites 1.1. Paris. 1922.
Hrozný, IHH = Bedřich Hrozný, Les Inscriptions Hittites Hiéroglyphiques 1. = Studies, Texts, and Translations, Issued by the Czechoslovak Oriental Institute, Vol. 1. Prague. 1933.
Hrozný, SH = Friedrich Hrozný, Die Sprache der Hethiter, ihr Bau und ihre Zugehörigkeit zum indogermanischen Sprachstamm, ein Entzifferungsversuch = BoSt. 1, 2. Leipzig. 1917.
HT = Hittite Texts in the Cuneiform Character from Tablets in the British Museum. London. 1920.
IF = Indogermanische Forschungen. Berlin and Leipzig.
JA = Journal Asiatique, recueil trimestriel de mémoires et de notices relatifs aux études orientales, publié par la Société Asiatique. Paris.
JAOS = Journal of the American Oriental Society. New Haven.
JRAS = Journal of the Royal Asiatic Society of Great Britain and Ireland. London.
JSFO = Journal de la Société Finno-Ougrienne = Suomalais-Ugrilaisen Seuran Aikakauskirja. Helsingfors.
JSOR = Journal of the Society of Oriental Research. 16 vols. Chicago. 1917–32.
KBo. = Keilschrifttexte aus Boghazköi. 6 parts = 30, 36. Wissenschaftliche Veröffentlichung der Deutschen Orient-Gesellschaft. Leipzig. 1921–3.
KlF = Kleinasiatische Forschungen. Weimar.
Korošec, Vert. = Viktor Korošec, Hethitische Staatsverträge = Leipziger Rechtswissenschaftliche Studien 60. Leipzig. 1931.
KUB = Staatliche Museen zu Berlin, Vorderasiatische Abteilung, Keilschrift-Urkunden aus Boghazköi. Berlin. (28 Hefte have been issued. 1921–35.)
Kurylowicz, EI = Jerzy Kuryłowicz, Études Indoeuropéennes 1 = Polska Akademja Umiejętnosci Prace Komisji Językowej, No. 21. Cracow. 1935.
Lang. = Language, Journal of the Linguistic Society of America. Baltimore.
Lang. Mon. = Language Monographs, published by the Linguistic Society of America. Philadelphia and Baltimore.
Marstrander, Car. = Carl J. S. Marstrander, Caractère Indo-Européen de la Langue Hittite = Videnskapsselskapets Skrifter, Hist.-Filos. Klasse, 1918.2. Christiania. 1919.

MDOG = Mitteilungen der Deutschen Orient-Gesellschaft. Leipzig.
Meissner, Beitr. = Bruno Meissner, Beiträge zum Assyrischen Wörterbuch 1 and 2 = Assyriological Studies, vols. 1 and 4, of the Oriental Institute of the University of Chicago. Chicago. 1931–2.
MSL = Mémoires de la Société de Linguistique de Paris. Paris.
MVAG = Mitteilungen der Vorderasiatisch-Aegyptischen Gesellschaft. Leipzig.
OLZ = Orientalistische Literaturzeitung, Monatsschrift für die Wissenschaft vom ganzen Orient und seinen Beziehungen zu den angrenzenden Kulturkreisen. Leipzig.
Pedersen, Group. = Holger Pedersen, Le Groupement des Dialectes Indo-Européens = Det Kgl. Danske Videnskabernes Selskab, Historisk-filologiske Meddelelser 11.2. Copenhagen. 1925.
RA = Revue d'Assyriologie et d'Archéologie Orientale. Paris.
Real. Ass. = Erich Ebeling and Bruno Meissner, Reallexikon der Assyriologie. Berlin and Leipzig. 1928–.
Real. Vorg. = Max Ebert, Reallexikon der Vorgeschichte. 15 vols. Berlin. 1924–32.
REAn. = Revue des Études Anciennes = Annales de la Faculté des Lettres de Bordeaux et des Universités du Midi, quatrième série. Bordeaux.
RHA = Revue Hittite et Asianique, organe de la Société des Études Hittites et Asianiques. Paris.
RO = Rocznik Orjentalistyczny. Lwów.
SBPA = Sitzungsberichte der Preussischen Akademie der Wissenschaften, phil.-hist. Klasse. Berlin.
Sommer, AF = Ferdinand Sommer, Aḫḫijavā-Frage und Sprachwissenschaft = Abhandlungen der Bayerischen Akademie der Wissenschaften, phil.-hist. Abteilung, NF 9. Munich. 1934.
Sommer, AU = F. Sommer, Die Aḫḫijavā-Urkunden = Abhandlungen der Bayerischen Akademie der Wissenschaften, phil.-hist. Abteilung, NF 6. Munich. 1932.
Stud. Orient. = Studia Orientalia Edidit Societas Orientalis Fennica. Helsingfors.
Symb. Gramm. = Symbolae Grammaticae in Honorem Ioannis Rozwadowski. Cracow. 1927.
TAPA = Transactions of the American Philological Association. Middletown, Conn.
Tenner, HAT = Ernst Tenner, Ein Hethitischer Annalentext des Königs Muršiliš II. Leipzig. 1926.

VBoT = Albrecht Götze, Verstreute Boghazköi-Texte. Marburg a.d. Lahn. 1930.
Walther, CH = Arnold Walther, The Hittite Code = John M. Powis Smith, The Origin and History of Hebrew Law, Appendix IV. Chicago. 1931.
Weidner, Stud. = Ernst Weidner, Studien zur Hethitischen Sprachwissenschaft 1 = Leipziger Semitistische Studien 7.1,2. Leipzig. 1917.
Witzel, HKU = P. Maurus Witzel, Hethitische Keilschrift-Urkunden in Transcription und Uebersetzung mit Kommentar 1 = Keilinschriftliche Studien 4. Fulda. 1924.
WZKM = Wiener Zeitschrift für die Kunde des Morgenlandes. Vienna.
ZA = Zeitschrift für Assyriologie und Verwandte Gebiete. Berlin and Leipzig.
ZDMG = Zeitschrift der Deutschen Morgenländischen Gesellschaft. Leipzig.

2. OTHER ABBREVIATIONS

abl. = ablative
acc. = accusative
act. = active
adj. = adjective
adv. = adverb
Bo. = Boghazköitexte (unpublished)
cf. = compare (literature thus referred to is partially or wholly inconsistent with the conclusions registered here; it is often of first rate importance. Cross references so introduced are less important than others)
dat. = dative
determ. = determinative
e.g. = for example
f. = following page
fem. = feminine
fn. = footnote
(G) marks matter that I owe to Goetze.
gen. = genitive
imper. = imperative
ind. = indicative
infin. = infinitive
inst. = instrumental

masc. = masculine
midd. = medio-passive
neut. = neuter
NF = Neue Folge
No. = Number
nom. = nominative
part. = participle
pl. = plural
prec. = preceding
pres. = present
pret. = preterit
q. v. = quod vide
sg. = singular
s. v. = sub voce
VAT = Vorderasiatische Abteilung Tontafel (unpublished)
verb. n. = verbal noun
w. = with
(W) marks matter that I owe to Walther.
[ ] Square brackets enclose parts of words not preserved on a tablet, but supplied by conjecture. They also enclose phonetic transcriptions.
< > Angular brackets enclose material erroneously omitted by a scribe.
( ) Parentheses enclose parts of words that are sometimes written and sometimes omitted. They also enclose forms cited immediately after the lemma to illustrate orthography and morphology. If the lemma is an inflectional form other than the nominative singular, it is followed by a label in parentheses.
+ In a Sumerian lemma a plus sign indicates the addition of the second sign to the first.
× In a Sumerian lemma a multiplication sign indicates the insertion of the second sign within the first.
⸢ The scribes sometimes prefix one or two diagonal wedges to foreign (chiefly Luwian) words.
· In phonetic transcription a high point indicates length of the preceding sound.

INTRODUCTION

This book treats Hittite words whose meaning is known or for which a probable or possible meaning has been or can here be suggested. Included are loan words which appear to function normally in a Hittite sentence. Akkadian and Sumerian words used ideographically are also included, but words occurring in Akkadian texts from Boghazköi and the Akkadian and Sumerian parts of Hittite vocabularies are omitted unless they occur also in a Hittite context.

The alphabetic arrangement is that which has become usual in Hittite word-lists. The mutes b and p are treated as a single phoneme in the alphabetic position of p. Similarly d is to be found in the position of t, while g and q are grouped with k. Words written sometimes with e and sometimes with i are listed with the former orthography. In Hittite words transcribed without hyphens I omit the diacritic from $ḫ$ and $š$, although they are employed in syllabic transcription (in the few places where this method is used) and always in Akkadian and Sumerian words. The double writing of consonants is recorded; in lemmata a variation between single and double consonant is indicated by parenthesis, e.g. $ak(k)$-; but if a word shows the double writing constantly between vowels, the necessary single writing in a written consonant group is not indicated, e.g. $assnu$- on account of $assanuzzi$, in spite of $asnuzi$. The pleonastic writing of a vowel sign beside an open syllabic sign is indicated by the macron, e.g. $ārri$ for a-ar-ri, $apās$ for a-pa-a-$aš$; similarly $āra$ stands for a-a-ra. In case the pleonastic vowel sign is sometimes employed and sometimes not in a given word I write $ărs$-, etc.

The reader is cautioned not to assume that the macron indicates vowel length; it is here employed merely as a record of the pleonastic writing of a vowel. In the cross references the macron and the indication of variation between single and double consonant are omitted.

Before a different vowel u, whether written by a vowel sign or by a syllabic sign, is transcribed w (e.g. $kwis$ for ku-$iš$), unless there is some reason for assuming syllabic value. In case of variation between w, uw, and uww (e.g. $ḫu$-i, $ḫu$-wi-, $ḫu$-u-i-, $ḫu$-u-wi-), I prefer the simplest recorded orthography, unless there is reason for thinking that another one represents the actual pronunciation.

The lemmata summarize the orthography of an entire paradigm as far as possible, while the variation between separate forms is indicated as far as seems useful in parentheses; thus the lemma *ak(k)-* is supported by citation in parentheses of the forms *aki, akkanzi, akkis, aggas,* and *akta.* The great variety of Hittite orthography often requires a choice in setting up the lemmata, and in such cases the spelling is chosen which I believe to correspond most closely with the pronunciation. No more phonetic interpretation is introduced into the lemmata, however, than is required by the varying orthography within a closely related group of words. The forms cited in parentheses follow the orthography as closely as possible (the letter *q* is employed in Hittite words only within parentheses). In a few words I have employed syllabic transcription to avoid ambiguity. On the other hand, phonetic transcriptions (in Roman type enclosed within square brackets) indicate the probable pronunciation, if the orthography is misleading. Even here, however, the phonetic interpretation is only tentative and approximate; e.g. [k·] stands for written *kk,* although it is not certain whether the stop was long or fortis (see HG 74 and fn. 78).

Nouns are entered in the nominative singular and adjectives in the nominative singular masculine if this is citable or if it can be reconstructed with certainty. Reconstructed forms are marked with an asterisk. If the nominative singular is unknown, the stem, or occasionally an oblique case form, is employed as lemma. If a noun form is cited without label it is nominative singular; an adjective form without label is nominative singular masculine. If there is no designation of number a form is singular, and masculine gender of an adjective form is to be assumed unless it is called neuter.

Verbs are listed in the stem form, except that a rare verb whose stem cannot be determined is necessarily listed in one of the forms actually citable. If a form is cited without indication of person or number, it is third singular; if there is no indication of tense, it is present; and when the mood is not named, it is indicative. Hence a form cited without any label is third singular present indicative.

Verb stems are indicated with some care, and if there is variation between two or more conjugation classes or if a conjugation is built up by suppletion, the several stems are separately listed, except that an isolated heteroclitic form is sometimes included under the main stem.

Thematic verb stems are designated in three different ways, as follows, *hatra(e)-, akkiske/a-, aniya/e-.* A different notation is required by the three groups of verbs: denominatives like *hatra(e)-* show a plus in the *e-* forms; verbs with a consonant except *y* before the thematic vowel show written *e* or *i* more often than *a*; verbs with *y* before the thematic vowel show written *a* more often than *e* or *i*.

I have indicated my doubts as to the correctness of a definition by interrogation points as follows: one interrogation point indicates some doubt, although I believe the definition to be correct; two points indicate that the definition is to be regarded as a mere suggestion; three points indicate that I consider the definition improbable although possible.

The etymological connection of Hittite words with one another is frequently indicated by cross references. Etymological connections outside of Hittite are not indicated, but references to etymological discussions are given.

Sumerian and Akkadian words used as ideograms in Hittite texts are included. Sumerian words are written in straight capitals, and I have tried to list each of them in all transcriptions that a beginner is likely to meet or to hit upon in his own attempts at transliteration. The definition is usually given only once, under the transcription that is preferred, while the other transcriptions are followed only by cross references. Sumerian words are translated into Akkadian if the Akkadian word occurs in Hittite texts, or if it is needed to explain a phonetic complement, and into Hittite if the Hittite equivalent is known. Finally comes the English translation. For convenience the alphabetic arrangement is the same as that employed for Hittite. My transcriptions follow Deimel's Šumerisches Lexikon except in a few details that will cause no inconvenience.

Akkadian words are written in slanting capitals. Verbs are listed in the forms actually used in the texts, not in the infinitive. Nouns are listed in the nominative singular. The construct state is listed separately with a cross reference, if this seems necessary. Here again the alphabetic arrangement is the same as that employed for Hittite words. References to scientific literature are given for Sumerian and Akkadian words only if some peculiarity of the Hittite documents makes this necessary.

In assigning Sumerian and Akkadian words an alphabetic position I have disregarded phonetic complements, whether Akkadian or Hittite. Repeated vowels are disregarded in Sumerian words precisely as in Akkadian and Hittite; A.AM stands next to AM.

Determinatives (see HG 37) are printed in small superior capitals. A determinative before a lemma indicates that the determinative is sometimes found in the documents, not necessarily that it is used constantly. Determinatives do not affect the alphabetic position of a word.

WORD-LIST

The alphabetic order is as follows:
a e h i k, g, q l m n p, b r s, š, ṣ t, ṭ, d u w y z

A = MŪ (oblique MĒ) = *watar* 'water'.
  LÚ.MEŠ A ŠA KUŠ.LAL 'water carriers'.
Â^{MUŠEN} = *haras* 'eagle'.
-a (-*ya* after final vowels and after ideograms; sometimes -*i* or -*iya* after z; precedes other enclitics except possessives) 'also, and, but' (connecting words or sentences). After an indefinite pronoun or adverb, equivalent to Latin -*que* in *quisque*, etc. After a personal pronoun, often merely a mark of emphasis. Ungnad, ZDMG 74.417–22; Götze, KlF 1.183, AM 277; Tenner, KlF 1.388 f.; Pedersen, AOr. 5.184; HG 192; Götze-Pedersen, MS 40 f., 46.
-ă 'ea'; see -*as*; *ta* = *ta* + *a* 'et ea'.
ā- (midd. *a-a-ri* — KUB 20.88.6.21, pl. *a-a-an-ta* — VBoT 58.1.24, part. *a-a-an-za*) 'be hot'. Friedrich, ZA NF 5.79; Eheloff, KlF 1.400 and fn. 1; Götze-Pedersen, MS 31 and fn. 1.
AḪĪTU 'bad luck'.
^{DUG}*ahrushi* (probably Hurrian), a vessel used in ritual. Götze-Pedersen, MS 43 and fn. 2.
Á.ḪU; read Â^{MUŠEN}.
aīn (acc.), something unpleasant, Sommer, Hirt Festschrift 2.294 fn. 2.
ais neut. (gen. *issas*) 'mouth'. Götze-Pedersen, MS 26, 55; Sommer, Hirt Festschrift 2.291–6.
A.QAR = *kweras* 'field, territory'. Ungnad ap. Sommer, BoSt. 7.30 fn. 1.
aki (gen. *akias*) 'death'?? Walther, HC 271 fn. 3; KBo. 3.34.2.12.
ăk(k)-, *ek(k)*- (*aki*, pl. *akkanzi*, pret. *ăkkis, aggas, akta*, 3 pl. *ekir*) 'die, be eclipsed'. Hrozný, BoSt. 3.139 fn. 7; Zimmern, OLZ 25.298; HG 75 fn. 79, 240 f.; Götze-Pedersen, MS 49; Sturtevant, Lang. 11.183; Pedersen, Hirt Festschrift 2.581.
  arha a. 'die off, die away'.
aggalan (acc.), some kind of animal? Friedrich, ZA NF 1.191. 'Victim'?? (W). Cf. *akk*-.

*akkantes (acc. akkandus, dat. aggandas, aggantas) 'the dead, Manes'. See akk-, ekk-.
akkātar (nom.-acc. aqqātar, UG₆-tar, gen. aggannas) 'death; pestilence'. Götze, Hatt. 59.
⁂aggatius 'net'? Friedrich, ZA NF 5.39 f.
akkiske/a- (akkiskizzi, pret. akkiskēt) 'die'. See akk-.
-ak(k)u ... -ak(k)u (also -kku, -ku; cf. takku) 'either ... or'. Hrozný, CH 2.2, 14.45, 76.53, ZA NF 4.175; Götze, ZA NF 2.268.
⁂akkusa 'pits'? Friedrich, ZA NF 5.39 f.; Sturtevant, Lang. 6.219.
akkuske/a- 'drink, give to drink'; see eku-, aku-.
AQBI = tenun, memahhun 'I said'.
ᴸᵁAGRIG = ᴸᵁABARAKKU 'steward, major domo'. Landsberger, AOF 10.150 fn. 48.
AGRIG-ahh- 'make (one) a steward'.
AKŠUD = eppun 'I captured'.
-aku; see -akku.
aku-; see eku-.
akugallit (instr.), a vessel in which water for washing the hands is carried. Carruthers, Lang. 9.153 f.; HG 144.
akuttaras (also ekuttaras) 'drinker, one who gives to drink'. Sommer, BoSt. 7.60; HG 156.
akuwakuwas 'toad' or 'frog'?? Forrer ap. Kretschmer, KlF 1.310 fn. 2; Carruthers, Lang. 6.160.
akuwanna; see eku-.
AG ZAB; read MÊ.
AL, construct state of ALLU.
alalamas, alalimas 'fear'?? Friedrich, ZA NF 5.75; HG 156.
ᴳᴵˢALAN, ALAM = essri 'form, statue'. See LÚ ALAN.KA×UD s.v. LÚ.
alel 'heart'??? Sayce, RA 24, 125. 'Middle' or 'beginning'?? (W). Cf. Götze, Hatt. 91 f.
alilas, a kind of bird. Götze, Kulturg. 149.
alis 'white'. Götze, Madd. 142 and fn. 4; Sturtevant, Lang. 6.156, HG 87. Cf. alpanza, alpas.
⁂allallā (dat.) 'war'??? Forrer, Altorient. Stud. 1.33. Rather a. pai- 'desert, revolt'? Sommer, AU 348 and fn. 3.
allaniya/e- 'become hot'?? Hrozný, AOr. 3.444.21.
allapa 'spittle'? KBo. 3.8.2.35.
allap(p)ahh- (allapahhi) 'spit'. Cf. Hrozný, BoSt. 3.68 fn. 5. KBo. 2.3.1.41; KUB 17.27.3.8–16 (G).

allappahhiske/a- 'spit'. See *allappahh-*.
al(l)iyas, an oracle bird; 'dove'? Götze, Madd. 142.
ᵁᴿᵁᴰ*ALLU* 'mattock, pick axe'? Güterbock, ZA NF 8.227 fn. 3.
alpanza 'bewitched'??? Götze, Madd. 112 fn. 2. 'Pale'?? KUB 7.1.1.1 f. Cf. *alis, alpas*.
alpas 'cloud'. Friedrich, Vert. 2.35 f., 166 f.; Mudge, Lang. 7.252. Cf. *alis*.
alsanza 'captive'. Friedrich, ZA NF 2.274.
ᴳᵁᴰ*ALŪ* 'the heavenly bull'. Friedrich, ZA NF 5.18.13.
ĀLU = URU = *happiris*(?) 'city, town'.
*alwanzah (abl. *alwanzahhaz*) 'witchcraft'. VBoT 120.3.4. See *alwanzahh-*.
alwanzahh- (part. *alwanzahhanza*, infin. *alwanzahhuwanzi*) 'bewitch'. Götze, NBr. 14 f.
alwanzahheske/a- 'bewitch'. See *alwanzahh-*.
alwa(n)zatar 'witchcraft, condition of one bewitched'. See *alwanzahh-*.
alwa(n)zessar = prec.
ᴳᴵˢA.AM; read ᴳᴵˢILDÁG.
ᴳᵁᴰAM; read GUD.AM.
AMA = *annas* 'mother'.
ˢᴬᴸAMA DINGIR-*LIM* = ˢᴬᴸ*siwanzannis*? 'mother of the god', a kind of priestess. Ehelolf, ZA NF 2.318; Götze, Kulturg. 159 and fn. 10.
AMA; read DAGAL 'broad, breadth'.
AMAR 'young animal', especially 'calf'.
AMAT, construct state of *AMTU*.
ᴸᵁ́AMA.A.TU, ᴸᵁ́AMA.A.AT 'member of one's household, house slave'. Friedrich, Vert. 1.79; Götze, AOr. 5.12.
AMĀTU = INIM = *uttar, memiyas* 'word, thing'. Cf. *AWĀTU*.
AMĒLU 'vir'. See LÚ.
AMĒLŪTU, AMĒLUTTU 'mankind'.
amiyaraza (abl.) 'from a canal'. Ehelolf, ZA NF 9.182 fn. 4.
AMMATU = *sekan*? 'ell'.
ammēl 'my', gen. of *uk*. Hrozný, SH 99; Götze, AM 277; HG 192.
ammētaz 'from me', abl. of *uk*. Hrozný, SH 103 f.
ammiyanza 'sharp'?? Götze, Kulturg. 135. 'Excellent, vigorous'? KUB 8.6.15b f. (W).
ammuk (before an enclitic w. initial vowel, *ammug-, ammuqq-, ammugg-*) 'I, me, to me'. Hrozný, MDOG 56.25, SH 100–5; Götze, AM 278; HG 192. See *uk*.

ambassis (nom. KUB 25.22. margin 2), a Hurrian word of unknown meaning. Friedrich, AOF 10.294. Cf. Ehelolf, KlF 1.142 f.

AMTU = GÍM 'slave woman'.

AN = *ŠAMŪ* = *nepis* 'sky, heaven'.

AN; read DINGIR 'god'.

-an 'eum', acc. of *-as*.

ANA (sometimes written by a vertical wedge) 'to', a sign of the dative.

anāhi, anāhita 'a little, a sample'? Sommer, BoSt. 10.66; Götze, KlF 1.229 fn. 5

anas-; read *ans-*.

ᴵᴹ*ANḪULLU* 'hot wind'? Friedrich, ZA NF 5.46.

anisiwat 'today'?? Hrozný, AOr. 1.284. Cf. *siwaz*.

aniur; see *anniur*.

aniya/e- 'work, perform, celebrate; till (a field); care for (animals); inscribe (a tablet)'. Götze, AM 224 f. Cf. *anneske/a-, anniur, aniyatar*.

appa a., arha a. 'undo, cancel; purify'.

aniyan 'performance, day's work'. Sommer, BoSt. 7.39 fn. 3; HG 148. See *aniya/e-, anniur*.

aniyaz (gen. *aniyattas, aniyaddas*) 'performance, report; service, use'. Götze, Madd. 79 and fn. 1, AM 225 f., HG 149.

-anki, multiplicative suffix. Götze, KlF 1.231; HG 104. See pp. 190 f.

anku 'together; separately, apart'. Ehelolf, ZA NF 9.176 f.

AN.NA; read NAGGA.

*annal(l)as (neut. *annalan, annallan*, abl. *annalaz, annallaz*) 'former, earlier'. Götze, Madd. 138 f.; Götze-Pedersen, MS 19, 47; Sturtevant, Lang. 10.267.

annalan, annalaz 'formerly'.

*annallis (pl. *annallius*) = *annallas*, q.v.

annanekus (acc. pl.) 'these'??? Hrozný, CH 144.32, 146.44. Rather a substantive; possibly 'daughters'??

annanu- 'cause to perform, instruct in a trade, train'. Ehelolf ap. Friedrich, Vert. 2.170.

ᴷᵁˢ*annanuz[zi]* 'rein'?? Hrozný, CH 116.26.

annanuhhas 'trained', of animals. Cf. Walther, HC 258.65 etc. Cf. *annanu-*.

annas 'mother'. Hrozný, SH 31; Marstrander, Car. 128; Sturtevant, TAPA 59.49–52, HG 87.

annas UD-*az* 'mother's day' i.e. 'day of one's death'. Friedrich, Vert. 2.90, 168.

?*annas* 'those'??? Hrozný, CH 144.33, 146.44. Rather *annan-sman*, 'their mother'?
?SAL*annawalanas* 'step-mother'?? Hrozný, CH 144.30; Zimmern, AO 23.2.30.76. Cf. Sommer, AU 51 fn.
annaw(a)lis 'of equal standing, equal'. Sommer, AU 51 fn., 101 f.; Götze, Kulturg. 90.
annaz 'olim'. Friedrich, Vert. 1.152.
an(n)eske/a- (also *anniske/a-*) 'perform'. See *aniya/e-*.
anningas (or ᴰ*ningas*), a sign in the sky. Götze, Madd. 118, KIF 1.405.
SAL*ǎnnin(n)iyǎmis* 'cousin'. Friedrich, Vert. 2.98.
annis 'that'. Friedrich, Vert. 1.152; HG 201 f.
annisan 'previously'. Friedrich, Vert. 1.151 f.
an(n)iūr (gen. *aniuras*, dat. *aniuri*) 'performance, rite'. Sommer, BoSt. 10.41; Götze, AM 226; HG 148. See *aniya/e-*.
anniyatar; *arha a.* 'purging, menses'? Götze, AM 225. See *aniya/e-*.
ANNŪ 'this'.
AN.BAR 'iron'.
ans- (*ānsi*, pl. *ānsanzi*, imper. *ānasdu*) 'wipe, cleanse'. Sommer, BoSt. 10.71.
ANŠU (also written ANŠE) = IMĒRU 'ass'.
ANŠU.GÌR.NUN.NA 'mule'.
ANŠU.KUR.RA 'horse'; pl. 'charioteers'. Götze, AM 278.
ANŠU.KUR.RA.SAL.AL(.LAL) 'mare'.
ANŠU.SAL; read EMÈ.
AN.TA = *ser* 'above'.
anda, adv. or preverb, 'in, within; together; into'; postposition w. dat. or gen. 'in, among, during; into; for the sake of'. Hrozný, MDOG 56.28, SH 17 fn. 4, 182; Götze, Hatt. 115 f.; Götze-Pedersen, MS 47; HG 104, Chrest. 121; cf. Götze, AOr. 5.22 f., 28 f., AM 278 f.; Kurylowicz, EI 74.
    anda parna 'in and out'?? Götze, KIF 1.224. Cf. s.v. *parnan*.
AN.TAḪ.ŠUMŠAR, a food plant. Ehelolf, SBPA 1925.267 fn. 3.
antakissi, variant for *antakitti*. KUB 11.20.1.13.
antakitt- (dat. *antakitti*, *andakitti*) 'middle, abdomen, waist'. Sturtevant, Lang. 12 No. 3.
andan, preverb and postposition, 'in, within, into'. Götze, AOr. 5.19 f. See *anda*.
*ǎndaras (acc. *ǎndaran*) 'blue' or 'red'?? Chrest. 118 f. Cf. *mitis*.
⁺*antaris* 'god; king'?? Sommer, AU 246 f.
*antiyanza (acc. ᴸᵁ*antiyantan*) 'husband'? Hrozný, CH 28.28; Chrest. 227; cf. Ranoszek, IF 52.166.

antuhhas; see *antuhsas*.
antuhsannanza; see *antuhsatar*.
antuhsas, antuhhas, antuw(w)ahhas 'human being, man'. Hrozný, SH 28 f.; Friedrich, Vert. 1.72, 180; Götze, Madd. 138; Benveniste, RHA 1.203-8; Götze-Pedersen, MS 57; Petersen, AJP 56.59 f.
antuhsatar, antuhsannanza 'humanity, mankind, people'. Hrozný, SH 72; HG 159.
ANDURĀRU 'freedom'.
*antŭris (gen. *antūriyas, anduryas*, pl. *antŭres*, dat. *andurriyas*) '(born) within, native'. Friedrich, Vert. 1.167-70; Sturtevant, Lang. 10.272.
andurza 'within'. Friedrich, Vert. 1.167-70; HG 128.
antuw(w)ahhas; see *antuhsas*.
^{LÚ}*antuwwasallis*, a dignitary? Sommer, AU 123 fn. 2.
ānza 'hot'; part. of *a-* 'be hot'.
*anzais (inst. ^{GIŠ}*anzait*), a cleansing or purifying instrument. KUB 24.7.2.11.
AN.ZA.QAR 'pillar'.
anzās 'us, to us; we'. Hrozný, SH 112-4; HG 104, 193, 196.
anzel 'our'. Hrozný, MDOG 56.26, SH 111 f.; HG 193, 196, 205.
anzedaz (*anzidaz, anzitaz*) 'from us'. Friedrich, Vert. 2.24; HG 196.
^{GIŠ}AB = ^{GIŠ}*luttais* 'window'. Friedrich, ZA NF 3.297-9.
^{GUD}ÁB; read GUD.ÁB.
ap-; see *epp-* 'take'.
^{DUG}ÁB × A; read ^{DUG}DU$_{10}$ × A.
-apa, -ap, -pa, an enclitic particle. Friedrich, Vert. 2.151.
ABAN, construct state of *ABNU*.
^{LÚ}*ABARAKKU* 'steward, major domo'. See ^{LÚ}AGRIG.
apăs 'is'. Hrozný, SH 137-9, JSOR 6.69 fn. 1; Götze, AM 279; HG 201, 208 f.
apăsel, apăsela 'is ipse'. See *-el, -ela*.
apasil, apasila; read *apasel, apasela*.
apăt 'id', neut. of *apas*.
apadda(n); read *abeda(n)*, dat. of *apas*.
apē 'ea', pl. neut. of *apas*.
apĕl 'eius', gen. of *apas*.
apĕnessan (*apēnissan, apinissan, apinessan*) 'thus'. Hrozný, SH 135, 139; Götze, ZA NF 2.14; Götze-Pedersen, MS 55.
apĕnessu(w)anza (acc. *apĕnessuwantan, apenissuwantan, apinessuandan*) 'such'. HG 161. See *apenessan*.
apenzan 'eorum', pl. gen. of *apas*.

apet (*apit*), inst. of *apas*.
apēda(*ni*), *apidani*, *abeda*(*ni*), *apidan* 'ei', dat. of *apas*; 'thither, for that reason'. Cf. Friedrich, ZA NF 2.274, Vert. 1.30, 2.85 f.; HG 206, 208.
apēdanda, inst. of *apas*. Ehelolf ap. Sommer, AU 389.
apĕdas, pl. dat. (rarely gen.) of *apas*.
apēz 'ab eo', abl. of *apas*. HG 206.
ᴳᴵᔆAPIN 'plough'.
ᴸᵁAPIN.LAL 'farmer'.
  ᴸᵁ ᴹᴱᔆAPIN.LAL-*ŪTU* = *ERRĒŠŪTU* 'position of a farmer, farmership; agriculture'.
apidda, *apiddan*; read *abeda*, *abedan*.
apiya 'there, then'. Hrozný, SH 138 fn. 2; Sommer, BoSt. 10.81.
  apiākku 'an Ort und Stelle'?? Götze, ZA NF 2.268.
APLU 'son'.
ABNĪ = *wetenun*, *wedahhun* 'I built'.
ABNU = *ZÁ* 'stone'.
app-; see *epp-* 'take'.
A.AB.BA = *arunas* 'sea'.
AB.BA = *attas* 'father'.
  AB.BA AB.BA(ḪI.A) = *huhhantes* 'forefathers'.
āppa (usually written EGIR-*pa*) adv. 'afterwards, again'. Hrozný, MDOG 56.27; Friedrich, ZA NF 2.276; Sommer, AU 214. Preverb 'back, again'. Götze, Hatt. 117; Sommer, AU 40 f.; Lohman, IF 51.324 f.; Götze-Pedersen, MS 49. Cf. Götze, AOr. 5.17, 21, 23, 26 f., 27 fn. 3, 29, AM 282; Kurylowicz, EI 75.
appāi- (*appāi*, pl. *appiyanzi*) 'be finished'. Friedrich, ZA NF 2.294 and fn. 2; HG 213, 247.
ᴳᴵᔆ*appalassas* (dat. pl.?) 'pillory' or the like? Hrozný, CH 110.12. Cf. Walther, HC 264.121 and fn. 3; cf. also the following words.
appaleske/a- (rather than *duppaleske/a-*) 'deride'? Friedrich, ZA NF 1.172.
appāli- or *appāla-* (dat. *appāli*) 'derision'? See *appaleske/a-*.
appaliyallas 'derider'? Cf. Forrer, Altorient. Stud. 1.32.
āppan (usually written EGIR-*an*) preverb 'behind, after'. Postposition w. dat. or gen. 'behind, after'; w. abl. 'concerning'. Adv. 'afterwards; secretly'. Friedrich, Vert. 1.147 and fn. 1; Sommer, AU 40 f.; Götze, AOr. 5.19, AM 282; Götze-Pedersen, MS 37 f., 38 fn. 2, 49.
  appanset 'behind him'; *appansmet* 'behind them, behind you'. Friedrich, ZA 3.182 f.

appanda (usually written EGIR-*an-da*) 'behind', with a suggestion of motion not to be expressed in English; 'afterwards'. Sommer, BoSt. 10.12; Götze, NBr. 50.35, AOr. 5.20 and fn. 1.

$^{LÚ}appās$, a workman of some kind. Friedrich, Altorient. Stud. 53.

appātar (gen. *appannas*) 'a taking, beginning'. Friedrich, ZA NF 1.10 and fn. 2, Vert. 1.88.

appatare/a-; read *appatre/a-*.

ăppatre/a- (*appatrizzi, appatarizzi,* infin. *āppatriwanzi*) 'hire, rent'?? Sommer, BoSt. 7.42. 'Borrow'?? Walther, HC 259.76, 268.164.

appatriya/e- = *appatre/a-*. KUB 13.8.1.10.

appiske/a- 'take, seize'. See *epp-, app-*.

appiya/e-; see *appai-*.

appizzis [ap'etsis] 'last, later; of lowest rank'. Lohmann, IF 51.319-28; Sturtevant, Lang. 10.268-73.

appizziyan, appizziyaz adv. 'behind, afterwards, finally'.

$^{UZU}appuzzi$ 'tallow'. Friedrich, ZA NF 3.191 and fn. 2; Ehelolf, ZA NF 9.173 fn. 1.

ABRIG; read IZKIM 'omen'.

^{LÚ}ABRIG; read ^{LÚ}AGRIG 'steward'.

ABU = *attas* 'father'.

ABU ABI = *huhhas* 'grandfather'.

?*ABU BĪTI* (written $^{LÚ}ABUBITUM$) 'householder', title of an official.

apūn 'eum', acc. of *apas*. HG 93 fn. 29, 201.

apūs 'ei, eos', pl. of *apas*.

ăr- (*artari, arta,* imper. 2 sg. *ărhut*) 'take one's stand, stand'. Friedrich, ZA NF 2.43, 163; Sturtevant, Lang. 3.165-7, HG 133, 289-91.

anda a.; anda aranda adv. 'all together'? Götze, AM 252.

appan a. 'stand behind, support'.

kattan arha a. 'stand apart from, desert'.

ăr-, ĕr- (*ări,* 2 pl. *ĕrteni,* pret. *āras,* 1 pl. *eruwen*) 'arrive'. Friedrich, ZA NF 2.18, 42 f.; Sturtevant, Lang. 3.165-7, HG 92, 93, 107 f., 239; Kurylowicz, EI 74.

^{ZA}ARĂ 'mill-stone, mill'.

É ^{ZA}ARĂ 'mill'.

LÚ ^{ZA}ARĂ, SAL ^{ZA}ARĂ 'pistor; miller, baker'.

āra (*a-a-ra*), usually after a negative, ' a good thing, right'. Hrozný, MDOG 56.28, SH 41; Götze, NBr. 30 fn. 4; Sommer, AU 97 f.

arā(e)- (*araizzi,* pl. *arānzi*) 'rise, rebel; give an oracle'. See *arai-*.

ARĂḪ (acc. ARĂḪ-*an*) 'granary'.

ARĀḪ (3 pl. ARĀḪ-anzi) 'store in a granary'.
arahhanius (acc. pl.) 'free (women)'?? Hrozný, CH 144.32.
arahza 'around, outside'. Friedrich, Vert. 1.167–70; HG 88, 174.
arahzanta 'around'. Hrozný, SH 6; Friedrich, Vert. 1.167; HG 88.
*arăhzĕnas (acc. *arahzinan*, dat. *arāhzēni*) 'foreigner, neighbor'. Friedrich, Vert. 1.170; HG 88.
arăi- (*arăi*, pret. *arăis*) 'rise, rebel; give an oracle'. Sommer, BoSt. 10..55; Götze, ZA NF 2.18, AM 254; Friedrich, ZA NF 2.43 f.; Sturtevant, Lang. 3.166 f., 220 f.
arallā(e)- (pret. *arallāit*) 'make (one) the consort of, marry to'. KUB 21.27.1.11 (G).
⁎*arannuhha* (pret. 1 sg.) 'I withheld'??? Götze, Hatt. 116. Rather 'I yielded'?
aranda; *anda aranda*, see *ar-* 'stand'.
arantalliya/e- (3 pl. *arantalliinzi*, *arandallienzi*, *arantalliyanzi*) 'murmur'? Friedrich, Vert. 1. 153, 2.90.
arantet (*a-ra-an-te-it*) = *āntet* (*a-a-an-te-it*)?? Götze-Pedersen, MS 31.
ᴸᵁ*arăs* 'companion, friend'. Sommer, AU 174 f., AF 83.
 ᴸᵁ*aras* ᴸᵁ*aran* 'alter alterum'.
aras-; read *ars-*.
araske/a-; read *arske/a-*.
ARAD, construct state of ARDU.
arăwēs- (pret. *arawēsta*, pl. *arāwĕsser*) 'become free'. Sommer, AU 344.
araw(w)ahh- (*arawwahhi*, *arawahhi*) 'set free'. Friedrich, ZA NF 1.16; HG 241 f.
arawwannis (nom. *arawwannes*, acc. *arawwannin*) 'free, noble'. Zimmern, OLZ 25.298; Hrozný, CH 146.45; Marstrander, Car. 150; HG 168 fn. 72.
arăw(w)ēs (nom. pl.) 'free, noble'. Hrozný, CH 46.4.
areske/a- (pret. 1 sg. *ariskēnun*, midd. *areskittari*) 'inquire by divination'. See *ariya/e-*.
arha preverb, rarely postposition, 'out, away, forth'. Sommer, BoSt. 4.7 fn. 1, AU 168; Forrer, Altorient. Stud. 1.33; Götze, AOr. 5.17 and fn. 2; HG 88; Götze-Pedersen, MS 76 f. Cf. Götze, AOr. 5.21 and fn. 5, 27 and fn. 3, 29 and fn. 2, AM 280.
arhayan 'what follows, sequel, addition'; as adv. 'additionally, separately'. KUB 24.3.4.7 f. (G). Cf. Sommer, BoSt. 10.17 f.
arhi (dat.) 'on a farm'. HG 88; Chrest. 225.
ᴳᴵˢ*arimpas*, an implement of bronze used in ritual. VBoT 58.4.28. Cf. *eripisa*, *irimpi*.
ariske/a-; read *areske/a-*.

ᴷᵁˢ*ARĪTU* 'shield'.
ăriya (dat.; *a-a-ri-ya, a-ri-ya*), a foreign word of unknown meaning. Götze-Pedersen, MS 47. Cf. Ehelolf, KlF 1.142 f.
ariya/e- 'inquire by divination'. Sommer, BoSt. 10.13, AU 401; Götze-Pedersen, MS 47 f.
ᴳᴵˢ*ariyala-* 'basket' or the like. Cf. Sommer, BoSt. 10.81.
ariyasessar 'inquiry by divination, divination'. Götze, KlF 1.135.
ark- (3 pl. *arkanzi*) 'shut in, ward off'. Hrozný, BoSt. 3. 153 fn. 6.
ārk- (*ārgi*) 'cut off, mutilate; cut up'. KUB 10.63.1.29 f. (G). Cf. Götze, NBr. 58 fn. 1.
arkamman-; see *arkammas.*
arkammanallas 'tributary'. See Götze, Madd. 139. Cf. *arkammas.*
arkammanallatar 'payment of tribute'. See *arkammanallas.*
⸰*arkammanallāwi*, a Luwian 1 sg.?? Sommer, AU 231.
*arkammanallis (acc. pl. *arkammanallius*) 'tributary'. See *arkammas.*
arkammanatar 'payment of tribute'. See *arkammas.*
arkām(m)as (gen. *arkammanas, arkamanas*) 'tribute'. Götze, Madd. 130 f.; HG 184.
ᴳᴵˢ*arkam(m)i*, a musical instrument. Götze, Hatt. 101.
argatiya/e- (pret. *argatiyēr*) 'come to blows'? KBo. 3.7.1.10 (G).
arkuwa- (pret. 1 sg. *arkuwanun*) 'plead, pray'. Sommer, BoSt. 10.40; Götze, Madd. 63 and fn. 1; HG 222.
arkuwēske/a- (1 sg. *arkuwēskimi, arkuwīskimi, arkwĕskimi*) 'plead, pray'. See *arkuwa-.*
arkuwessar 'plea, prayer'. Götze, Madd. 63 fn. 1.
arkuw(w)ar 'plea, prayer'. Sommer, BoSt. 10.40, AU 133 f.

> a. w. *essa-, dai-,* or *ya/e-* (usually preceded by *-za*) 'pray'. Friedrich, OLZ 39.308.

armahh- (3 pl. *armahhanzi*) 'impregnate'?? Götze, AM 199; HG 242. Rather 'join, copulate'. Cf. *armezzi, armezziya/e-.*
*armahhanza (dat. *armahhanti*) 'joined; pregnant'. Hrozný, CH 136.33.
*armahhatar (dat. *armahhanni*) 'impregnation'? Rather 'copulation'. Götze, Hatt. 92. See *armahh-.*
armaniya- (midd. *armaniyatta*) 'become ill'??? Ehelolf ap. Boissier, Mantique 22 f., ZA NF 9.182 fn. 2. Rather 'be joined; become pregnant'. Cf. *armahh-, armanza.*
armannis (perhaps pl.) 'crescent'? KUB 17.21.2.14. Cf. *armas.*
NINDA *a.* 'crescent-shaped loaf'?? KUB 2.13.1.15.
*armanza (acc. *armandan*) 'joined; pregnant'. Hrozný, CH 66.15, 68.17. Cf. *armahh-, armaniya-.*

*armaš 'moon'? Götze, NBr. 18. Cf. armannis.

*armaw(w)anza (acc. armawandan, pl. armawwantes) 'pregnant'. Hrozný, CH 62. 78; Götze, AM 199. Cf. armanza.

ᴳᴵˢarmĕzzi (also armizzi), ᶻᴬarmizzi 'bridge'?? KUB 17.10.3.26; 19.9.4. 11; 20.2.4.19 (G).

armezziya/e- (written armizziya-) 'join, connect by a bridge'. Cf. Sayce, JRAS 1930.315. See armezzi.
   parā a. 'spread (a rumor)'. KUB 26.1.3.28 (G).

arnu- 'move, bring; bury'. Hrozný, SH 12 fn. 5. 130 fn. 2; Friedrich, ZA NF 2.41–3; Sturtevant, Lang. 3.166 f., HG 234; Götze-Pedersen, MS 48; Kurylowicz, EI 74.
   anta a. 'bring in'.
   kattan a. 'bring down'.
   parā a. 'carry forward, transmit'. Sommer, AU 31.
   ZI-aš a. 'fulfill (one's) wish'. Sommer, AU 31 f.
   ZI-ni a., w. dat., 'go before, approach'? Sommer, AU 28–31.

arnuške/a- 'move, bring'. See arnu-.

arnuwalaš 'foreign'?? Hrozný, CH 150.25, 151 fn. 6; Götze, Madd. 63.

*arnwanza (acc. arnwandan) 'pregnant'. The word is a variant for armawwanza in three passages in the Code. Hrozný, CH 62.78 and fn. 14, etc.

arpan (acc.) 'bad luck'. Forrer, Forsch. 1.129 f.; Friedrich, IF 49.225; Sommer, AU 62; Sturtevant, JAOS 50.127, HG 93.

arpašă- (arpašăi, pret. ⁺arpasatta) 'be unlucky'. See arpan.

*arpuw(w)anza (neut. arpuwwan, pl. arpuwantes) 'unlucky'. HG 160. See arpan.

ārr- (ārri), ărra- (ărrai, pl. ărranzi, infin. arrumanzi) 'wash'. Ehelolf, KlF 1.145 and fn. 3, 152, 157 f.; HG 244; Götze-Pedersen, MS 48; Sturtevant, Lang. 11.40.
   arha a. 'wash (clothes)'.

arra- (acc. arran), arrašš-? (acc. arrassan?, dat. arrissiya-ssi?) 'anus'. Friedrich, IF 41.376; Benveniste, BSL 33.139; Götze-Pedersen, MS 50; Sturtevant, Lang. 11.39 f.; Kurylowicz, EI 74.

arreške/a- 'wash'. HG 238. See arr-.

arrissiyassi; see arra-.

arruwe/a-, arrume/a-; see arrwe/a-.

arrwe/a- (arrwizzi, 3 pl. arruwanzi, arrumanzi) 'wash'. Sommer, BoSt. 10.74.

ărs- (ăraszi) 'flow'. Friedrich, ZA NF 3.190 fn. 7, 5.45 and fn. 4; Sturtevant, Lang. 8.120; Götze-Pedersen, MS 48. Cf. arse/a-.

arsā(e)- (*arsāizzi*), *arse/a-* (*arsezzi*) 'plant'. Hrozný, CH 102.12, 20; HG 227 f.

ārsake/a-; see *arskke/a-* 'plant'.

arsanat(t)allas 'envier'. Götze, Hatt. 66; HG 157.

arsaniya/e- 'envy'. Götze, Hatt. 66; HG 107 and fn. 55, 225; Benveniste, BSL 33.139.

arse/a- 'plant'; see *arsā(e)-* 'plant'.

arse/a- (*arsizzi*) 'flow'. Ehelolf, OLZ 36.6 fn. 3. Cf. *ars-*.

*ārsēsur (dat. *ārsēsuri*) 'current (of a river)'? Forrer, RHA 1.149.22.

arsikke/a-; read *arskke/a-* 'plant'.

arsis 'a planting, planted field'. Hrozný, CH 102.11–13; Götze, Madd. 99 and fn. 14.

ārske/a- (*āraskizzi*, pret. *āraskit*) 'come to, reach'. See *ar-, er-*.
    parā a. 'make incursions'. Chrest. 68.13, 92. Otherwise Götze, Hatt. 116.

ărsk(k)e/a- (*ārsakizzi*, pret. *arsikkit*) 'plant'. Götze, Madd. 60 and fn. 2. Cf. *arsā(e)-*, *arse/a-*.

ārtattar 'arrival (in a foreign country)'? Hrozný, Congr. 1.158. Cf. *arzana-*.

ARDU = ERUM 'slave'.

arum(m)a 'very much'. Götze, KlF 1.220.

ărunas 'sea'. Sommer, OLZ 24.197–201; Kretschmer, WZKM 33.1–22; Benveniste, RHA 1.206 f.

arwă(e)- (*aruwăizzi*, *aruwwāizzi*, pl. *aruwānzi, arwanzi*, pret. 1 sg. *arwānun*) 'bow before, worship'. Ehelolf, OLZ 27.580 f.; Sturtevant, Lang. 5.10, HG 87.

arwīske/a- (*arwīskizzi, aruwiskizzi*) 'bow before, worship'.

arzana- (part. *arzananza*) 'settle in a foreign country'. Götze, Madd. 63 and fn. 4. Cf. *artattar*.

AŠ = *INA*, a sign of the dat.

AŠ; read 1 (see p. 189).

ÁŠ; read ZÍZ.

-as (follows *-ma, -a,* or *-wa;* precedes *-za, -kan,* or *-san;* may be repeated after an intervening reflexive enclitic) 'is, ea'. Hrozný, MDOG 56.38 and fn.4; Ungnad, ZDMG 74.417–22; Götze, NBr. 19, AM 276 f., AOr. 5.3; HG 198–200; Götze-Pedersen, MS 46; Chrest. 95, 174; Friedrich, RHA 3.157–62. Cf. *-at* 'id, ei', *e* 'ei, ea', *ta = ta + a* 'et ea'.

ăs- (*āszi*, pret. *āsta*) 'remain'. Sommer, AU 254 and fn. 1; Bechtel ap. Chrest. 91.

as-; see *es-* 'set'.
as-; see *es-* 'be'.
A.ŠA(G) = *EQLU* 'field'.
asallu, imper. 1 sg. of *es-* 'be'.
AŠAMŠUTU 'hurricane'.
*asandul (dat. *asanduli*) 'a remaining; a being left as a garrison, garrison duty'. Götze, AM 199-201.
asandula(e)- 'delay, tarry; be on garrison duty'. Götze, AM 199 f.
*asandulas (acc. *asandulan*, abl. *asandulaz*) 'garrison'. Originally a gen. of *asandul*, the word developed a complete declension.
*asandulatar (dat. *asandulanni*) 'garrison duty'. Götze, AM 200.
asanduleske/a- 'delay, tarry; be on garrison duty'. See *asandula(e)-*.
*asandulis (acc. *asandulin*) = *asandulas*. Götze, AM 199 fn. 3.
asănza (neut. *asān*) 'true'. Sommer, AU 69.
AŠAPPAR = *hatrami* 'I send (word), I shall send (word)'.
AŠAR, construct state of *AŠRU*.
asăras 'wool'?? Chrest. 119.
AŠARĪDU 'first in rank, prominent'.
asăs-, asĕs-, eses- (*asăsi*, 3 pl. *asesanzi, asisanzi*, pret. *asasta, asesta, esesta*, pl. *asĕser*) 'set, conduct to one's place; cause to dwell, found (a city); beset (a city)'. Sommer, BoSt. 10.50-2; Götze, Madd. 103; Sturtevant, HG 241, Lang. 11.182.
AŠ.AŠ.ḪI.A, plural suffix used with URU 'city'.
asătar 'a sitting'. Götze, Hatt. 53.
asauni; see *asawar*.
asawar (dat. *asauni*, abl. *asaunaz*) 'sheepfold, goat pen'. Friedrich, IF 43.258 fn. 5; Götze, NBr. 67; HG 187.
ases-; see *asas-*.
asesanu- 'cause to dwell, cause to be inhabited'. Hrozný, BoSt. 3.146 fn. 5.
asesanuske/a- (*asisanuske/a-*) 'cause to dwell, cause to be inhabited'. See *asesanu-*.
asessar 'assembly, population'. Sommer, BoSt. 10.51; Friedrich, ZA NF 2.294 fn. 2; HG 152; cf. Forrer, Caucasica 9.15 fn. 4.
^{LÚ}A.SI-*as*; read *A-SI-RUM*.
asi 'is, ea, id'. Friedrich, ZA NF 2.286-9; HG 201.
$^{LÚ}ASIRU$ = $^{LÚ}hipparas$ 'captive'. Feigin, AJSL 50.228.
asiwanteske/a- 'obey'?? See *asiwanza*.
*asiwanza (gen. $^{LÚ}asiwandas$) 'slave'?? Cf. Forrer ap. Kretschmer, KlF 1.312 fn. 1.

LÚAŠGAB 'shoemaker'. Hrozný, CH 134.25; Friedrich, Vert. 1.58.29. But cf. Deimel, No. 4.1.

āska- (acc. āska, dat. āski, āska, āsga) 'gate, court'. Friedrich, ZA NF 5.73; Götze, Kulturg. 102 fn. 6.

áskaz(a) 'foris'. Friedrich, Vert. 1.168 f., AOr. 6.374 fn. 5.

AŠ. ME = sittar? 'sun disk.' Ehelolf, ZA NF 9.187 fn. 2.

AŠMĒ, AŠMĪ = istamassun 'I heard'.

asnu-; see assnu-.

AṢBAT = eppun 'I captured'.

AŠPUR = hatranun 'I sent (word)'.

AŠRU = pedan 'place'.

AŠAR-ŠU 'his place'.

AŠRI-ḪI.A 'places'.

assanu-; see assnu- 'prepare'.

āssiske/a- 'love'? Sommer, AU 304. Cf. assiya/e-.

ās(s)iya/e- 'love'. Götze, NBr. 17.

ás(s)iyatar 'love, affection'. See assiya/e-.

*āssiyawwatar (inst. āssiyawwannit) 'love, affection'. Sayce, RA 27. 165; HG 151.

assnu- (asnuzi, assanuzzi) 'prepare, institute; supply, serve'. Götze, Madd. 63, 103 and fn. 17; Ehelolf, Berl. Mus. Berichte 49.34. Cf. es-, as- 'set'.

*assnum(m)ar 'preparation'; asnumas ki 'these supplies'. KUB 17.28.4.42.

ássul, ássulas 'favor, kindness; greeting'. Götze, Hatt. 66; Sommer, AU 80.

AŠŠUM 'for the sake of'; sign of the dat.

ássus 'good, kind'; neut. 'property; favor, greeting'. Friedrich, IF 41.370 f.; Kurylowicz, EI 30, 74.

assutar (SIG₅-utar) 'welfare'.

ássuwa(e)- 'be good'. Götze, Madd. 82; HG 226 f.

*āssuwatar (dat. āssuwanni) 'goodness'. Götze, Madd. 95.

āssuzēri (3 sg.) 'can'. Ehelolf, KUB 27 preface p. V.

-asta, -sta 'then, afterwards'. Friedrich, ZA NF 2.273; Sommer, AU 89 fn. 1.

astiras 'star'. Weidner and Friedrich, AOF 6.223.

at-; see et-.

-at (neut. sg. and masc. nom. pl. of -as) 'id, ei'.

Á.DAḪ 'helper'.

GIŠA.DA.GUR 'spoon'? Sommer, BoSt. 10.42 fn. 3; Deimel, No. 579. 313.

URUD*ates* 'plate, dish'? Hrozný, CH 122.1, 124.14, 16.
ATḪŪTU 'relationship, household'. Cf. Götze, AM 263.
AD. KID 'wickerwork'. Sommer, BoSt. 10.5, 54. 55.
 LÚAD.KID 'wickerworker'.
AD. LÍL; read AD.KID.
attas (also *addas*) 'father'; pl. 'forefathers'. Hrozný, SH 31; Sommer, BoSt. 10.47, AU 304; Forrer, JA 217.243.
ADDIN = *pehhun* 'I gave'.
adduwala-, adduwali-, Luwian for *idalus* 'bad'? Sommer, AU 51 fn.
TÚG*adupli* 'breeches'?? Hrozný, CH 138.49.
au-, aus-, ū- (*auszi*, 2 sg. *autti*, 3 pl. *uwanzi*, pret. 1 sg. *ūhhun*) 'see; read'; w. *-za* 'see for oneself; experience, dream, be conscious of' Friedrich, ZA NF 3.186 and fn. 1, 202 f.; Sommer, AU 281 fn. 1; Götze, AM 281 f.; Sturtevant, Lang. 6.34 f., 7.115 f., 8.120 f., HG 103, 228, 247, 288 f; Friedrich, OLZ 39.308. Cf. *uwa-* 'appear, be seen'.
 anda a. 'attend to'. Sommer, AU 232.
 arha a. 'look out (from)'.
 katta a. 'examine, take care of'.
 parā a. 'overlook, neglect, be indulgent toward'.
 ser a. 'observe'.
aulis (1) a part of the body. KUB 17.24.3.4 (G). (2) 'Celebration, festival' or the like. KUB 24.1.2.5 (G).
aumani, Arzawan infin. 'to see'. HG 154.
auris 'frontier garrison, outpost, sentry'. Tenner, HAT 24; Götze, Madd. 109. Cf. *awwaris*.
LÚ*auriyalas* 'member of a frontier garrison, sentry, sentry post'. Götze, Madd. 106–10; HG 159.
aus-; see *au-*.
awan 'apart, off'. Hrozný, MDOG 56.28, SH 35; Götze, Madd. 135 f.; Sturtevant, Lang. 7.5, HG 101, 212; Kurylowicz, EI 75.
AWĀTU = INIM = *uttar* 'word, affair'. Cf. *AMĀTU*.
 AWĀTE-MEŠ 'words'.
 AWAZ(Z)U 'his word'.
awēr, pret. 3 pl. of *au-* 'see'.
*awwaris (gen. *awwariyas*), variant for *auris* 'frontier garrison', q.v.
ayali; EZEN × ŠE *a.*, name of a festival. Sommer, AU 50.
ayawalas 'personal representative (of a king)'?? Sommer, AU 41–54.
ay(y)ari; EZEN × ŠE *a.*, name of a festival. Sommer, AU 276, 355.
AZ 'bear'. Landsberger, Die Fauna des alten Mesopotamiens 80–3.

az-; see *et-*, *at-*.
AZAG; read KU(G).
AZAG.GA: read KU(G).GA.
AZAG.GI; read GUŠKIN.
AZAG.GIM; read KU(G).DÍM.
AZAG.UD; read KUBABBAR.
AZ.BAT; read *AṢBAT*.
^{LÚ}AZU 'seer'.
^{LÚ}A.ZU 'physician'.
azzasteni; 2 pl. of *et-*.
azzik(k)e/a- [*atske-*] (*azzikizzi*, 3 pl. *azzikkanzi*) 'eat, cause to eat'.

É = *BĪTU* = *pir* 'house'; also determinative.
    É EN.NU.UN 'prison'.
    É ḪI.ÚS.SA = É *tarnu*-?? 'bath-house, laundry'.
    É IN.NU.DA 'storage for straw, barn'.
    É GAL = *ÉKALLU* 'palace'.
    É GUD 'stable'.
    É LUGAL 'palace'.
    É NIM.LÀL 'bee-hive'.
    É DINGIR-*LIM* 'temple'.
    É ZÁ, É ZÁ.KIŠIB = É *siyannas* 'house of seals, storehouse, treasury'. Eheloff, OLZ 29, 988; Götze, ZA NF 2.258, AM 231, Kultur. 102.
É-*na* = *parna*; É-*nas* = *parnas*. Friedrich, ZA NF 5.78. See *parna-*.
-*ē* (nom. pl. masc. and neut. of -*as*) 'ei, ea'. (G). Cf. HG 198 f.
    nē 'et ei, et ea'.
ě-; *ěsta* 'postea ei'. KBo. 3.28.2.5; 3.38.1.15 (G).
É.A; ^{Ú}*zuhris* É.A 'green fodder'. Cf. Sommer, BoSt. 7.16.
    ^{GIŠ}GEŠTIN.É.A 'grape(s)'.
ehu 'agedum, up, come'; introducing another verb. After -*kan*, 'come, go'. Sommer, ZA 33.92 f., AU 166; Sturtevant, Lang. 6.26, 7.245, HG 100; Güterbock, ZA NF 9.323 f.
    anda e., 'come in'. Chrest. 125, 230.
    arha e., 'come away'. Sommer, AU 166.
    parā e., 'go forth'. Chrest. 108.28, 120.
ehuradā(e)- 'fill (the ears with wool)'. KUB 7.53.1.16, 18. Cf. *ehuratius*.
^{SIG}*ehuratius* (acc. pl.) 'bits of wool put into the ears'. KUB 12.58.2.19. See *ehurada(e)-*.

34   WORD LIST

^{TÚG}E.ÍB 'girdle'.   Sommer, BoSt. 10.82 s.v. E.TUM; Götze-Pedersen, MS 44.
ek-; see *akk-*, *ekk-*.
ega(ē)- (pret. *igait*, midd. 3 sg. *igaētta*, *egattaru*) 'burst, cause to burst'???   Ehelolf, KlF 1.400 and fn. 5. Rather 'quench, cool; be quenched, become cool'? Cavaignac, RHA 1.104 and fn. 20.
É.GAL; read É GAL and see s.v. É.
^{SAL}É.GE$_4$. = *KALLĀTU* 'bride, daughter-in-law, young woman'.
^{SAL}É.GE$_4$.A = *KALLĀTŪTU* 'the state of being a bride, daughter-in-law, or young woman'.
EGIR = *appa* 'afterwards, again, back'.
EGIR = *appan* 'behind, after'.
EGIR = *appanda* 'behind, afterwards'.
EGIR = *appizzis* 'last, later'.
EGIR = *appizziyaz* 'behind, afterwards, finally'.
EGIR-*ŠU* 'after him, after it, next'.
EGIR.UD(.KAM) = *ARKĀT ŪMI* 'future, eternity'.
ekk-; see *akk-*.
eku-, aku- (*ekuzi*, 3 pl. *akwanzi, akuwanzi, akuwwanzi*) 'drink, give to drink; pour a libation'. Hrozný, MDOG 56.33, SH 42 f.; Pedersen, Group. 40; Sturtevant, Lang. 6.219 f., HG 90; Benveniste, BSL 33.142 and fn. 1; Götze-Pedersen, MS 49; Juret, RHA 2.251 f. Cf. *akkuske/a-*.
ekunas 'cold, chilly'. Götze, KlF 1.186 and fn. 8; Sturtevant, Lang. 6.219.
ekunimas 'cold, coolness'. Götze, KlF 1.186 and fn. 8; HG 156.
É.GUD; read É GUD and see s.v. É.
ekuttaras; see *akuttaras*.
ekuzazzi; probably error for *ekuzzi*. Götze, Madd. 126 fn. 5.
-el, -ela (also *-ila*), particles appended to pronouns, 'ipse'. Sommer, BoSt. 7.48 fn. 1; HG 203; Götze, AM 246.
-ēl, -ēla, particles or phonetic complements appended to numerals. Friedrich, ZA NF 5.56 f.; Götze, AM 246.
elaneske/a- 'destroy'??   KUB 7.53.2.12, 17.
ELKU = *sahhan* 'goods and services due an overlord'.
   LÚ *ELKI* 'vassal, dependent, tenant farmer'.
^{D}ELLAT; read ILLAT.
ELLU (pl. *ELLŪTI*) 'free, noble'. Friedrich, Vert. 2. 183.
^{IM}*ELTĀNU* 'north wind'.
É.LUGAL; read É LUGAL and see s.v. É.

ᴳᴵˢēlzi, a kind of tree.
ᴷᵁˢÊ.MÁ.ÙRU = ᴳᴵˢMÁ.URU.ÙRU 'quiver'.   Ehelolf, ZA NF 1.47.
EME = tissatu? 'tongue'.
EMÈ 'female ass'.
EMÈ.AL.LAL 'female pack-ass'.
EMṢU 'sour'.
ᴸᵁ*EMU* 'father-in-law'.
EN = BĒLU = eshās 'master'.
   EN É = BĒL BĪTI 'master of the house'.
   EN KARAŠ 'general'.
   EN *QĀTI* 'artisan'.
   EN SISKUR 'sacrificer, person who has a sacrifice performed'.
   EN *DĪNI* 'opponent at law'.
   EN UTÚL 'master of the pots, kitchen worker'.
EN = BĒLŪTU = EN-atar, EN-izna-, EN-iznatar 'lordship, mastery'. Götze, AM 252 f.
É.NA₄; read É ZÁ and see s.v. É.
enandan (acc.) 'tame'?   Walther, HC 258. 65.
É.NA₄ DUB; read É ZÁ.KIŠIB and see s.v. É.
enessan, enissan 'ita; as just stated'.   Friedrich, Vert. 1.73 f.
eni, enin 'is, the above-mentioned'.   Friedrich, Vert. 1.73 f.; HG 201, 207.
ˢᴬᴸEN.ME.LI; read ˢᴬᴸENSI.
EN.NU.UN 'watch, watchman'.
   EN.NU.UN MÚRUB 'the middle watch' of the night.
   É EN.NU.UN 'prison'.
ˢᴬᴸENSI 'female seer'.
enumandari (midd. pl.) 'they rest, recover'?   Sommer, BoSt. 10.45; Hrozný, AOr. 3.446.37
enumassiya (dat.) 'for appeasement'???   Sommer, BoSt. 10.45; Götze-Pedersen, MS 42 f., 49.
ēp(p)-, app- (ēpzi, pl. appanzi) 'take, occupy; marry, rape; begin'. Hrozný, SH 75, 170 f., JSOR 6.69 fn. 1; Götze, AM 283; Meillet; MSL 23.276; HG 91.
   anda e. 'pack up; take in, include'.   Götze, AM 252; Götze-Pedersen, MS 45; Friedrich, OLZ 39.306.
   appa e. 'withdraw, retire'.
   appan e. 'pursue'.   Götze, AM 282.
   arha e. 'remove'.
   parā e. 'hold out, offer'.

piran e. 'shut one off, block one's road'.
sarā e. 'raise, lift up'.
ser e. 'hold out, offer'.
ĒPIŠ (construct state of ĒPIŠU); LÚ ĒPIŠ 'maker'.
LÚ ĒPIŠ GA 'milkman, cheesemaker', or the like.
EBUR; read ŠIBIR.
er-; see *ar-* 'arrive'.
EREM, ERÉN; read ERÍN.
EREN; read ERIN.
ᴳᴵˢERIN 'cedar'.
ᴸᵁERÍN; ERÍN.MEŠ = *tuzzis* 'troups'.
ERÍN.MEŠ-*za* = *tuzziyanza* 'army'.
ᴳᴵˢ*eripisa*, an implement used in ritual; cf. *arimpas, irimpi.* Sommer, BoSt. 10.48.
ERṢETU (IR-ṢE-TUM) = *tekan* 'earth'.
ERUM 'slave'.
ERUM-ŪTU = ERUM-*atar* 'slavery'.
ERUM-*nahh-* 'enslave, subject'.
ᴰEŠ; read ᴰSIN.
ēs-, as- (*ēszi*, pl. *asanzi*) 'be, exist, amount to; be possible'; w. the particle -*be* 'remain, continue'; w. dat. *es-* denotes possession; w. the part. *es-* forms a perfect (act. if the verb is intransitive, pass. if the verb is transitive—cf. *hark-* 'have'). Hrozný, MDOG 56.28, 33, SH 78 fn. 8; Götze, AM 284; HG 88, 99, 267 f.; Pedersen, AOr. 7.82; Kurylowicz, EI 74.

ēs-, as- (*ēszi*, pl. *asanzi, esanzi*) 'set, sit; beset; do'. Götze, Madd. 100–2; HG 221 f. Cf. *ās-* 'remain'.
GAM *e.* 'settle, take up residence'. Sommer, AU 168.
parā e. 'station ahead'.

ēs-, as- (*esa, esari*, 2 sg. *estari*, pret. *esat, esati, ēstat*) without -*za* 'remain'; w. -*za* 'seat oneself; alight'. Götze, Madd. 104 f., AM 257 f., 284 (Götze separates *ēstat* from the other middle forms).
appa e. w. -*za* 'become hostile, rebellious'. But cf. Weidner, Stud. 110.
parā e. w. -*za* and acc. 'sit down before, beset, besiege; be stationed in advance'. Götze, AM 254.

É.ŠA(G)=É *tunnakkessar* 'interior'.
ᴮᴬᴸEŠERTU, a secondary wife. Götze, AOr. 2.155–9; Feigin, AJSL 50.228–34; Landsberger, AOF 10.144 f.
eses-; see *asas-*.

eseske/a-; see *esske/a-*.
eshahru (also *ishahru*) 'tears, weeping'. Friedrich, ZA NF 5.45 f. and fn. 1; HG 143.
eshahruwe/a- (pret. *ishahruit*, midd. pret. *ishahruwattat*) 'weep'. See *eshahru*.
eshanittarātar (*ishanittarātar*) '(blood) relationship'.
eshananza (*ishananza*) 'blood, murder'. Friedrich, Vert. 1.86; Götze, KlF 1.192.
ēshanuwanta [eshanwanta] 'bloody (clothes)'. Hrozný, Encyc. Brit. 603; Götze-Pedersen, MS 35 fn. 1.
ĕshar (nom. *ēshar, ishar, ēssar*, gen. *ēshanas, ēsnas*?, dat. *ēshani, ishanī*, inst. *ēshanta*) 'blood; murder'. Sommer, BoSt. 10.18; Friedrich, Real. Vorg. 1.131; HG 142 f.
ĕsharnu- (also *isharnu-*) 'make bloody'. Götze, Madd. 110.
esharnumaizzi (*isharnumaizzi*) 'makes bloody'. Sommer, BoSt. 10.18.
ēsharwēl (? *e-eš-ḫar-ú-i-il*) 'a bleeding'? KUB 9.4.2.5.
esharwēske/a- (? *iš-ḫar-ú-i-eš-ki-iz-zi*) 'bleed'? Sommer, BoSt. 10.18 fn. 3.
eshās (*ishās*, dat. *eshe*) 'master'. Zimmern, OLZ 25.297; Carruthers, Lang. 6.161; HG 88; Sommer, AF 83. See *ishassarwatar*.
eshizziya/e- (*ishizziyazi*) 'master, overpower'? Götze, AM 252 f.
ᴷᵁˢE.SIR 'shoe'.
eske/a-; see *esske/a-*.
ēslut, imper. 1 sg. of *ēs-* 'be'.
esnas, gen. of *eshar*?
esnas; see *essnas*.
esri; see *essri*.
ēssā- (*ēssāi, īssai*, pl. *ēssanzi*) 'make, do, perform, prepare; celebrate'. Götze, Hatt. 91 f.; Friedrich, ZA NF 2.51; Sommer, AU 303 f., 404; Götze-Pedersen, MS 49 f. Used as durative of *ya/e-* 'make'
essanas; see *essnas*.
essar; see *eshar* 'blood'.
essari; see *essri*.
ēsses- (pret. *ēssesta*) 'make, do, perform'. HG 230. See *essa-*.
essikir, see *esske/a-*.
ĕs(s)ke/a- (pl. *ēskanzi*, pret. pl. *eseskir, ēssikir*) act. 'make, perform, treat; finish'; midd. 'remain'. Friedrich, Vert. 2.160 and fn. 1; but cf. Götze, AOr. 2.155 fn. 2.
ĕs(s)nas (*issanas*, gen. *isnas, ēssanas*) 'dough'. Chrest. 120.
ēssri (*ēsri, ēssari*) 'form, picture, statue'. Friedrich, ZA NF 5.33 f.

ēsta = e + sta. See e-.
ět-, at-, ēz-, az- (ēzzazzi [etstsi], pl. adanzi, atānzi, 2 pl. azzasteni [atsteni], pret. pl. eter) 'eat, give to eat'. Hrozný, MDOG 56. 33 f., SH 61 f.; Götze, Madd. 126 fn. 5; HG 49, 88, 98 f., 129, 269 f.; Götze-Pedersen, MS 50; Sturtevant, Lang. 11.183 f.; Kurylowicz, EI 74.
etas 'eius'; edani 'ei'; etez 'ab eo, on that side'. Friedrich, Vert. 1.160; Götze, AM 260 f.; HG 200, 207; Kurylowicz, EI 101. Cf. edi.
ᴸᵁE.DÊ.A 'smith'.
edi (also idi) 'on that side, yonder'? Sommer, BoSt. 10.12. Cf. etas.
É.DINGIR-*LIM*; read É DINGIR-*LIM* and see s.v. É.
ētreske/a- 'feed'. Walther, HC 262.100.
ēdri, idri-ḪI.A (neut. pl.) 'kinds of food, viands'. Sturtevant, TAPA 58.22.
E.TUM; read E.ÍB.
ᴳᴵˢeya(n), a pole (?) set up as a symbol of freedom. Götze, NBr. 74 and fn. 1, AM 203 fn. 1.
ez-; see et-.
É.ZÁ(.KIŠIB); read É ZÁ(.KIŠIB) and see s.v. É.
EZEN × ŠE (some transcribe EZEN) = *ISINNU* 'festival, feast'. Cf. Sommer, AU 391.
ēzză- (ēzzāi, imper. pl. ēzzandu) 'eat, give to eat'. HG 246.
ēzzan 'food'? Chrest. 99.
ezzazzi; see et-.

ḪA; read KU₆.
ḪÁ = ḪI.A, a sign of the collective plural.
ḪA.A; read ZAḪ.
hā (1 sg. hāmi) 'trust, believe'? Hrozný, JA 218.314.
hahharsananza 'corrupted, seduced'? Götze, Madd. 129.
hahharske/a- (pret. ḫa-aḫ-ḫar-aš-ki-it) 'corrupt, seduce'? See hahharsananza.
hahhimas 'Starrheit'?? Götze, KlF 1.403 and fn. 2. 'Schwäche'?? Forrer, RHA 1.155.34.
ᵁᶻᵁhahhri- (dat. hahhari, hahri), a part of the body. Cf. Sayce, RA 24.124; Sturtevant, Lang. 4.124 f.
hahreske/a- (hahreskizzi) 'corrupt'? See hahharsananza.
*hakkunnais (pl. ᴰᵁᴳhahkunnaēs, acc. ᴰᵁᴳhakkunnaus), a vessel for oil. Hrozný, SH 23, 49.
ᴸᵁḪAL 'seer'.
ḪA.LA = *ZITTU* 'share, portion'.
    LÚ.MEŠ ḪA.LA 'sharers'; LÚ.MEŠ ḪA.LA-*ŠUNU* 'their coheirs'.

ᴷᵁˢ̌halaliya, a container for gold.   VBoT 1.15, 30.
halanta 'head'.   Hrozný, SH 43 and fn. 2.
halantuwa (dat.) = ᴱhalentuwwa.   Ehelolf, ZA NF 9.188 and fn. 1.
ᴱhalentuw(w)a, a room in a temple often used by the king and the queen. Friedrich, ZA NF 3.177 f.; Götze, Kulturg. 155.
É *halentuw(w)as*, 'house of *h*', is equivalent to *halentuwwa* alone or with determinative É.
halessiya/e- (also *halissiya/e-*) 'enclose, surround, set (a gem)'.   Ehelolf ap. Sommer, AU 186; cf. Hrozný, SH 80 fn. 1; Götze, Hatt. 65, 85, 118.
halhaltŭm(m)ari- (dat. *halhaltūmari*, pl. *halhaltummarēs*) 'corner, corner stone'??   Friedrich, ZA NF 3.191.   Perhaps 'wall'??
ḪAL.ḪI.A; read AŠ.AŠ.ḪI.A.
halihlā- (*halihlāi*, 2 sg. *halihlatti*) 'disgrace'?   Götze, Madd. 133.
*hălis (acc. *halen*, dat. *hăli*, *hăliya*) 'enclosure, halo about the moon; (temple) precinct, court; pen, corral, fold'.   Götze, Madd. 107, NBr. 67 and fn. 1; Sturtevant, JAOS 54.402, Chrest. 172; Milewski, L'Indo-Hittite et l'Indo-Européen 4 fn. 2.
NINDA *h.*, a kind of bread.   2 BoTU 23 B. 4.2; KUB 20.28.1.7.
haliske/a- (*haliskittari*) 'kneel, bow down'.   See *haliya/e-* 'kneel'.
hăliya/e- (*haliyazi*, pret. *haliyat*, *hāliyēr*, midd. *hāliya*, *hāliyari*) 'kneel, bow down'.   Ehelolf, Stud. Orient. 1.9–13; cf. Götze, Madd. 106–8. *kattan h.* 'kneel, bow down'.
haliya/e- (pl. *halienzi*) 'protect, keep'.   See *halis*.
hāliyattallās 'keeper, guardsman'.   See *halis*.
halkis 'grain'.   Hrozný, SH 12.
halkwĕssar (gen. *halkwesnas*, *halkwissanas*) 'offering, contribution'?? KUB 13.1.4.2 f.; 13.2.4.11 f.; 22.27.4.25–7 (G).
*halliyaris (pl. ᴸᵁ́·ᴹᴱˢ̌halliyarĕs, *hallēres*, *hallires*), priests of a certain kind.   Sommer, BoSt. 10.69 fn. 1.   'Singers'???   Götze, Madd. 98 fn. 1.
hallu-; see *halluwais*.
halluwa(e)- 'quarrel'.   Götze, Madd. 82 f.
*halluwais (acc. *halluwāin*, abl. *halluwaz*, *halluwayaza*) 'a quarrel'. Götze, Madd. 118.   The forms that Götze (p. 83 fn.) ascribes to the stem *hallu-* belong rather to this word.
halluwamus (pl.) 'cleft, precipitous'?? (W). Cf. Ehelolf, KlF 1.396 and fn. 1.
halluwanu- (pret. *halluwanut*, pl. *halluwanwēr*—KUB 24.7.1.32, 3.26) 'cause to quarrel'.   Götze, Madd. 82 fn. 1.

halluwātar (dat. *halluwanni*) 'anger, quarreling'. Götze, Madd. 95 and fn. 3.
halluwiske/a- 'quarrel'. Götze, Madd. 83.
ᴳᴵˢ*halmas(s)wittis*, ᴰ*h.* (nom. DAG-*tis*, acc. *halmasswittan*, dat. *halmaswitti*, DAG-*ti*) 'throne'. Ehelolf, ZA NF 2.312 f.; Friedrich, ZA NF 3.181 and fn. 5.
ᴰ*ḪALMAŠŠUIDDŪ* and ᴰ*ḪALMAŠŠUTTUM* appear to be attempts to treat the name of the deified throne as Akkadian.
ḪALṢU 'fortress'.
halugas (acc. *halugan*, dat. *haluki*) 'message; courier service, messengers'. Hrozný, SH 56, BoSt. 5.26 f.; Sturtevant, JAOS 52.8 fn. 21. Cf. Ehelolf, KlF 1.400 and fn. 4; Šmieszek, Eos 30.257–60.
ᴸᵁ́*halugatallas* 'messenger'. Hrozný, SH 56.
halwamnaz (abl.) 'with enthusiasm'?? Götze, AM 262.
halwanis, a vessel for liquids. KUB 20.35.3.9, 22.
halzāi-, halze- (*halzāi*, 1 sg. *halzihhi*, pret. *halzāis*) 'recite, pray, read'; w. *-za* 'name, call'. Hrozný, SH 40 fn. 5; Sommer, BoSt. 4.10 f., 10.58, 69; Friedrich, Vert. 1.179; Hrozný, JA 218.316. Cf. *halzessa-, halziya/e-*.
halzeske/a- 'recite, pray, read'. See *halzai-, halze-*.
halzĕs(s)a- (*halzissai, halzisai*, pl. *halzessanzi*, pret. *halzessesta*, pl. *halzessir*) 'recite, pray, read'. HG 230, 246, 286 f. See *halzai-*.
?*halzis* (or *ḪALṢU*?) 'stronghold'. Friedrich, Vert. 2.139.
halziya/e- (pl. *halziyanzi*, midd. *halziya, halziyari, halziyattari*, verb. n. gen. *halziyawas*) 'recite, pray, read'. KUB 25.15.2.4; 25.24.2.13; 25.41.5.11. See *halzai-*.
ḪALZU; read *ḪALṢU*.
hamank-, hamenk- (*hamanki*, pl. *hamankanzi, hamanganzi, haminkanzi*, part. *hamenkanza, hammenkanza*) 'bind; promise (a girl) in marriage'. Weidner, Stud. 53 f.; Sommer, AU 274, 404; Chrest. 226. Cf. Götze, Kulturg. 104.
   anda h. 'harness (horses)'.
   piran h. 'keep away, hinder'.
hamenkiske/a- (written *haminkiske/a-*) 'bind'. KBo. 3.1.3.48.
hameshanza 'spring'. Ehelolf, SBPA 1925. 267 fn. 2; Friedrich, Vert. 1.80 fn. 1; Kurylowicz, Symb. Gramm. 101. See *hameshas*.
*hameshas (acc. *hameshan*, dat. *hameshi, hamishi*) 'spring'. Götze, KlF 1.179; Benveniste, Origines de la Formation des Noms 157. See *hameshanza*.
hamik-, hamink-; see *hamank-, hamenk-*.

hān- (*hāni*) 'draw, dip'. Götze, KlF 1.201 and fn. 1.
haness- (imper. pl. *hanissandu*) 'clean, trim'? Götze, NBr. 62 f.
ᴰᵁᴳ*hānes(s)ăs* (also *hanissăs, hanisas*), a vessel for liquids. Götze, KlF 1.201 fn. 1; Sommer, AF 83; Chrest. 124.
hanessuwar 'fragments trimmed from a wall'. See *haness-*.
⁎*hanhaniyai* 'observes, is observant'? Sturtevant, JAOS 54.398.
ᴰᵁᴳ*hanissas*; read ᴰᵁᴳ*hanessas*.
hannā- (*hannāi*, pl. *hannanzi*) 'litigate, decide a law suit, judge'. Sommer, ZA 33.93 and fn. 1; HG 213, 237.
hannas 'grandmother'. Friedrich, Vert. 2.88 and fn. 2; Sturtevant, Lang. 4.163, TAPA 59.52, HG 87, 146; Kurylowicz, EI 74.
hanneske/a- (also *hanniske/a-*) 'decide a law-suit'. Friedrich, Vert. 2.160.
hannessar 'justice, court, law-suit'. Friedrich, OLZ 26.45 f.; HG 152.
hannitalwaessir 'they became opponents at law'. See *hannittalwas*.
*hannitalwatar; gen. *hannitalwanas* 'opponent at law'. Cf. Friedrich, ZA NF 3.195; Furlani, RHA 3.40. See *hannittalwas*.
hannittalwas 'opponent at law'. Götze ap. Chrest. 227.
hansatar 'family, descendants'. Götze, NBr. 14 fn. 2; Sommer, AU 136-8. Cf. Götze, AOr. 2.159-61.
handa 'according to, for the sake of'. Friedrich, IF 49.226; Götze, AM 222; HG 87. Cf. *handas*.
handă(e)- (*handăizzi*) 'establish, determine, fix; set in order, prepare; get married, cause to marry'; midd. 'be established, be determined'. Sommer, BoSt. 10.25, 31, AU 254; Götze, AM 285.

anda h. (act. and midd.) 'attach oneself to, join, make common cause'. Sommer, AU 348 f.

arahza h. (midd.) 'be reversed'.

parā h. 'rule, control' (said of a god). Chrest. 85 f., 229. Cf. Sommer, BoSt. 10.30 f. Others would translate 'bestow divine favor upon, fill with divine power' or the like. Ehelolf, Berl. Mus. Ber. 49.34; Götze, KlF 1.226, Kulturg. 138 and fn. 2.

handais 'heat'. Friedrich, IF 49.230 fn. 1.
handalliya/e- (pret. pl. *handalliyēr*) 'dare'? Götze, AM 249.
handa(n) 'really, actually; to be sure'. Götze, AM 222.
handanda- (pret. *handantĕsta*); *para h.* seems to be nearly equivalent to *parā handa(e)-*, q.v. Götze, Hatt. 60.
handandătar; *parā h.* 'numen, divine power'. Sommer, BoSt. 10.30 f.; Götze, Hatt. 52-5, 60, Kulturg. 138; Ehelolf, Berl. Mus. Ber. 49.34

fn. 3; Chrest. 85 f., 229 (in line 7 from the bottom of the page, read *handandatar*).
handas 'firm, loyal, true'. Götze, Hatt. 91-3; Sommer, AU 70, 81, 126, 160. Friedrich, IF 49.226, and Götze, AM 222, consider *handas* a variant for *handa* 'according to'.
handātar; *parā h.* is a variant for *parā handandātar*, q.v.
*handaz (gen. *handattas*) 'truth'. Götze, Madd. 79 and fn. 6.
hante/a- (*hantezzi*) = *handa(e)-*, q.v. HT 1.3.7.
hanteske/a- 'establish'. Götze, Madd. 131.
hantezzis (sometimes written IGI-*zis*) 'first'. Hrozný, SH 19-21; Götze, AOr. 2.158 fn. 2; Kurylowicz, Symb. Gramm. 101, EI 74; Pedersen, AOr. 5.180; Lohmann, IF 51.319-28; Sturtevant, HG 87, Lang. 10.268 f.
hantī 'in front, before, separately'. Sommer, AU 185-7; HG 87; Kurylowicz, EI 74. Cf. *hanti tiya/e-*; see s.v. *tiya/e-* 'take one's stand'.
hantitiyatallas; see *tiyatallas*.
hantiyā(e)- (*hantiyāizzi*? pret. 1 sg. *hantiyanun*) 'be true to; worship (a god)'? Sommer, AU 160. 'Establish, support'??? Forrer, Forsch. 1.178; Friedrich, IF 49.229; cf. Götze, KlF 1.232.
hanza (dat. *hantī*, *handa*, *handi*) 'front'. Forrer, Forsch. 1.167-9; Götze, OLZ 33.291 fn. 1; Sommer, AU 140 f.; HG 87, 172.
hanza ēp- 'receive kindly'?? Sommer, AU 140 f.
hanzan hark- 'keep the peace'?? Sommer, AU 141.
hanzassa; see *hassas* 'grandson'.
hap-; see *happ-*.
hapallasa(e)- (*hapallasaizzi*) 'break'. Hrozný, Encyc. Brit. 602.
*hapātis (acc. *hapātin*) 'vassal'. Götze, Madd. 98, 105 f.; Sturtevant Lang. 4.164, HG 88, 146; Sapir, Lang. 10.274-9.
hapatiya/e- 'obey'. See *hapatis*.
hapiriyas; see *happiris*.
LÚ*ḪABIRU* 'robber; Bedouin'. Landsberger, KlF 1.321-34.
happ- (midd. pret. *haptat*, verb. n. *happuwar*) 'be joined (to)'? KUB 21.27.1.12 (G).
happar 'price, purchase money'. Götze, Lang. 11.268 f.
   h. ya/e- 'make a price, perform a business transaction'.
happarā(e)-, *happirā(e)-*, usually preceded by *-za*, 'sell'. Friedrich, Vert. 1.92-4; Sturtevant, Lang. 5.11; Friedrich, OLZ 39.308.
   parā h. 'sell'.
happarius (acc. pl.) 'price'? Friedrich, Vert. 1.93 fn. 1. Otherwise Hrozný, CH 120.21; Walther, HC 266.146.

happariya/e- (pret. 1 sg. *happarienun*) 'surrender, give over'?? Friedrich, Vert. 1.93.

happarranzi (3 pl.) 'they pronounce (judgment)'?? Friedrich, Vert. 1.93.

happesna(e)- (3 pl. *happesnanzi*, part. *happesnanza*) 'dismember'. Götze ap. Chrest. 121. See *happessar*.
  arha h. 'cut into bits'.

*happessar (dat. pl. *happisnas*) 'joint, member, part of the body'. KUB 9.4.1.18-21 (G).

happina (dat.), *happinit* (inst.) 'fire' or 'heat' or a cooking utensil. Friedrich, ZA NF 1.178.

happinahh- (imper. 2 sg. *happinahhi*) 'make powerful'?? KBo. 2.9.1.35.

happinanza 'powerful'?? KUB 24.8.1.11.

happira(e)-; see *happara(e)-*.

**hăp(p)iris* (nom. URU-*as*! gen. URU-*yas*, *hapiriyas*? dat. *hăppiri*, URU-*ri*) 'town, city; subdivision of a city, district'. Götze, KlH 31 fn. 2, AOr. 5.17 and fn. 1, AM 50.29; Götze-Pedersen, MS 72.
  LÚ.MEŠ *hapiriyas* 'merchants' or 'townsmen'? Cf. Sturtevant, JAOS 54.404.

hăpusas (pl.) 'stalks, stems, trunks'?? Götze, AOr. 5.11.

hapus(s)- (pl. *hapus(s)anzi*, imper. *hapusdu*) 'repeat (a neglected ceremony)'. Götze, AM 201 and fn. 8.

ḪAR 'ring'.

ᴳᴵˢḪAR 'symbol, document, list, inventory'.

har-; see *har(k)-*.

harak-; see *hark-*.

harakzel; see *harkzel*.

hăras (gen. *hăranas*, acc. *hăranan*) 'eagle'. Friedrich, ZA NF 5.64; Mudge, Lang. 7.252 f.; Sommer, AU 318 fn. 2; HG 93, 184.

harassanaza; see *harssan*.

harătar (inst. *haranet*) 'punishment'?? Hrozný, CH 144.29. 'Crime'?? Sommer, BoSt. 10.44 f.

ᶻᴬḪAR.ḪAR; read ᶻᴬARÀ.

ᴰᵁᴳ*harharān*, a vessel for beverages. KBo. 3.34.2.1; KUB 10.60.4.

ᴳᴵˢ*hariuzzi* (dat.) 'on a wicker table'. Eheloff, ZA NF 9.172.

hăriyas 'valley'. Götze, Kulturg. 149 and fn. 5.

har(k)- (*harzi*, 3 pl. *harkanzi*) 'have'; w. part. (acc. sg. neut.) *har(k)-* forms perfects and pluperfects, chiefly from transitive verbs (cf. *es-*, *as-* 'be'). Sommer, BoSt. 7.7 and fn. 2; Götze, AM 285 f.; HG 220, 268, 272 f.; Götze-Pedersen, MS 50; Sturtevant, Lang. 11.41.

appa h. 'occupatum habere'.
pē h. 'have with one; carry'. Götze, Hatt. 83 f.; Sturtevant, Lang. 7.5-9, HG 90.
arha pē h. 'carry away'.
sarā pē h. 'carry up'.
hark- (*harakzi*, pl. *harkanzi*) 'be destroyed, be lost'. Friedrich, ZA NF 2.50, IF 49.224; Götze, NBr. 27 fn. 1; Sommer, AU 24-8; Cuny, RHA 2.205; HG 232 and fn. 34; Götze-Pedersen, MS 50.
harganu- 'destroy'. Friedrich, Vert. 2.163; Götze, NBr. 8-10; Sommer, AU 27 f.; HG 236.
arha h. 'destroy utterly'.
katta h. 'destroy utterly'.
?*kattan arha h.* 'destroy utterly'.
hargas 'destruction, ruin'. Götze, NBr. 9 f.; Sommer, AU 26 f.
*harkatar (gen. *harkannas*, dat. *harkanna*) 'destruction'. HG 151, 166.
harkēs- (*harkēszi*) 'become white'. HG 231. See *harkis*.
harkis 'white'. Friedrich, ZA NF 3.184 f.; Kurylowicz, Symb. Gramm. 101; EI 74; HG 87; Götze-Pedersen, MS 50.
harkiske/a- (pl. *harkiskantari*) 'be destroyed'. Cf. *hark-*.
harkiya/e- 'be destroyed'. KUB 17.10.1.18. Cf. *hark-*.
harkzel (*harakzi*[*l*]) 'destruction'. 2 BoTU 10 β 31. Cf. *hark-*; HG 156.
harnā- (part. *harnān*) 'ferment'. Friedrich, ZA NF 1.176.
harnāis (acc. *harnāin*) 'pertaining to the birth-chair'? KUB 9.22.2.31; but cf. 9.22.2.28. Cf. HG 169.
harnammar 'yeast' (originally 'fermentation'). Friedrich, ZA NF 1.176; Chrest. 122 (on 3.7).
harnamniya/e- 'ferment, instigate'? Friedrich, Vert. 1.154 f.
kattan h. 'corrupt, make rebellious'.
harnāus (acc. *harnāu*, gen. *harnāwwas*, dat. *harnāu, harnāwi*) 'birth-chair'. Sommer, BoSt. 10.3 f.; Cuny, REAn. 32.311 f.; HG 168, 171 f., 181 f.
harnenk- (*harnikzi*, pret. 1 sg. *harninkun*, imper. pl. *harnenkandu*) 'destroy'. Götze, ZA 34.186, Hatt. 72; HG 232, 274 and fn. 116.
arha h. 'destroy utterly'.
harnenkiske/a- (written *harninkiske-*) 'destroy, devastate'. See *harnenk-*.
harnik-, harnink-; see *harnenk-*.
harp- (*harapzi*, pl. *harpănzi*), act. 'join, cause to unite'; midd. 'unite, be associated, agree, help'. Hrozný, CH 58.52, 108 fn. 9; Götze ap.

Chrest. 226. Cf. Friedrich, ZA NF 1.175 and fn. 3; Sommer, AU 382 fn. 4; HG 130, 213; Couvreur, Hitt. *h* 13.

harpanallis (*harpanalli*[*s*], acc. pl. *harpanallius*) 'enemy'??? Friedrich, ZA NF 1.175. Rather 'conspirator'? See *harpus*.

harpiske/a- 'join'. KUB 27.16.4.26.

harpiya/e- = *harp-*. Götze, KlF 1.409 fn. 2.

*harpus (acc. pl. *harpus*, neut. *harpu*) 'hostile'??? Friedrich, ZA NF 1.175. 'Joined, conspirator'; neut. 'conspiracy'? Cf. *harp-*.

harră- (*harrai*, pl. *harranzi*, part. *harrănza*) 'break, pulverize; ruin; make harmful'. Friedrich, ZA NF 1.16, 179, Altorient. Stud. 53.

harran 'destroyed'; inserted in a text to indicate that the corresponding portion of the copy was illegible. Forrer, ZDMG 76.181; Friedrich, Vert. 2.105, 144.

harranis (nom. *harranes*, acc. *harranin*), a kind of bird. Sommer, AU 318 fn. 2.

harranu-, *harranuske/a-* 'pulverize'. Friedrich, ZA NF 1.16, 164.23, 179 f.

hars- (*haraszi*, infin. *harsuwanzi*) 'spade, hoe, harrow', or the like. Götze, NBr. 62.

harsal(l)anza 'angry'. Hrozný, SH 86; Holma, JSFO 33.30 f.

harsanalanzi 'they crown, wreathe'; *harsan(n)al(l)anza* 'wreathed'. See *harssan-*.

harsanalli (dat.) 'wreath'. See *harssan-*.

harsanas; see *harssan-*.

harsiharsi (gen. *harsiharsiyas*) 'thunder-storm'. Götze-Pedersen, MS 16 f., 50 f.; Sturtevant, Lang. 11.39 f., 41.

harsis 'ordinary, usual'. Götze, KlF 1.199 f.

harsiske/a-, durative from *hars-*, q.v.

^{LÚ}*harsiyal(l)as* 'sacrificer of ordinary offerings'. Götze, KlF 1.200.

**harsiyal(l)is* (gen. *harsiyalliyas*, abl. *harsiyallaz*, pl. *harsiyalliyas*) 'pertaining to, suitable for a sacrificer'. Cf. Götze, KlF 1.238.8; Lang. 10.272 f.

^{DUG}*harsiyal(l)i* 'a sacrificer's vessel', a technical term in the rituals.

harssan- or *hurssan-* (gen. *harsanas*, dat. *harsani*, abl. *harassanaza*, *harsanaza*) 'head'. Götze, ZA NF 2.265; Friedrich, ZA NF 2.275.

harsanas aggatar 'death penalty'. Chrest. 152.11.

harsanas wastul 'capital crime'. Chrest. 156.16.

?*hartuwas* 'great-great-grandchild'?? Cf. Forrer, AJSL 48.167; Meriggi, RHA 2.23.

*harwāsis; *harwāsī pēdan* 'a secret place, secrecy'. Cf. Sommer, BoSt. 7.40 fn. 2, 45; Ehelolf, KlF 1.146 fn. 6.

has-; see *hass-*.
hās (acc. *hassan*) 'soap'? Friedrich, Vert. 1.166, ZA NF 3.191.
hāsaw(w)as 'of opening' or 'of bearing'. See *hass-* 'open', *hass-* 'bear'. SAL *h.* (also analogical acc. SAL *hāsawan*) 'midwife'? Sayce, RA 24.123. 'Woman in child-birth'??? Forrer, RHA 1.157.44.
hashass- (part. *hashassan*, verb. n. *hashasswar*) 'open'. Götze, AOr. 5.36; HG 214. See *hass-* 'open'.
ᴳᴵˢḪAŠḪUR, a kind of palm. Cf. Deimel, No. 146.
ᴳᴵˢḪAŠḪUR KUR.RA 'pomegranate'?
haske/a- 'bear'. Ehelolf. OLZ 36.5. See *hass-* 'bear'.
haske/a- 'open'. See *hass-* 'open'.
haske/a-; see *hasske/a-* 'decide a law-suit'.
haske/a-; see *hasskke/a-* 'sate oneself'.
⁕*hasp(a)-* (pret. 1 sg. *haspaha*, pl. *haspir*) 'destroy'. Götze, Madd. 118 f.; Sommer, AU 71; Güterbock, ZA NF 9.325.
hăs(s)- (*hāsi*, pret. *hasta*, part. *hassanza*) 'bear, beget'. Sommer, BoSt. 7.6-11.
hăs(s)-, *hēs-* (*hāsi*, pl. *hassanzi*, *hēsanzi*, part. *hassanza*, verb. n. gen. *hēsuwas*) 'open'. Ehelolf, KlF 1.141 fn. 2, 395 fn. 5; Friedrich, ZA NF 3.298 and fn. 7, AOF 5.108; HG 240.
hassa- (acc. *hassan*, gen. *hassas*, dat. *hassī*) 'hearth, stove'. Sommer, Bost. 10.24 fn. 3.
hassa; see *hassas* 'grandson'.
hassan; see *has* 'soap'?
hassana- (acc. *hassanan*, dat. *hassanai*) 'family'. KBo. 3.1.2.49, KUB 11.1.4.23. See *hassatar*.
hassannasas (acc. *hassannasan*) 'member of the (royal) family'? Chrest. 199.
[*hass*]*antis* 'family'? Götze, NBr. 48.16.
hassas 'grandson'. Forrer, Altorient. Stud. 31; Friedrich, Vert. 2.36 f. *hassa hanzassa* 'grandson and great-grandson'? HG 167. Cf. Götze, Madd. 43, AOr. 2.162 f.
has(s)ātar (gen. *hassannas*) 'reproduction; kin, family'. Sommer, BoSt. 7.8 f. Cf. Götze, AOr. 2. 159-61; Sommer, AU 136 f.
hassike/a-; see *hasske/a-* 'decide a law-suit'.
hassikkanu-; see *hasskkanu-*.
hassik(k)e/a-; see *hasskke/a-* 'sate oneself'.
hasske/a- (imper. *hassikandu*) 'decide a law-suit'. Ehelolf, OLZ 29.989.
hasskkanu- (pret. *hassiqqanut*) 'cause to sate oneself, soak (the earth with rain)'. KUB 25.23.4.59.
hassk(k)e/a- (pret. *hassikkir*) 'sate oneself'. Ehelolf, KlF 1. 137-42.

hassus (LUGAL-*us*) 'king'. Hrozný, BoSt. 3.99 fn. 15; Sommer, BoSt. 7.9 fn. 2; Götze-Pedersen, MS 57.
hassuwe/a- (pret. *hassuwēt*, LUGAL-*wēt*) 'become king'. Friedrich, ZA NF 2.276. See *hassus*.
hassuwezna(e)- (pret. LUGAL-*wiznanun*) 'be king, rule'. Götze, AM 253.
hassuwĕznas (LUGAL-*wĕznas*) 'ruler'? or 'kingship'??? Cf. Götze, AM 253.
*hassuwĕznatar (dat. LUGAL-*wĕznanni*) 'kingship'. See *hassuwezna(e)-*
hassuwezziya/e- (LUGAL-*izziyat*, midd. pret. 1 sg. LUGAL-*izziyahhat*, LUGAL-*izziyahhahat*) 'become king'. See *hassuwezna(e)-*.
hastăi (gen. *hastiyas*, inst. *hastiyit, hastit*, pl. *hastae*—KUB 17.28.1.23— G) 'bone; strength, force'. Sommer, AU 181; Benveniste, BSL 33. 139; HG 93, 180; Götze, AM 240 f.; Kurylowicz, EI 112, 255.
hastiyas per 'mausoleum'. Chrest. 82. 75.
hastiyet 'with firmness'. Sommer, AU 181.
ᴳᴵˢ*hasdwĕr* (also *hasdwir*) 'branches'. Sturtevant, TAPA 58.23, Chrest. 123 f.
hăt- (*hazzizzi* [hatstsi], pret. *hăzzasta* [hatst], 3 pl. *hăter*) 'dry up, wither'. Götze, Madd. 126 and fnn. 3, 4; HG 129, 269.
ᴳᴵˢ*hatalkessar* (*hatalkis*<*sar*>, gen. *hatalkesnas, hatalkisnas*) 'stick'. Chrest. 120 f. Cf. Güterbock, OLZ 35. 721.
hatalwa(e)- (imper. pl. *hatalwandu*) 'bolt (a door)'. See *hattalu*.
hatalwalas; see *hattalwalas*.
hatalwas; see *hattalu*.
ᴸᵁ*ḪATĀNU, ḪATNU* 'son-in-law, wife's relative'.
hatk- (*hatki*) 'close'. Sommer, BoSt. 7.1-6; Sturtevant, Lang. 6.218, HG 117.
hatganu- 'shut in, oppress'. Friedrich, ZA NF 1.16; HG 236.
hatkesnu- (*hatkisnuzzi*, 1 sg. *hatkesnumi*) 'shut in, oppress'. Sommer, BoSt. 7.2-5.
anda h. 'invest, blockade'.
ᴸᵁ*ḪATNU*; see *ḪATĀNU*.
hatnu- 'cause to dry up'. VBot 58.1.8. See *hat-*.
hatră(e)- (pret. *hatrāit*, 2 sg. *hatrāes*, imper. 2 sg. *hatrăi*) 'send (word), write'. Hrozný, SH 71 fn. 3; Meriggi, OLZ 36.76 fn. 2; HG 282.
appa h. 'write back, answer'.
hatreske/a- 'send (word), write'. See *hatra(e)-*.
hatressar 'message, order'. Hrozný, SH 71; HG 152.
hatriyassar 'message, order'. Götze, Hatt. 94; HG 152.

hattă- (*haddāi*, pl. *hattanzi*, midd. *hatta*, pl. *hattanta*) 'pierce, stick, stab; butcher'. Friedrich, ZA NF 3.186 f.
hattalas 'moonlight'??? Forrer, JA 217.242.
ᴳᴵˢ*hat(t)alu* (gen. *hattalwas, hatalwas*) 'bolt (of a door)'. Friedrich, ZA NF 3.181 f., 5.48 f., 49 fn. 1; Sommer, OLZ 33.755. Cf. *hatalwa(e)-*.
ᴸᵁ́*hat(t)alwalas*, ᴳᴵˢ*hatalwalas* 'doorkeeper'. (Originally gen. of the prec. ?) Sommer, AU 50.
hattannir (pret. pl.) w. double acc. 'they struck (one) with (something)', or the like. KBo. 3.34.1.3 f.
hattăta (*hattata-smet, hattada-met*) = *hattatar*.
hattatar (gen. *hattannas, haddannas*) 'wisdom'? Sommer, BoSt. 10.4 fn. 1; cf. Götze, Hatt. 54 fn. 2, 119; Friedrich, ZA NF 3.186 f.
**hattessar* (abl. *hattesnaz*, dat. pl. *hattesnas*) 'hole, den'. Forrer ap. Kretschmer, KlF 1.310 fn. 2; Friedrich ap. Porzig, KlF 1.382 fn. 3. Cf. *hatta-*.
ᵁᴿᵁ*Hattīli* 'in Hattic'. Götze, Madd. 53 and fn. 5; HG 28, 160.
hattīyaniya/e- 'assemble'?? KBo. 3.7.1.13 (G).
hattulahmi 'I make well'. Forrer, JA 217.242.
hattulătar (also *haddulatar*) 'health'. Sommer, ZA 33.99 fn. 1; Forrer, JA 217.242.
hattules- (pret. *hattulista* 'become well'). Forrer, JA 217.242; HG 232.
?**hattus* (Hattic; cf. ᵁᴿᵁ*Hattusas*) 'silver'. Hrozný, SH 60 fn. 1; Forrer, JA 217.242; Sommer, AF 55.
ᵁᴿᵁ*Hattusas* (also ᵁᴿᵁKUBABBAR-*sas*) (1) the name of the Hittite capital; (2) 'Hittite'. Götze, Hatt. 136. See *hattus*.
hatuga; see *hatukis*.
hatugătar 'frightfulness'. See *hatukis*.
hadukes- (*hadukiszi*) 'become terrible'. See *hatukis*.
**hatukis* (dat. *hatugaya, hatuga*, pl. *hatugaēs*) 'terrible'. Friedrich, ZA NF 3. 189 f.; Götze-Pedersen, MS 17 f., 18 fn. 2, 50 f.; Sapir, Lang. 12, No. 3.
hatugaya, hatuga 'terribly'.
hazilas; see *hazzilas*.
ḪAZINNU 'axe'.
hazke/a-; see *hazzke/a-*.
hazzasta, hazzizzi; see *hat-* 'dry up'.
hazzike/a-; see *hazzke/a-*.
haz(z)ilas 'handful'? Götze, KlF 1.228 fn. 4; cf. Hrozný, AOr. 3.447 and fn. 17.
hazzis 'dry'? Sturtevant, Lang. 10.270 f. Cf. *hat-*.

hazziske/a-; see *hazzke/a-*.

hazziya/e- 'cut, write (on a clay tablet); kill'. Sommer, BoSt. 7.57; Hrozný, AOr. 1.278.51. Cf. *hatta-* 'pierce'.

hazzizziyas 'of dryness'? Sturtevant, Lang. 10.270 f. Cf. *hat-*.

haz(z)ke/a- [hatske-] (*hazzikizzi*, pl. *hazikanzi, hazziskanzi*) 'play (a musical instrument)'. Götze, Hatt. 101 and fn. 2.

ᶻᴬ*hekur* (also *hegur*) 'summit, peak; stronghold'. Sommer, AU 317 f.

ᴱ*hēlas* (also *hīlas*) 'forecourt' or 'antechamber' of a temple. Friedrich, ZA NF 3.179-81; Sommer, AF 84.

henk- (*hinikizi, hingazi, hikzi*, pret. *henikta, hinikta, hingata*, midd. *hinga, hingari, hinkatta*) 'fix, assign, devote; fasten (a door)'; act. and especially midd. 'devote oneself, show reverence'. Sommer, BoSt. 10.27 f.; HG 116, 273 and fn. 114; cf. Götze-Pedersen, MS 33-8, 51; Chrest. 228.

appa h. 'determine finally'.

appan h., act. or midd., 'determine, give a signal, show reverence'. Götze-Pedersen, MS 34 f.

henkan (more often *hinkan, hingan*) 'fate, death; pestilence'. Friedrich, ZA NF 1.19 f.; Kurylowicz, Symb. Gramm. 101; HG 148 f.; Couvreur, Hett. *h* 14; Pedersen, Hirt Festschr. 2.381 fn. 1. See *henk-*.

henganu- (written *hinganu-*) 'cause to show reverence'. Götze-Pedersen, MS 36.

hes-; see *hass-* 'open'.

heske/a- (1 sg. *hesikēmi*) 'open'. Götze, KlF 1.189. See *hass-, hes-*.

heus, hewwas; see *heyus*.

hēyawwaneske/a- (pret. *heyawwanes[kit]*) 'to rain'. Friedrich, Vert. 2.33. See *heyawwatar, heyus*.

hĕyūs (*hēūs*, acc. *hĕūn, heyūn*, gen. *hĕyawwas, hēwwas*, pl. *hēuēs*) 'rain'. Friedrich, Vert. 2.32-6, 166; HG 53, 55, 111.

?*hēyuwaneske/a-* (pret. *hēuwaneski[t]*) 'to rain'. See *heyawwaneske/a-, heyus*.

ḪI.A, sign of a (collective or impersonal) pl.; sometimes appended even to Akkadian and Hittite words.

ḪI.ḪI 'producing lightning'? Friedrich, Vert. 2.101 f.

hik-; see *henk-*.

ḪI.GA; read DÚG.GA.

hikanni, dat. of *henkan*.

ᴱ*hilammar* (dat. *hilamni, hilamna*), a porch or anteroom at the outer door of a temple. Friedrich, ZA NF 3.179 f.; Götze, AM 204 fn. 1, Kulturg. 155. Cf. *hilatar*.

hilamnanza 'all the *hilammar*'.   Cf. Friedrich, ZA NF 3.299 and fn. 2.

hilas; see *helas*.

*hilatar (gen. *hilannas*) 'door-yard'?   Hrozný, CH 66.13, 67 fn. 23, 70.26. Cf. *hilammar*.

himma- (acc. *himman*, gen. *himmas*, dat. *himmi*, pl. *himmus*), a kind of sacrifice.   KUB 24.3.1.24 (G).   Cf. Friedrich, ZA NF 1.187.

hink-; see *henk-*.

hingan; see *henkan*.

hinganiyawar 'dance, merry-making'.   Sommer, BoSt. 10.28.

$^{LÚ}hipparas$ 'captive'.   Walther, HC 256.48 f.; Feigin, AJSL 50.228.

^{É}ḪI.UŠ.SA; read É ḪI.UŠ.SA.

^{DUG}ḪI.UŠ.SA; read DUG ḪI.UŠ.SA.

hiyaras 'pertaining to rain'??   Chrest. 169.

ḪU; read MUŠEN.

ḪU × A; read ŠE$_{12}$.

huek-; see *hwek-*.

huelpis; see *hwelpis*.

huenu-; see *huwenu-*.

hues-; see *hwes-*.

hueske/a-; see *hweske/a-*.

huesus; see *hwesus*.

hueswa(e); see *hweswa(e)-*.

huhhahannis 'grandfather and grandmother'.   Friedrich, AOF 4.95; HG 145, 165.

huhhantes 'forefathers'.   Friedrich, Vert. 2.88.

*huhhartis (acc. $^{UZU}huhhartin$) 'throat'???   Sayce, RA 24.124; cf. Sturtevant, Lang. 4.124.

huhhas 'grandfather'.   Friedrich, Vert. 2.88 and fn. 2, 168; Sturtevant, Lang. 9. 278 f.; Pedersen, AOr. 5.183–6; HG 101; Kurylowicz, EI 74.

⸘*huhhupas* 'neutral'.   KUB 26.12.2.8 (G).

ḪU + ḪI; read MUD.

hūhūpal, a musical instrument.   Götze, Hatt. 101 and fn. 3.

huik-; see *hwek-*.

huinu-; see *huwenu-*.

huis-; see *hwes-*.

huisas; see *hwisas*.

huisnu-; see *hwesnu-*.

huisnuske/a-; see *hwesnuske/a-*.

huisus; see *hwesus*.

huiswa(e); see *hweswa(e)-*.
huiswatar; see *hweswatar*.
huitar; see *hwitar*.
huittiya/e-; see *hwittiya/e-*.
huittiyanna-; see *hwittiyanna-*.
huittiyanneske/a-; see *hwittiyanneske/a-*.
huiya/e-; see *huwiya/e-*.
huk-; see *hwek-*.
ḪU.GAG; read MUŠEN.DÙ.
huk(k)eske/a- 'conjure, charm, cure'. See *hwek-, huk-*.
hŭkmăis 'magic, incantation'. Friedrich, ZA NF 4.188 fn. Cf. *hwek-, huk-*.
?*hukmattalas* (pl. ᴸᵁ̂·ᴹᴱˢ*hukmattal[es]*) 'magician, sorcerer'. See *hukmais*.
ḪUL = *idalus* 'bad'.
ḪUL- = *idalawahh-* 'injure'.
ḪUL = *idalawes-* 'become bad'.
*hūlalēssar (dat. *hūlalēsni*) 'ligament, band'. Ehelolf, Berl. Mus. Berichte 49.34.
hŭlăli 'band, winding sheet'. Sommer, BoSt. 10.72; Sturtevant, Lang. 4.164.
ᴳᴵˢ*hŭlăli* 'distaff'. Sommer, BoSt. 10.72; Götze, Madd. 98; Sturtevant, Lang. 4.164.
hŭlăliya/e- 'wrap, wind'. Sommer, BoSt. 10.72; Madd. 98; HG 225.
hulhuliya/e- 'fight' (intransitive?). Delaporte, Voc.; HG 214. Cf. Weidner, Stud. 115; 2 BoTU 14α 12.
hŭllă- (*hullāi*, pret. *hullis*, pl. *hullumen*) 'smite, destroy, annul'. Sommer, BoSt. 10.68 f.; HG 218 f., 231. Couvreur, Hett. *h* 14, 24 f. Cf. *hulle/a-, hulliya/e-*.
hullanzais 'battle'. Cavaignac, RHA 1.12; Chrest. 186.19.
hullanzan (acc.) 'battle'? KBo. 3.22.1.11. Cf. Hrozný, AOr. 1.276.
hullas- (midd. pret. *hullasat*) midd. 'be defeated'. Götze, AM 287, AOr. 5.2.
hŭlle/a- (*hūllazzi*, pret. *hullit*, 1 sg. *hullănun*, pl. *hullir*) 'smite, destroy, annul'. See *hulla-*.
hulli, hullis, something sacrificed upon bread. Sommer, BoSt. 10.68 f.
hulliske/a- 'smite, destroy, annul'. Götze, AM 130.60.
hŭlliya/e- (*hūlliyazzi*, pret. *hulliyat, hulliyet*) 'smite, destroy, annul'. See *hulla-*.
huldalā (pret. 1 sg. *huldalānun*) 'respect, honor, preserve, spare (a temple in a captured town)'. Cf. Götze, AM 263.

ᴳᴵᏚḫūlugannis (acc. ḫūlukannin, ḫūlugannin, abl. ḫuluganaz) 'litter'? Sommer, AU 81 and fn. 2.

hūmanza (rarely human etc.) 'whole, all, every'. Hrozný, SH 83 f.; Götze, AM 287; HG 188 f.; Couvreur, Hett. h 14, 24 f.

    hūmandaz 'completely'.

⋆ḫūmma (nom. or dat.?) 'pig-sty'. Götze, Hatt. 101; Chrest. 97.

ḫūnenk- (ḫūnikzi, part. ḫūninkanza, ḫūnikanza, midd. ḫūniktari) 'cause to be bewitched'. HG 233 and fn. 35, 274 and fn. 116.

hunhuessar; see hwnhwessar.

hunhuwanas; see hwnhwatar.

huntariya(e)- or huntariya/e- (midd. huntariyaitta) midd. 'fart'? KUB 17.28.2.8 (G).

hūnu-; read huwenu-. HG 59.

hupala-; see huppala-.

hūpp- (pret. hūppir) 'hold, fasten'. HG 222, Chrest. 121.

    anda h. 'pile together, heap up'.

⋆ḫūp(p)ala- (acc. huppalan, abl. hūpalaza) 'net'? Sommer, BoSt. 10.56, AU 260.

ᴰᵁᴳḫūppar (gen. hūpparas) 'large jar'. Sommer, BoSt. 10.19, 40; HG 183.

ḪUPPI (pl.), a valuable metal part of a garment, especially of the ritual garment of the priest-king. (G).

ᴳᴵᏚhūppulli 'chair'?? Walther, HC 269.171.

ᴸᵁhupralas 'potter'?? Witzel, JSOR 9.124.

huprus (pl. acc.), name of an article of clothing? Götze, Kulturg. 115 fn. 2.

ḫūprushis, a cult object, possibly a temporary altar. Sommer, BoSt. 10.25; Götze-Pedersen, MS 43.

ᴰᵁᴳḫūpuwāi, a kind of small cup. Witzel, HKU 106.

ḪUR; read ḪAR.

ḫūrkel (also hurkil) 'death penalty'? Götze, ZA NF 2. 255 fn. 1.

ᵁᴿᵁHurlas 'Hurrian, Hurrite'. Götze, Madd. 53, and fn. 3, Kulturg. 57 fn. 2; Sommer, AU 42–8.

Hurlili 'in Hurrian, in Hurrite'. See Hurlas.

hurn- (pl. hurnanzi, infin. hurnwanzi) (1) 'hunt (wild animals)'; (2) 'sprinkle'? Ehelolf, KlF 1.146–50. Cf. hurniya/e-, hurnu-.

*hurnāis (acc. hurnāin) 'spray' or the like. KUB 10.91.2.10; HG 147.

ᵁᶻᵁhurnius if pl. acc., 'arms'?? If sg. nom., 'penis'?? Friedrich, ZA NF 5.37.

hurniya/e- 'sprinkle'? See hurn-.

hurnu- 'sprinkle'? See hurn-.

*_Hurris_; GUD _Hurrin_ (acc.), a divine bull. Götze, Kulturg. 133 and fn. 3.

ḪURRU 'cave'.

MUŠEN _ḪURRI_; see s.v. MUŠEN.

ḪUR.SAG 'mountain'; also a determinative before names of mountains.

hurssan-, a possible transliteration for _harssan_-.

hurta-; see _hwrta_-.

hurtais; see _hwrtais_.

hurzake/a-; see _hwrzke/a_-.

ᴷᵁˢ_hŭsan_, a part of a harness or a kind of harness. Hrozný, CH 64.3, 114.9; Walther, HC 260.78, 265.125.

hŭske/a- 'await'. Ungnad, OLZ 26.572 and fn. 3; Friedrich, Vert. 1.170; HG 54; Kurylowicz, EI 74. Cf. Götze-Pedersen, MS 51. Cf. _hweske/a_-, _hwes_-.

hŭsselli- (dat. _hŭssiliya_, abl. _hŭsselliyaz_), some kind of a field or garden. Walther, HC 263.110.

hūswandus (KBo. 3.55.2.8); read _hweswandus_. HG 58–60; cf. Friedrich, Vert. 2.167.

hūdāk 'immediately, at once'. Hrozný, SH 180; Sommer, BoSt. 7.15 fn. 2.

⁎_hūtas_ 'agility, activity (in battle)'?? Sommer, AU 324 f.

ᴰᵁᴳ_hūtnikkis_, a vessel that may contain honey. Sommer. BoSt. 10.8*. 45, 83.

ˢᴵᴳ_huttulli_ (dat. _huddulli_, inst. _huddullit_) 'fleece'. Sturtevant, TAPA 58.21, Chrest. 123.

huwăi-, _huwa(e)_- (_huwăi_, _huwwăi_, _huwwaizzi_, pl. _huwwanzi_) 'flee, run, go, march'. Hrozný, SH 30 f., BoSt. 3.175 fn. 11; Götze, ZA 34.1.177 f.; HG 94, 223, 234, 237. See _huwiya/e_-.
    appan h. 'go behind, hinder'.
    piran h. 'go ahead of, help'.

huwăi- (_huwāi_, pret. _huwaīs_) 'grow'. Friedrich, ZA NF 1.182; KUB 17.10.1.13 (W).

huwal(i)yar 'luxuriant growth'. Weidner, Stud. 67; Götze, ZA 34.188.

huwaliyazi (written _huwalyaz[i]_) 'grows luxuriantly'. See _huwaliyar_.

huwallis (pl.) 'glowing coals'? KUB 7.53.2.26 + 12.58.2.1. Cf. _huwwallissananza_.

huwanhuessar; see _hwnhwessar_.

*_huwantas_ (gen. _huwandas_, pl. _huwwantes_, acc. _huwwadus_) 'wind'. Forrer, ZDMG 76.244; Mudge, Lang. 7.253; HG 97; Sommer, AF 84 f.; Kurylowicz, EI 74 f.

huwanzi; see _huwai_ and _huwwa_-.

huwapp- (1 sg. *huwappahhi*, 2 sg. *huwapti*) 'be malicious' or the like. Götze, Hatt. 119, Madd. 143; Chrest. 89.

huwappas (acc. *huwappan*, dat. *huwwappi, huwappi*) 'malicious'. Hrozný, SH 40.

huwappinanza 'malicious'. Götze, ZA 34.188.

huwappiske/a- 'be malicious'. KUB 21.17.1.9.

huwarta-; see *hwrta-*.

^{ZA}*huwǎsi* (commonly *huwwǎsi*), a cult object of stone. Götze, Kulturg. 158; Chrest. 99. 'Statue'??

huwek-; see *hwek-*.

huwelpis; see *hwelpis*.

huwenu- (*huwinuzi*, pl. *hwinuwwanzi*) 'cause to flee, run, go, march'. Sommer, BoSt. 10.8 fn. 1; Friedrich, Vert. 1.77; HG 58–60, 234, 237. See *huwai-*.

huwes-; see *hwes-*.

huwesus; see *hwesus*.

huweswa(e)-; see *hweswa(e)-*.

huwigatar; see *hwegatar*.

huwinu-; see *huwenu-*.

huwis-; see *hwes-*.

huwisa-; see *hwesa-*.

huwisas; see *hwesas*.

huwissuwe/a-; see *hweswe/a-*.

huwisus; see *hwesus*.

huwiswa(e)-; see *hweswa(e)-*.

huwitar; see *hwitar*.

huwittiya/e-; see *hwittiya/e-*.

huwittiyanna-; see *hwittiyanna-*.

huwittiyanneske/a-; see *hwittiyaneske/a-*.

huwiya/e- (*huwiyazi*, 1 sg. ⁎*huwiyami*, pl. *huwiyanzi, huyanzi*) = *huwāi-* 'flee, run, go, march', q.v. HG 56 and fn. 46.

huwiyatallas; ^{LÚ}*piran huwiyatallas* 'helper'. Götze, Hatt. 119. Cf. *huwai-*.

huwwa- (pl. *huwwanzi*) 'wait, await'??? Götze-Pedersen, MS 51. Rather this is the 3 pl. of *huwai-* 'march'.

huwwai-; see *huwai-*.

huwwallissananza 'glowing'? Eheolf, KlF 1.400. Cf. *huwallis*

huwwanhwesar; see *hwnhwessar*.

huwwandus; see *huwantas*.

huwwappas; see *huwappas*.

huwwarta-; see *hwrta-*.
huwwarzake/a-; see *hwrzke/a-*.
huwwasi; see *huwasi*.
huwwadus; variant for *huwwandus*.
huya/e-; read *huwiya/e-*.
hwĕk-, hŭk- (*hwikzi, hwēkzi, huwĕkzi, hukzi,* pl. *hŭkanzi*) 'bewitch, charm, cure by magic'. Friedrich, ZA NF 4.187 fn. 3; HG 96, 121, 221.
hwegatar (*huwigatar*) 'incantation, magic'. KUB 24.8.1.14.
hwelpis (acc. *huwelpin,* dat. *hwelpi, huwelpi*) 'bearing for the first time; first produced'; neut. 'first-fruits'. Ehelolf, OLZ 36.6.
hwĕs- (*hwīszi,* 2 pl. *hwisteni*) 'live'. Götze, Madd. 80 f.; Kurylowicz, Symb. Gramm. 101, EI 74; HG 89. Cf. *hwesus, huske/a-*.
hwesa- (verb. n., gen. *huwisawas, huwwisawes*) 'live'. HG 153, 169. Cf. *hwesus*.
hwesas (pl. *hwisas, huwisas*) 'alive, raw (of meat)'. KUB 7.1.1.13, 2.32. Cf. Götze, Madd. 80 fn. 3. Cf. *hwesus*.
hweske/a- = *huske/a-,* q.v. KBo 3.34.2.23.
hwesnu- (*hwisnuzi*) 'cause to live, keep alive'. Friedrich, OLZ 26.46 f.; HG 235. Cf. *hwesus*.
hwesnuske/a- (*hwisnuskizzi,* pret. *hwisnuskēt*). 'cause to live'. Götze, Hatt. 95 f.
hwesus (neut. *huwesu, huwisu, hwisu, hwesu*) 'alive, raw'. Sommer, BoSt. 10.20; Kurylowicz, Symb. Gramm. 101; HG 89.
hweswă(e)- (pret. *hwiswait,* part. pl. *hūswandus*) 'be alive, remain alive'. Götze, Madd. 81. Cf. *hwesus*.
hweswătar (*hwiswătar,* gen. *hwiswannas*) 'life'. Götze, Madd. 81. Cf. *hwesus*.
hweswe/a- (*huwissuwizzi,* pret. 2 pl. *hwisweten*) Friedrich, Vert. 2.186; HG 227 f. Cf. *hwesus*.
hwis-; see *hwes-*.
hwisas 'raw'; see *hwesas*.
hwisas 'mirror'. Zimmern, ZA NF 1.183 fn. 1.
hwisnu-; see *hwesnu-*.
hwisnuske/a-; see *hwesnuske/a-*.
hwisus; see *hwesus*.
hwiswa(e)-; see *hweswa(e)-*.
hwiswe/a-; see *hweswe/a-*.
hwitar (*hwitar, huwitar,* gen. *hwitnas*) 'animals'. Friedrich, ZA NF 5.61 f.; HG 150, 186.

hwĭttiya/e- (*hwittiyēzzi, hwittiyai*, pret. 1 sg. *huwīttiyanun*) 'draw, lead; string (a bow), shear (a fleece)'. Götze, Hatt. 89 f.; HG 75 fn. 79, 129; Milewski, L'Indo-Hittite et l'Indo-Européen 4 fn. 2.
    appa h. 'draw back, injure, delay'.
    arha h. 'draw away, take away'.
    parā h. 'draw forth, prefer; close'. Friedrich, Vert. 2.145, 147.
    sarā h. 'draw up, cause to stand'. Friedrich, ZA NF 2.292.
hwittiyanna- (1 sg. *hwittiyannahhi*) 'draw, lead'. Götze, Hatt. 89 f.
hwittiyaneske/a- (1 sg. *hwittiyanneskimi*, 1 pl. *huwittiyanneskiwani*) 'draw, lead'. Götze, Hatt. 90 fn. 1, Madd. 130.
*hwnhwatar (gen. *hunhuwanas*) 'flood' or the like. KBo. 3.7.2.16 (G).
hwnhwes(s)ar (*huwanhwessar, huwwanhwesar*, gen. *hunhwesnas*, dat. *huwanhwisni*) 'flood' or 'wave'. Ehelolf, KlF 1.395 f. Cf. *hwnhwatar*.
hwrta- (*hurdai*, 1 sg. *huwwartahhi*, pret. *huwartas, hurtas*, 1 sg. *hurtahhun*) 'curse'. Friedrich, ZA NF 1.189, 5.60 fn. 1; Sturtevant, JAOS 50.128, HG 105 f.
hwrtăis (*hurtāis*, acc. *hurtain*) 'curse'. HG 180. See *hwrta-*.
hwrtal(l)iya/e- (*hurtaliizzi*, pl. *hurtalliyanzi*) 'speak incantations; curse'? 2 BoTU 8.3.38; VBoT 3.6.10 (W). Cf. Ehelolf, OLZ 32.323 fn. 1.
hwrzke/a- (*hurzakizzi*, verb. n. *hurzakiwwar, huwwarzakiwwar*) 'curse'. HG 237. See *hwrta-*.

I, properly the figure 1, used as determinative with the names of men. See p. 189.
Ĭ = YĂ, q.v.
-*I* = -*mes* 'my'. Cf. -*YA*, ᴅUTU-*ŠI*.
-*i*; read -*e* (nom. pl. masc. and neut. of -*as* 'is').
ĭ- (imper. 2 sg. *ĭt*, 2 pl. *ĭtten*) 'go'. Hrozný, SH 4 fn. 2; Friedrich, Vert. 1.163; HG 95; Kurylowicz, EI 74.
IĂ; read YĂ.
-*IA*; read -*YA*.
-*ia*; read -*ya*.
iet; see *ya/e-*.
ᴳᴵˢIG 'door'.
iga(e)-; see *ega(e)-*.
IGI 'eye'; IGI.ḪI.A = *sakwa* 'eyes'.
IGI-*zis* = *hantezzis* 'first'.
IGI-*anda* = *menahhanda* 'opposite, against'.

IGI-*wantariya/e-* = *sakuwantariya/e-*, q.v.
ᴸᵁIGI.MUŠEN 'augur'.
IGI.NU.GÁL 'blind'.
ᴳⁱˢIGI.DÙ; read ᴳⁱˢŠUKUR.
IGI.DU₈.A 'choice'.
IGI.DUB; read IZKIM.
ᴸᵁIGI.DUB; read ᴸᵁAGRIG.
IKKIR = *waggariyat* 'he rebelled'.
ikniyanza 'paralyzed, lame'. Ehelolf, KlF 1.393 f.; Benveniste, BSL 35.102 f.
IQBÎ = *tet, memas* 'he spoke'.
IKRIBU 'prayer, votive offering'.
IKRUB 'he prayed'.
iktas, a case form of *ikza*.
IKU = *IKŪ*, a measure of surface and of length; 100 *IKŪ* = 1 DANNA. Hrozný, AOr. 3.437 f.
ikunas; see *ekunas*.
ikza, an attribute of a god. KBo. 3.21.2.14–18.
-il, -ila; see *-el, -ela*.
ilaliske/a- 'desire, covet'.
ilāliya/e-, usually w. *-za*, 'desire, covet'. Sommer, BoSt. 7.55 and fn. 1; HG 215; Friedrich, OLZ 39.308.
ilasni, archaic dat. of *ilessar*.
ilatar 'desire'. Chrest. 97 f. Cf. Götze, NBr. 32 f.
ilessar (dat. *ilasni, ilesni*) 'desire'. Götze, NBr. 33.
ILKU; read *ELKU*.
ᴰILLAT 'military post'? Friedrich, Vert. 2.187.
ᴳⁱˢILDÁG = *ILDAQQU*, a kind of wood.
ILU = *siunas, siunis, sius, karimn-* 'god, goddess'.
IM 'clay, earth'.
   IM GÍD.DA 'long tablet'? Götze, RHA 1.19.10. Cf. Ehelolf ap. Landsberger, ZA NF 7.199.
IM = *huwantas* 'wind, storm'; also determinative.
ᴰIM; read ᴰIŠKUR.
imiya/e-; see *immeya/e-*.
imma 'really, actually; besides, after all; rather'. Götze, ZA NF 2.266–8; Friedrich, Vert. 2.157–60; Sommer, AU 87 f.; Götze-Pedersen, MS 51, 77–9.
   kwis i. kwis 'whoever actually, whoever else'.
   natta i. 'not really, almost'. Sommer, AU 138 f.

immak(k)u seems to be nearly equivalent to *imma*. Sommer, AU 265.
ᴸᵁIM.ME, an official in a temple.
im(m)eya/e- (*immiyazzi*, pret. 1 sg. *imienun*, midd. 2 sg. *immeatti*) 'mix'. Friedrich, Vert. 2.94 and fn. 1.
    anda i. (midd.) 'become involved in (a matter)'. Cf. Friedrich, Vert. 2.94.
IM.NUN 'woodshed' or the like. Deimel, No. 399.76.
IMBARU 'tornado'. Landsberger, ZA NF 8.157 fn. 5.
impawwar; *anda i.* 'suffering'? Hrozný, SH 183 f.
IM.BU.DA; read IM GÍD.DA.
IM.ŠU.(GAR.)RIN.NA; read ᴵᴹŠU.GAR.RIN.NA.
IM.TE; read NÍ.TE.
IM.ZU; read NÍ.ZU.
IMZU; read *EMṢU*.
INA 'in, into'; sign of the dat. 'From'; sign of the abl. KUB 11.35.1.13.
INAKKIZU = *kuranzi* 'they cut off'. Hrozný, CH 132.14.
inan (gen. *inanas*), a disease. Friedrich, ZA NF 1.177; Götze, Madd. 72 fn. 2.
ᴰINANNA 'Ishtar'.
    GIŠ ᴰINANNA, a certain musical instrument.
inarahh- 'make strong'? Sommer, AU 21. Cf. Forrer, Altorient. Stud. 31.
INIM = *AMĀTU* = *uttar*, *memiyas* 'word, saying, rumor, plan, affair'.
innara (acc., gen. *innarās*, dat. *innarā*) 'strength'? Kretschmer, KlF 1.301; Sommer, AU 21, AF 49 fn. 1, 84. Cf. Ehelolf, OLZ 37.721; Chrest. 118.
innarawatar; see *innarawwatar*.
innarawes- (*innaraweszi*) 'become strong'? Götze, Hatt. 69 fn. 2, 100 fn. 2.
innarawwanza (acc. *innarawwandan*, *inrawwandan*) 'strong, manly'? Kretschmer, KlF 1.302; HG 160 f., Chrest. 118.
innaraw(w)atar (dat. *innarawanni*, *innarawani*) 'strength, manliness'? Kretschmer, KlF 1.303; Götze, Madd. 95; Sommer, AU 21.
IN.NU 'straw'.
IN.NU.DA 'straw'. Götze, Hatt. 80 fn. 3; Deimel, Nachträge No. 626.
INBU = *iyata*? 'fruit'.
inrawwandan; see *innarawwanza*.
inuske/a- 'roast'? Friedrich, ZA NF 1.180.
IBILA 'heir'.
    IBILA-*atar* 'heirship, position as heir'.

IBNÎ = *wetet* 'he built'.
IR = *ilaliya/e-* 'crave, desire'.
ÌR; read ERUM 'slave'.
ÌR; read NITÁ 'male'.
irhă(e)- (*irhăizzi*, midd. *irhāitta, irhaittari*) 'finish'; midd. 'come to an end, wane'. Götze, Madd. 84 and fn. 3, 93 and fn. 3. Cf. Forrer, Altorient. Stud. 33; Ehelolf, ZA NF 9.184.
irhăs 'boundary'. Forrer, Altorient. Stud. 33; Sommer, AF 84. Cf. Götze, ZA 34.186.
irhiske/a- 'finish'. See *irha(e)-*.
ᴳᴵˢ*irimpi*, an implement used in ritual. Sommer, BoSt. 10.48 and fn. 1, 84. Cf. *arimpas, eripisa*.
irmalanza 'ill'. Friedrich, Vert. 2.188; HG 159.
irmalas 'ill'. Götze, AM 198 f.; HG 159. Cf. *irmas* 'ill'.
irmaliya- (midd. pret. *irmaliyattat*, once *irmalliyattat*) 'be ill'. Götze, Hatt. 106, 120, AM 198 f.; HG 225.
irmananza 'ill'? Ehelolf ap. Boissier, Mantique 23, ZA NF 9.182 fn. 3.
irmaniyawwar 'illness'? Hrozný, SH 205; Ehelolf, ZA NF 9.182 fn. 2.
irmas [*ermas*] 'ill'. Hrozný, BoSt. 3.166 fn. 2; Friedrich, ZA NF 5.79; Carruthers, Lang. 9.159; Götze, AM 198 f.; HG 91.
irmas (GIG-*as*) 'illness'. Götze, AM 198 f.
*irmatar (dat. *irmani*) 'illness'. See *irmas* 'ill'.
IRṢETU; read *ERṢETU*.
IRDÎ 'he pursued, he went'.
ÎRTU 'omen'.
IŠ; read SAḪAR.
ᴸᵁIŠ 'groom, horseman, esquire'.
IṢ; see *IṢU*.
IŠERTU; read *EŠERTU*.
ishahru; read *eshahru*.
ishāi- (*ishāi*, pl. *ishiyanzi*, pret. 1 sg. *ishihhun*) 'bind, fix (a penalty), levy (troops), make a treaty with'. Hrozný, SH 55; Friedrich, ZA NF 1.174 f.; Götze, Hatt. 68; Kurylowicz, Symb. Gramm. 101, EI 74; HG 142; Götze-Pedersen, MS 52.
?*ishaltuhmeyanza* 'sacrificing, instituting a festival'?? Chrest. 158.36; 172.
*ishamais (acc. *ishamain*, pl. *ishamis*) 'song'. Götze, Madd. 98 and fn. 2.
ishamaiske/a-; see *ishamiske/a-*.
ᴸᵁ·ᴹᴱˢ*ishamatalles* 'singers'. KUB 17.21.2.11.
ishamina- (acc. *ishaminan*) 'cord'. Götze, KlF 1.222. Cf. *ishimanta*.

ishamiske/a- (*ishamaiskizzi*, pl. *ishamiskanzi*) 'sing'. See *ishamiya/e-*.
ishamiya/e- 'sing'. Götze, Madd. 98 and fn. 1.
ishananza; read *eshananza*.
ishanittaratar; read *eshanittaratar*.
ishar, ishar-; read *eshar, eshar-*.
ishas; read *eshas*.
*ishassaras (dat. *ishassari*) 'mistress (of a house)'. Ehelolf, ZA NF 9. 184-6. See *eshas*.
ishas(s)arwatar 'friendliness' or the like? Sommer, AU 258 f. But cf. *ishassaras*.
ishēnius (nom. sg. or pl.) 'hair'? Ehelolf, KlF 1.150.
ishihhun; see *ishai*.
ishimanta (inst.) 'by means of cord'. Ehelolf, IF 43.316. See *ishai-*. Cf. *ishamina-*.
ishiske/a- 'bind'. KUB 25.17.1.5. See *ishai-*.
ishiūl (gen. *ishiūlas*) 'obligation, contract, treaty'. Hrozný, SH 55 f.; Korošec, Vert. 21-35; HG 148; Götze-Pedersen, MS 52. Cf. *ishai-, ishiya/e-*.
ishiūl(l)ahh- (pl. *ishiulahhanzi*, pret. 1 sg. *ishiūllahhun*) 'draw up (an army), instruct (a person), prepare (a thing)'. Götze, AM 249 f.
ishiya/e- = *ishai-*, q.v. HG 223.
ishiyal 'bond'. VBoT. 120.3.2. Cf. *ishiul, ishiya/e-*.
ᵀᵁᴳ*ishiyal* 'girdle'? KBo. 3.34.1.20.
ishizziya/e-; read *eshizziya/e-*.
ishuessar; see *ishwessar*.
ishunā- (pl. *ishunānzi*) 'bind'?? Hrozný, CH 134.19. 'Pelt'??? Walther, HC 269.175. Cf. Sommer, AU 317.
ishunahh- (pret. 1 pl. *ishunahhuwen*) 'oppose, resist' or the like? Sommer, AU 317. Perhaps originally 'cause to sweat'. Cr. *ishunas*.
ᵁᶻᵁ*ishunas* 'sweat'?? Sturtevant, Lang. 10.271. Cf. Sommer, AU 317.
ishunawwanza 'sweaty'?? See *ishunas*.
ishūnawwas 'of sweating'?? See *ishunas*.
ishuwa-; see *ishwa-*.
ishuwanna-; see *ishwanna-*.
ishuwessar; see *ishwessar*.
ishuwiske/a-; see *ishwiske/a-*.
ishuwwaiske/a-; see *ishwiske/a-*.
ishuwwanna-; see *ishwanna-*.
ishuwwiske/a-; see *ishwiske/a-*.
*ishuzzis (acc. *ishuzzin*, pl. *ishuzziyas*) 'band, girdle'. Sommer, AU 317 and fn. 1; HG 155.

ishuzziya/e- 'gird, girdle'. Götze, NBr. 77 fn. 3; Sommer, AU 317 fn. 1.
ishw- (ishwi) = *ishwa-,* q.v.
ishwă- (ishuwai, ishuwwăi, pl. *ishuwanzi, ishuwwanzi)* 'throw, scatter, pour; lay (a foundation)'. Sommer, BoSt. 10.53 f.; Götze, Hatt. 103 f.; Kurylowicz, Symb. Gramm. 102; Sturtevant, Lang. 6.151. Cf. *ishw-, ishwa(e)-.*
   arha i. 'throw away'.
   kattan i. 'throw down, put underneath'. Ehelolf, ZA NF 9.191 fn. 2.
   parā i. 'throw out'.
ishwa(e)- (ishuwwaizzi) = *ishwa-,* q.v.
ishwanna- (1 sg. *ishuwannahhi, ishuwwannahhi)* 'throw, scatter, pour'. Sommer, BoSt. 10.22. See *ishwa-.*
*ishwĕssar (dat. *ishwĕsni,* inst. *ishwēsnit)* 'a pouring out, abundance'. Götze, Madd. 62–4.
ishwiske/a- (ishuwwaiskizzi, pl. *ishwiskanzi).* 'throw, scatter, pour'. Götze, Hatt. 120.
isihh-; read *isiahh-* and see *isiyahh-.*
isiyahh- (isiyahhi, pret. *isiyahta, isiahhis)* 'spy out, trace; declare, disclose'. Friedrich, ZA NF 3.197–9; HG 73; Kurylowicz, EI 75 fn. 1.
isiyahheskattal(l)as (also *isiyahhiskattalas)* 'spy'. Friedrich, ZA NF 3.198 f.
isiyahheske/a- (written *isiyahhiske/a-); āppa i.* 'investigate'. Götze, Madd. 139, 164.
isga- (1 sg. *isgahhi)* 'anoint'. See *iske/a-.*
iskallă- (iskallai, midd. *iskallāri);* act. and midd. 'split' or the like? Hrozný, CH 12.37; Benveniste, BSL 33.139; HG 117.
iskalla(ē)-; ser katta iskallaīzzi 'tears to bits'? KUB 12.58.2.17.
^{TÚG}*iskallessar* 'a slashed garment'? Hrozný, CH 138.50; Walther, HC 270.182.
isgăr- (isgāri, pl. *isgaranzi)* 'place, fasten'. Götze, KlF 1.409 and fn. 5.
isgarā- (isgarāi) 'place, fasten'. See *isgar-.*
iskarrit 'with a chain'??? Hrozný, AOr. 1.85.
isgaruh (also *isqaruh),* a vessel used in libations; possibly the libation was poured into it. Götze, Lang. 11.185 f.
iske/a- (iskizzi, 1 sg. *isgāmi)* 'anoint'. Hrozný, SH 12, 62; Sommer, BoSt. 7.1; HG 224. Cf. *iskiya/e-.*
iskeske/a- 'anoint'. Ehelolf, KlF/ 1.145 fn. 3. See *iske/a-, iskiya/e-.*
^{UZU}*iskĭsa-* (acc. *iskisan,* gen. *iskisas,* dat. *iskĭsa, iskisi)* 'back'. Acc., dat., or abl. 'behind'. Sommer, BoSt. 10.52 f.; Götze, AM 232 f.

iskismit = *iskisa(n)-smet* (cf. Friedrich, IF 49.229); or = *iskissmet* (acc. of an *s*-stem; Götze, AM 232).
iskiske/a-; read *iskeske/a-*.
^{GIŠ}*iskissanan* 'bed'?? Hrozný, CH 132.5, 133 fn. 5. 'Head rest'??? Walther, HC 269.171. Cf. Götze, AM 233.
iskiya/e- 'anoint'. HG 224. See *iske/a-*.
ISQU 'a share'. Ungnad ap. Sommer, OLZ 38.280. Cf. Chrest. 227.
IŠKUN = *dais, yet* 'he put, he placed, he made'.
iskunahh- (pret. *iskunnahhis*) 'set, appoint'. Forrer, 2 BoTU 22* fn. 2.
*iskunanza (neut. pl. *iskunanta*) 'dirty'? Friedrich, ZA NF 3.192.
^{D}IŠKUR (often written ^{D}IM), a storm god; there were several of them. Götze, Kulturg. 125. Cf. ^{D}U.
^{LÚ}IŠ.GUŠKIN 'golden groom', title of certain officials at court.
IŠMĒ = *istamasta* 'he heard'.
ismeriyas (pl.) 'charioteers'? KUB 23.11.3.5.
isnas; see *essnas*.
isnŭra- (acc. *isnūran*, gen. *isnuras*, dat. *isnūri*) 'dough'. Chrest. 122 f., 230.
DUG *isnuras* 'dough pan'.
isnūras (acc. *isnūran*) 'pertaining to dough'. Chrest. 122 f.
ispāi- (imper. 2 sg. *ispāi*, 2 pl. *ispisten*) 'sate oneself'. Ehelolf, KlF 1.137–42; Sturtevant, Lang. 4.2, HG 130. Cf. *ispiya/e-*.
ispant- (acc. *ispandan*, abl. *ispantaz, ispandaza*) 'night'. Sommer, BoSt. 7.29, 30 fn. 3; Götze-Pedersen, MS 60.
ispantius (acc. pl.) 'nights' or 'nocturnos'. Sommer, BoSt. 7.30 fn. 3; Götze, AM 289. See *ispant-*.
^{DUG}*ispandu-* (abl. *ispanduwaz* [sp·antwats]) 'libation bowl'. Götze, KlF 1.201. Cf. *sippant-*.
$^{LÚ.MEŠ}$*ispa(n)tuzzēlas* (pl.) 'libation pourers'. Hrozný, SH 54; Cf. *ispantuzzi, ispantuzziyalas*.
^{DUG}*ispantuzzessar* (also *ispantuzzisar*) 'libation bowl'. HG 152 fn. 28. See *ispantuzzi*.
ispa(n)tuz(z)i- [sp·antutsi-] (acc. *ispanduzzin*, nom.-acc. *ispantuzi, ispanduzzi*) 'libation'. Götze, KlF 1.200–3, 214.8; HG 155. Cf. *sippant-*.
^{DUG}*i.* 'libation bowl'. Sturtevant, JAOS 54.400.
^{LÚ}*ispantuzziyali-* (pl. *ispantuzziyalēs*, acc. *ispantuzziyalius*) 'libation pourer'. HG 159. See *ispantuzzi-*.
*ispanduzziyassar (inst. ^{DUG}*ispanduzziyassarit*) 'libation bowl'. See *ispantuzzessar*.

?*ispanza*; see *ispant-*.
ispăr- [sp˙ar-] (*ispāri*, 1 sg. *isparhi*, *isparahhi*) 'spread, cover; trample'. Götze, Madd. 143 f.; Sturtevant, Lang. 4.2 f., HG 130. Cf. *isparra-*, *isparriya/e-*.
ispareske/a- 'spread'. KUB 7.5.2.19. See *ispar-*, *isparriya/e-*.
isparnu- 'cause to spread, destroy'. Cf. Götze, Madd. 143. See *ispar-*.
isparra- (2 sg. *isparratti*) 'spread, cover; trample'. See *ispar-*.
isparriya/e- 'spread, cover; trample'. Götze, Madd. 143 f.; Sturtevant, Lang. 4.2 f., HG 130.
ispart- (*isparzazi*, *isparzazzi* [spartstsi] or [ispartstsi], pret. *isparzasta* [spartst] or [ispartst], pl. *isparter*) 'arise, come out; escape; occur'. Sommer, BoSt. 7.12 fn. 2 end; Götze, Hatt. 80, 105, Madd. 126; Friedrich, Vert. 1.38; HG 49, 84, 129, 220.
sarā i. 'arise, ascend the throne'.
isparza- (*isparzai*, pret. 1 sg. *isparzahhun*, 3 pl. *isparzir*) 'arise, escape'. Sommer, AU 408; HG 129 fn. 92, 246.
IṢBAT = *epta* 'he took'.
^{URUD}*ispătar* (*ispātar*, inst. *ispannit*), an implement used in eating and in taking things from the hearth. Götze, Madd. 100 and fn. 1; KUB 7.1.2.3 f. See *ispai-*.
ispataza, abl. of *ispant-*, q.v. Götze, NBr. 5.
ispatuzi; see *ispantuzzi-*. Götze, NBr. 5.
ispatuzzelas; see *ispantuzzelas*.
ispis-; see *ispai-*.
ispiya/e- (pl. *ispiyanzi*, imper. *ispiya*) = *ispai-* 'sate oneself', q.v. HG 223.
ispiyatar 'satisfaction, abundance'. See *ispai-*, *ispatar*.
IŠPUR = *hatraet* 'he sent word, he wrote'; cf. *IŠṬUR*.
issa-; read *essa-*.
*issallis 'of the mouth'.
issalli 'spittle'. Ehelolf, OLZ 36.6 fn. 3. See *ais*.
issanas; read *essnas*.
issas, gen. of *ais* 'mouth', q.v.
istalk- (*istalakzi*) 'make even, smooth' or the like? KUB 24.9.2.20 (G). Cf. *istalga(e)-*, *istalkiya/e-*.
istalga(e)- (*istalgaizzi*) 'make even, smooth' or the like? KBo. 4.2.1.40. See *istalk-*.
istalkiya/e- (midd. *istalkiyattari*) 'make even, smooth' or the like? See *istalk-*, *istalga(e)-*.

*istămanas (acc. istamanan [st·amanan], inst. GEŠTUG-it, istamanta, pl. acc. istāmanus) 'ear'. Hrozný, CH 12 fn. 2; Sturtevant, Lang. 4.123, HG 93.
istamaske/a- 'hear'. Götze, ZA 34.179; Sommer, AU 69, 83.
istamass- [st·amas·-] (istamaszi, isdammaszi, pl. istamassanzi) 'hear'. Hrozný, MDOG 56.35, SH 77 fn. 2, 79; Forrer, JA 217.243; HG 133, 229.
    anda i. 'hear near at hand, hear in confidence'? KUB 26.1.3.49, 55 f.
    arha i. 'exaudire'. Friedrich, Vert. 2.139.
istammas-; see istamass-.
istam(m)as(s)uwar (istamassuwar, isdammasuwar, GEŠTUG-ar) 'obedience' or the like. Sommer, AU 391.
^{GIŠ}istanănas (dat. istanăni, isdanani, ^{GIŠ}ZAG.GAR-ni, abl. istananaz), something employed in ritual. 'Altar'?? Götze, AOr. 5.35.37. 'Stand'? Chrest, 166.69.
istantă(e)- (pret. istantait, istatāit, istandāit [st·antaet]) 'tarry, delay'. Hrozný, SH 79; Friedrich, Vert. 2.86; HG 124; Götze-Pedersen, MS 52.
    istantanza 'too late, obsolete'.
istantanu- 'cause to tarry, neglect'. Friedrich, Vert. 2.86.
istantanuske/a- 'cause to tarry, neglect'. Tenner, HAT 20.
^{D}Istanus (^{D}UTU-us, acc. ^{D}Istanun) 'sun'? Götze, Kulturg. 129; Sommer, OLZ 38.277.
istanza(istanza-ssas, ZI-anza, dat. ZI-ni) 'breath, heart, soul; wish, desire; self'. Ehelolf, KlF 1.144 fn. 2, 397 fn. 3, ZA NF 9.176.
ista(n)zanas, = istanza, q.v.
istăp(p)- (istappi, istāpi, isdăpi [st·ap·i]) 'shut, enclose, cover, store up'; midd. 'stop' (intransitive). Götze, Hatt. 80 f.; Sturtevant, Lang. 4.3, HG 88; Benveniste, BSL 33. 139.
?istappinu- 'cause to shut'. Friedrich, ZA NF 5.48.
istarkiske/a- 'be ill'. KUB 8.36.4.20. See istarkk-.
istarkiya/e- 'be ill'; impersonal 'it goes ill with'. See istarkk-.
istarkk- (istarakzi, pret. istarakkit, istarkta) act. 'be ill'; impersonal w. acc. of the person 'it goes ill with one, one is ill'. Götze, Hatt. 72; Friedrich, Vert. 1.31; Sturtevant, Lang. 4.5 f., HG 233 and fn. 37, 255.
istarna, istarni 'between, among'. Friedrich, ZA NF 1.140-4; Sturtevant, Lang. 4.5, HG 90.
    istarni-smi 'among them'. Friedrich, Vert. 1.81 fn. 2.

istarna pete 'around, upon'. KUB 20.59.5.19–25, 6.4–24; VBoT 24.1.12 (G).
istarna arha 'through'. Sommer, AU 187 fn. 3.
istarnenk- (*istarnikzi*, 1 pl. *istarninkwen*) 'injure, make ill'. Götze, Hatt. 72; HG 233 and fn. 37, 274 and fn. 116.
istarniya = *istarni* 'between, among', q.v. Friedrich, ZA NF 1.144.
istatait; see *istanta(e)-*. Götze, NBr. 5.
IŠTĒN = *sanas* 'one, only, alone'.
IŠTĒNŪTU (with pluralia tantum) 'one'. Götze, ZA NF 6.79 f.
IŠTU (once written IŠ-TA) 'from; with'. A mark of the abl. or inst. Sommer, AU 295.
IŠTU ŠA, a mark of the inst. Chrest. 78.11, 97.
IŠṬUR = *hatraet* 'he wrote'; cf. IŠPUR.
isduwā- (*isduwāri*, pret. *isduwāti*) 'become known'. Friedrich, ZA NF 3.198 and fn. 2; Sturtevant, Lang. 4.4, 6.31.
IṢU = *taru* 'wood, (wooden) implement'. Some scholars write IṢ for the determinative GIŠ.
isuwan (acc.) 'fold'??? or 'stable'??? Walther, HC 268.163.
isuwanalli (dat.) 'fold animal'??? See *isuwan*.
ÍD 'river, canal'; also determinative before river names.
īt, imperative of *i-* 'go', q.v.
idalamus (acc. pl.) 'bad'. Götze, Madd. 120 fn. 4.
idālāw(w)ahh- (*idalawahzi*, pl. *idālawahhanzi*, 2 sg. *idalawahti*, *idālāwwahti*) 'injure'. Friedrich, ZA NF 1.17; Kurylowicz, Symb. Gramm. 102; Sturtevant, Lang. 6.153, HG 72 fn. 72, 242, 285.
*idālāwatar (dat. *idālāwanni*, *idalawwanni*, *idalawanna*?) 'harm, injury'. Friedrich, Vert. 1.175–7; HG 151.
idālāwēs(s)- (*idālāwēszi*, pl. *idālāwēssanzi*, *idalawesanzi*) 'become malicious'. Götze, Hatt. 69; HG 231.
idalawwahh-; see *idalawahh-*.
idalawwatar; see *idalawatar*.
idālus 'malicious, bad'. Hrozný, MDOG 56.37, SH 5 f.; Sturtevant, Lang. 6.25; Sommer, AU 51 fn.; HG 181 f.
itar 'road'??? Forrer, RHA 1.146; HG 150.
ID.ḪU; read Á^{MUŠEN}.
IDĪ = *saggahhi* 'I know'; = *sakki* 'he knows'; = *sakkis* 'he knew'.
idi; read *edi*.
IDIGNA 'flowing'; ÍD IDIGNA 'the Tigris'.
ID.DAḪ; read Á.DAḪ.
īten, imper. 2 pl. of *i-* 'go', q.v.

ITTI 'with, to'. Usually equivalent to the Hittite dat. w. *kattan*; but sometimes a mark of the dat. Götze, Madd. 165; Sommer, AU 38.
IDDIN = *pesta* 'he gave'.
ITU; ITU.KAM 'month'.
^{LÚ}I.DU$_8$ 'porter'.
ITU.BÍL 'new moon, beginning of a month'? KUB 8.1.2.5.
iukan; read *yukan*.
iugas; read *yugas*.
iwar (with the gen.) 'as, in the manner of'. Sommer, BoSt. 7.11–22; Ehelolf, OLZ 36.7.
iwaru 'a share of one's father's estate received in his lifetime; dowry; inherited feudal property'. Götze, NBr. 58, Kulturg. 97; Speiser, JAOS 55.436 fn. 17.
iwārwā(e)- (pret. pl. *iwārwāir*) 'give an *iwaru*'. Friedrich, ZA NF 2.48 fn. 1.
-iya; see *-a*.
iya/e-; see *ya/e-* 'make'.
iya-; see *ya-* 'go'.
iyanna; see *yanna-*.
iyanne/a-; see *yanne/a-*.
iyanniya/e-; see *yanniya/e-*.
iyanza; see *yanza*.
iyasha- (pret. 2 sg. *iyashatta*) 'trust'? Götze, Madd. 61.
iyăta (*iyada*) 'fruit, abundance'? Ehelolf, KlF 1.144 fn. 1; KUB 4.4.1.14; 12.63.2.29 (G, W).
iyatniyanza 'neighbor'?? Hrozný, CH 104.26.
IZ; read *IṢ* and see *IṢU*.
IZI = *pahhur* 'fire'.
IZI; read BIL 'burn'.
^{DUG}IZI.GAR = ^{DUG}NŪRU = ^{DUG}*sasannas* 'lamp'.
IZKIM = *sagais* 'omen'.
IZKIM = *sakiyahh-* 'give an omen'. Götze, KlF 1.403.
IZBAT; read *IṢBAT*.
IZ.ZI 'wall, enclosure'. Deimel, No. 296.49; KBo. 6.29.2.32. (G).
IZZI, gen. of *IṢU*, q.v.
īzzi; read *yezzi* and see *ya/e-* 'make'.

GA 'milk'.
KA = *ais* 'mouth'.

KA; read INIM 'word, affair'.
KÁ 'gate, door'.
KA₈; read KAŠ.
-KA = -tes 'tuus'.
KA × A, read NAG.
-ka; see -kki.
kā 'here'. Hrozný, SH 141; Sommer, BoSt. 7.39; AU 14.55.
ka- 'this'; see kas.
*kaenanza (dat. ᴸᵁkaenanti) 'affinis, wife's relative'. See kaenas.
ᴸᵁkaenas (gainas, acc. kainan, pl. gainas, gaenes) 'affinis, wife's relative'.
    Hrozný, BoSt. 3.100 fn. 6; Friedrich, Vert. 1.36, 2.163; Götze,
    AOr. 2.161 f.
KA × IM = tethessar 'thunder'. Friedrich ZA NF 3.196 f.
KA.IZI 'flame'. Deimel, No. 15.170; Sturtevant ap. Götze, Lang.
    11.189 fn. 10.
GAG (KAK); read DÙ.
ᴳᴵˢGAG (KAK) 'stick, pet'.
KA × GAG = tititas 'nose'.
KA.GAG = PĪḪU, a kind of beer. Sommer, AU 132.
KÁ.GAL 'Tor, city gate'.
GA.KALAG.GA 'coagulated milk'.
KA × GAR; read KÚ.
GA.KIN.AG 'cheese'.
*kak(k)apas (acc. gaggapan, pl. kaqqapis, kakkapus), an instrument for
    striking?? Friedrich, Altorient. Stud. 48 fn. 5, 51. Cf. KBo.
    3.34.2.13; 3.36.1.19, 20.
QAQ(Q)ARU 'land, domain'.
ᴳᴵˢGAG.Ú.TAG.(GA) 'arrow'.
GAL = sallis 'great, noble; chief'.
    LÚ GAL 'leading citizen, chief'.
    GAL LÚ.MEŠ 'chief of men, commander'.
ᴰᵁᴳGAL (acc. GAL-AM), a vessel for liquids; sometimes = ispanduzzi
    'libation bowl'. Sturtevant, JAOS 54.400.
    GAL GIR₄ 'bowl made of asphalt'.
GÁL; see NU.GÁL.
GA.AL 'cream'.
KAL, KALA(G) 'strong, manly'. (On the Hittite equivalent, see
    Ehelolf, OLZ 37.721 f.; Chrest. 118.)
ᴸᵁKAL 'vir'.

KAL-*atar* 'manliness'. Sommer, AU 21.

ᴰKAL (sometimes transcribed ᴰLAMA), a designation of several gods. Sommer, AU 20–4, 382 f.; Ehelolf, OLZ 37.721 f.

ᴸᵁGALA, a kind of priest. (On the Hittite equivalent, see Sommer, BoSt. 10.69 fn. 1; Götze, Madd. 98 fn. 1.)

KALA(G); see KAL.

KALAG.GA = KAL.

galaktar 'appeasement; means of appeasement'? Chrest. 230.

KALĀM 'kidney'.

ᴳᴵˢ*galāma* 'door handle'??? Forrer, Forsch. 1.166. Cf. Sommer, AU 134 fn. 1.

kalănk- (part. *galănkanza, kalănkanza*) 'appease'? KUB 17.10.2.13; 24.1.1.15, 2.13.

kalēlē- (pret. *kalēlēt*) 'tie, bind'. Ehelolf, IF 43.316 and fn. 2.

ᴸᵁKA × LI, a kind of priest. Deimel, No. 16.1; Delaporte, Voc.

KALĪLU = *harsanallis* 'wreath'.

KAL.GA; read KALAG.GA.

GAL.GEŠTIN 'chief of the cup-bearers'.

GAL.GIR₄; see ᴰᵁᴳGAL.

kallăr- (acc. *kallaran*, neut. *kallăr*, inst. *kallarit*) 'bad, monstrous'? Friedrich, ZA NF 3.188 f.; HG 162.

*kallaratar (dat. *kallaranni*) 'badness, monstrousness'. See *kallar*-.

kallarates (pl.?) 'monstrous'? See *kallar*-.

kallares- 'become bad'. See *kallar*-.

kalles- (pret. *kallista*, infin. *kallesuwanzi*) 'invite, entice'. Forrer, RHA 1.146.22; KUB 17.5.1.6; 20.88.6.22 (G). Cf. *ules*-.

ᴸᵁGÀL.LU; read LÚ.GÀL.LU.

kalmanas = *kalmis*? Götze, AM 213.

*kalmaras (abl. *kalmaraz*, pl. *kalmarus*) 'horizon' or 'east' or 'ocean'. Friedrich, KlF 1.295, ZA NF 5.73, 80.

*kalmas (acc. pl. ᴳᴵˢ*kalmus*) = *kalmis*, q.v.

ᴳᴵˢ*kalmēsnas* (*kalmisnas, kalmisanas*, pl. *kalmēsnis*) = *kalmis*.

*kalmis (acc. ᴳᴵˢ*kalmin*, pl. ᴳᴵˢ*kalmēs*) 'stick of wood, fire-brand; thunder bolt'. Forrer, Forsch. 1.49–52; Götze, AM 212–4. Cf. *kalmanas, kalmas, kalmesnas*.

GALU; read LÚ.

*kalulupas (dat. ᵁᶻᵁ*kalulupi*, pl. ᵁᶻᵁ*kalulupes, kalulupus*) 'finger; inch'. Forrer, ZDMG 76.254, RHA 1.161 fn. 43; Sturtevant, Lang. 4.127.

kalute- (*kalutezzi*) 'offer the *kalutis*'. Cf. Sommer, BoSt. 10.21.

*kalutis (acc. *kaluten*, gen. *galudas*), a kind of sacrifice. Friedrich, ZA NF 5.63.

kalutiya/e- (*kalutiyēzzi, galutiyazi*) 'offer the *kalutis*'. Friedrich, ZA NF 5.63 fn. 1.

GAM = *katta, kattan* 'down, with, under, together; along, according to, accordingly'.

GAM = *kattanta* 'down, in'.

KAM, a suffix appended to ordinals and expressions of time.

KAM 'gall bladder'.

KAM; read UTÚL 'pot, pottage'.

gamarsuwanzan (acc.) 'having a full bladder'?? Sturtevant, Lang. 12, No. 3 fn. 7.

KA × ME; read EME.

KAMKAMMATU 'ring (for finger or foot)'.

kammarăs 'vapor, smoke, dust, darkness'? Götze, NBr. 69 and fn. 1, AOr. 5.8. 'Sunshine'??? Ehelolf ap. Friedrich, ZA NF 5.80.

kammari (dat.) 'in smoke'?? Götze, NBr. 69 fn. 1. 'In the hive'?? Hrozný, CH 70.29.

GĂN, KĂN; read IKU.

-*kan* (after -*ta* 'tibi' and *ta* = *nu*, written -*kkan*), a particle of unknown meaning appended to the first word (or phrase) of a sentence, always in the final position. It is particularly frequent with verbs of motion and verbs that imply a change (figurative motion?); but it is used also with such verbs as *as-* 'remain', *es-* 'be', *au-* 'see, observe', and in sentences that contain no verb at all. Ungnad, ZDMG 74.417-22. Cf. Götze, AOr. 5.16-30, AM 291 f.; Götze-Pedersen, MS 53 f. See Sturtevant, JAOS 54.402.

KA.NE; read KA.IZI.

kaness- (*ganeszi, kaneszi,* pl. *kanissanzi*) 'find, obtain; favor'. Götze, Hatt. 64 f.; HG 116.

KA × NÍG; read KÚ.

kanina- (part. *kaninanza*); *kattan k.* 'bow down, make obeisance'. VBoT 120.2.17, 19; cf. *kaniniya-*.

kaninanza (pl. *ganinantes*) 'thirsty'. Götze, Madd. 77 f.

kaniniya/e- (verb. n. *kaniniyawwar*) 'bow down, make obeisance'. Hrozný, SH 78 and fn. 10.

KA × NINDA; read KÚ.

*kăninza (dat. *kăninti*) 'thirst'. Götze, Madd. 78; KlF 1.188 fn. 7.

kaniss-; read *kaness-*.

kank-, kanka- (*ganki, gangai,* imper. 3 pl. *kankandu*) 'hang'. Sommer, BoSt. 10.35, 44 fn. 2; HG 93, 116.

kanganu- 'cause to hang'. KUB 21.27.3.42.

gangadā(e)- (*gangadāizzi*) 'offer sacrificial gruel'? Sommer, BoSt. 10.44; Götze, Madd. 99.
gangāti^ŠAR^, a vegetable. KBo. 5.2.1.15, 4.55.
gangăti, a kind of pottage (UTŬL) employed in ritual. Sommer, BoSt. 10.44; Chrest. 124.
^GIŠ^*kangur* 'hanger' or the like. KUB 25.36.2.20–37 (W). Cf. *kank-*.
kankuw(w)ar (*kankuwar*, *gankuwwar*) 'weight'. Sommer, BoSt. 10.44. fn. 2.
^GIŠ^*KANNU*, a vessel for liquids.
ganut, inst. of *genu* 'knee'.
kanza, a kind of grain or grass. Sommer, BoSt. 10.55; Hrozný, AOr. 3.440.9, 441 fn. 16.
^UZU^GAB 'chest, breast'.
GAB; read DU₈ 'loose' or 'without hesitation'.
KAB; read GÙB 'left'.
^DUG^KAB.KA.GAG, a vessel for liquids.
^TÚG^*KAPALLU*, a kind of clothing worn in pairs. Cf. Hrozný, CH 134.25; Walther, HC 270.176 B; Delaporte, Voc.
**kăpinas* (acc. ^SIG^*kāpinan*, pl. *gapinus*) 'curtain'?? Walther, HC 265.126. Cf. Hrozný, CH 114.15.
GAB.LÀL 'honeycomb, beeswax'.
QABLĪTU = *taksan sarras* 'half'.
KAPPI INI (written *E-NI*) 'eyelid'. Ehelolf, ZA NF 9.192 fn. 1.
kappilā(e)- (pret. pl. *kappilāir*) 'cause to quarrel'? Götze, AM 262 f.
kappilahh- (pret. pl. *kappilahhir*) 'make hateful'? Götze, AM 262.
kappilallis 'hateful, hated'. Götze, KlF 1.226, AM 261–3; Sturtevant, Lang. 10.267.
**kappilazza-* (midd. *kappilazzata*) 'grow angry'? Götze, KlF 1.225 f., AM 263.
kappis 'small'. Friedrich, ZA NF 1.18 f.; Sturtevant, Lang. 10.266.
^DUG^*kappis*, a vessel used as a measure; contrast ^DUG^GAL.
KAPPU 'pan'.
kappūske/a-, variant for *kappuweske/a-*. Götze, AM 220.
kappuwa(e)- (pret. *kappuwwait*, imper. 2 sg. *kappuwai*; *kappuwwai*) 'count, pay; take account of, care for'. Götze, Madd. 121–4; Sommer, AU 73, 166.
 appa k. 'reconsider, examine'.
 appan k. 'count again, check over, check up; deduct'.
kap(p)uwe/a- (*kappuwwizzi*, 2 sg. *kapuwesi*, pret. *kappuwet*) 'count, pay; care for'. HG 219. See *kappuwa(e)-*.

kappuweske/a- 'count, pay; care for'. See *kappuwa(e)-*.
kappuwwa(e)-, *kappuwwe/a-*, *kappuwweske/a-*; see *kappuwa(e)-*, *kappuwe/a-*, *kappuweske/a-*.
QABŪ = *mema-* 'say'.
kapunu, a measure of length. Friedrich, ZA NF 5.56.
kapuwe/a-; see *kappuwe/a-*.
GAR = *ŠAKĀNU* = *dai-* 'place, put'.
GAR = *ki-* 'be placed, lie'.
GAR; read NINDA 'bread, loaf',
KAR = *wemiya/e-* 'find'.
karăiz (dat. *karaitti*) 'sand'??? Forrer, Altorient. Stud. 32. Cf. Friedrich, Vert. 2.147.
kărăp- [krap-], *karĕp-* [krep-] (*karāpi*, *kārapi*, pl. *karipanzi*, pret. pl. *karēpir*) 'fressen, devour'. Götze, Madd. 79 f.; Sturtevant, JAOS 52.3, Lang. 8.130, HG 91, 118, 239 f., 283.
karapp-, see *karpp-*.
karappiya/e-; see *karppiya/e-*.
KARAŠ = *tuzzis* 'army, camp'. Ehelolf, SBPA 1925.268 fn. 6.
karasnu-; read *karsnu-*.
karas(s)-; read *kars(s)-*.
GIŠ*karassanis*, an alkaline plant. Friedrich, AO 25.2.14 fn. 10.
karasse/a-; read *karsse/a-*.
karassiya, dat. of *karssi-*.
karătes (pl.; less frequently *garātes*), something which, if eaten, causes illness?? Götze, Madd. 139. Perhaps rather 'undigested contents of the stomach'? Cf. Friedrich, Vert. 2.147.
karaz(z)a; see *karza*.
karep-; see *karap-*.
kāri (dat.); *kāri tiya/e-* 'comply, yield'. Friedrich, Vert. 2.28 and fn. 2.
karianza; read *kariyanza*.
karimn-, *karimm-* (gen. *karimnas*, dat. *karimmi*, *karimni*, 'god'. Ehelolf, ZA NF 2.313 f.
karimnas, *karimmas* (adj. developed from gen. of *karimn-*) 'of a god, divine'. É *karimni*, É *karimme* (dat.) 'in a temple'. Cf. Friedrich, ZA NF 2.313 f. (G).
karinu-; see *kariyanu-*.
karip-; see *karap-*.
karitashi 'grass'?? KUB 17.28.2.36 (G).
TÚG*kariulli* 'hooded gown'. Götze, OLZ 33.291 and fn. 5, NBr. 77 and fn. 3.
kariw(w)ăriwar, *karuw(w)ariwar* 'fog, mist'? KUB 8.12.5 f. (G).

'Early, in the morning'. Hrozný, SH 79 fn. 5; Götze-Pedersen, MS 54.

kăriya/e- 'cover, close; keep an army behind defenses'. Friedrich, ZA NF 1.18, IF 49.224; Forrer, Forsch. 1.123 f.; Sommer, AU 38 f.

kariya/e- (midd. pret. 1 sg. *kariyahhat*) 'yield, gratify'. Friedrich, Vert. 2.28; HG 118.

kari(ya)nu- 'cause to close; keep (an army) behind defenses; cause to be silent'. See *kariya/e-* 'cover'.

kariyanza (karianza) 'grass'?? KUB 17.28.2.42 (G). Cf. *kariya/e-* 'cover'.

^{LÚ}GAR.GAG.GAG; read ^{LÚ}NINDA.DÙ.DÙ.

QAR.QAR; read ALAN or ALAM.

⁑*kargaranti* 'gladly, willingly'?? Sommer, AU 51, 153.

^{UZU}GAR.GIG; read ^{UZU}NÍG.GIG.

GAR.GÍL.RA; read NINDA KUR₄.RA.

^{GIŠ}GAR.GUL; read ^{GIŠ}NÍG.GUL.

^{SAL}KAR.LÍL 'whore'.

karmalassai 'remains crippled'?? Hrozný, CH 82.28. 'Causes suffering'?? Walther, HC 249.10.

^{GIŠ}*karnas(s)-* (dat. *karnasi, karnasiya*, abl. *karnassaza*), an implement upon which something may be placed. Götze, NBr. 63.

^{TÚG}GAR.NE; read ^{TÚG}NÍG.LÁM.

karp-; see *karpp-*.

GAR.BA; read NÍG.BA.

karpessar 'entirety, totality'? Hrozný, SH 71; Götze, Madd. 45.

^{GIŠ}*karpinas* 'pear tree'??? Hrozný, CH 100.1.

karpis 'anger'. Friedrich, ZA NF 3.189 f., 5.35 fn. 1; Chrest. 125.

karpiwāla (neut. pl.) 'angry'? Sommer, AU 387 and fn. 3.

karpiya/e-; see *karppiya/e-*.

karp(p)- (*karapzi*, pl. *karappanzi, karpanzi*) 'raise, muster, take; complete'. Friedrich, ZA NF 1.185 f.; Sommer, BoSt. 10.73 f.; Götze, Hatt. 98 f.; Sturtevant, Lang. 6. 155 and fn. 23, HG 120, 271 f.

sarā k. 'lift up, take'.

karp(p)iya/e- (*karpiyēzzi*, pl. *karpianzi, karpiyanzi, karappianzi*) 'raise, muster, take; complete'. See *karpp-*.

GAR.RA 'inlaid, trimmed (with silver or gold)'.

kars-; see *karss-*.

karsanu-; read *karsnu-*.

karsanuske/a-; read *karsnuske/a-*.

?*garsaramna-, ?garsaramma-*, a kind of seat. Götze, AM 220 fn. 1.

karsattar 'castration'. Sturtevant, JAOS 54.406. See *karss-*.
karsaddas (dat. pl.?) 'castrated animals'? See *karsattar*.
karsaya; see *karssi-*.
GAR.SIG; read NINDA SIG.
karsike/a-; read *karske/a-*.
karsin; see *karssi-*.
GAR.SI.DI; read NÍG.SI.DI.
karsiya/e-; see *karsiya/e-*.
karske/a- (pl. *karsikanzi*) 'cut off'. See *karss-*.
karsnu- (*karsanuzi*, pret. pl. *karasnuir*) 'forget, neglect (a rite)'. Sommer, AU 228 f. Cf. *karss-*.
karsnuske/a- (pret. pl. *karsanuskir*) 'forget, neglect (a rite)'. See *karsnu-*.
karss- (*karaszi*, pl. *karsanzi*, part. *karassanza*, *karsanza*) 'cut, cut off, mark off; castrate; stop (a disease), cure; stop (a rite), neglect'. Friedrich, ZA NF 2.46 f., 5.42, 9.191 fn. 3; Sommer, AU 226-9; HG 120, 228. Cf. *karsse/a-*, *karssiya/e-*.
   appan arha k. 'get rid of'. Sommer, AU 226.
   appan katta k. 'cut off, renounce; keep away'.
karsse/a- (*karassezzi*) 'cut off'. HG 229. See *karss-*.
karssi- (acc. *karsin*, neut. *karsi*, dat. *karsaya*, *karassiya*, *karsi*) 'unchecked, free, frank, clear, true; without reservation, sure'. Friedrich, Vert. 1.37; Götze, Madd. 112; Sommer, AU 109 fn. 1.
karssiya/e- (*karssiyĕzzi*) 'cut off'. KBo. 6.2.1.8; 6.3.1.15. See *karss-*.
kart-; see *karza*.
karta(e)- (pret. 1 sg. *kartānun*, part. *kartantes*) 'make clean' or the like. Cf. Ehelolf, KlF 1.151; Friedrich, AOr. 6.262 and fn. 7.
kardammiyaw(w)anza 'angry'. See *kartimmiyawwanza*.
QARTAPPU; LÚ Q. 'groom'. Sommer, AU 128 f.
kardi- (gen. *kardiyas*) 'heart'. See *karza*.
kartimiyawwanza; see *kartimmiyawwanza*.
kartimiyaz; see *kartimmiyaz*.
kartimmēs- (TUKU.TUKU-*eszi*, pret. *kartimmēsta*) 'become angry'. Friedrich, ZA NF 5.18.15.
kartimmiya/e- (pret. 1 sg. *kartimmiyanun*, midd. 2 sg. TUKU.TUKU-*atti*, pl. *kartimmiyantari*) 'be angry, quarrel'. Sommer, BoSt. 10.14 f.; Götze, Madd. 59; Chrest. 218.32.
kartimmiyanu- 'make angry'. Friedrich, Vert. 1.28 fn. 1, ZA NF 5.51.
kartim(m)iyaw(w)anza (also TUKU.TUKU-*wanza*) 'angry'. Sommer, BoSt. 10.14 f., Ehelolf, KlF 1.148; Götze, KlF. 1.188; HG 160. Cf. *kardammiyawwanza*.

kartim(m)iyaz (also *kardimiyaz*) 'anger'. Götze, Madd. 79 and fn. 4; HG 141, 149.
kartimnu- 'make angry'. Friedrich, ZA NF 5.51 fn. 1.
GAR.TUG; read NÍG.TUKU.
karū 'formerly, already, long since'. Hrozný, SH 79 fn. 5; Götze, Hatt. 106; Götze-Pedersen, MS 54.
karūlis; read *karuwilis*. HG 59.
karŭssiya/e-, act. and midd., 'be quiet, inactive, indifferent; endure'. Friedrich, Vert. 1.172 f., 2.165.
karussiyantili 'quietly, secretly'. KUB 22.70.1.72.
karussiyanu- 'cause to be silent'. Friedrich, Vert. 1.173.
*karuwilas (neut. pl. *karuwila*) 'previous, primitive, ancient; eternal'. Friedrich, ZA NF 5.36. See *karuwilis*.
*karuwilis (acc. *karuwilin*, abl. *karuwiliyaz*, pl. *karuwilēs*) 'previous, primitive, ancient; eternal'. Hrozný, BoSt. 3.88 fn. 5; Friedrich, Vert. 1.47 f.; Götze, KlF 1.178; Sturtevant, Lang. 10.267. See *karu*, *karuwilas*.
karuwiliya/e- (midd. *karuwiliyatta*) 'become as before'. Ungnad, ZA NF 2.105 fn. 1; Götze, KlF 1.240.
karuwwariwar; see *kariwwariwar*.
karza (*karaz*, *karazza*, dat. *kardi*, ŠA(G)-*ta*) 'heart'. Hrozný, JSOR 6.69 fn. 1; Götze, ZA 34.183, NBr. 65 fn. 3; HG 106 and fn. 50; Ehelolf, ZA NF 9.176 f. Cf. *kardi-*.
KAS; read KASKAL 'road, journey; campaign'.
KAS₄; read KAŠ₄.
KAŠ = *siyessar* 'beer'.
KAŠ₄ 'run'.
kās 'hic'. Hrozný, MDOG 56.26, SH 140 f., ZA NF 4.174; Friedrich, Vert. 2.95, 141 fn. 1; HG 116, 207 f. For enclitic -*kas*, see *nakkus*.
kāsa 'ecce'. Zimmern, Streitberg Festgabe 439; Sommer, BoSt. 10.31 f., AU 156.
GAŠAN = BĒLTU = *parassis*? 'mistress, lady'. Chrest. 97.
ᴸᵁKAŠ₄.E 'runner, courier'. Cf. Deimel, No. 202.10.
⸔*gasin* (acc.) 'obeisance'?? Sommer, AU 246 f.
KASKAL = ḪARRĀNU = *ursan* 'road, journey; campaign'.
ŠA KASKAL-*NIM* 'viaticum'. Friedrich, AO 25.2.10.47.
KASKAL-*siahh-* (or KASKAL-*sihh-*) 'put on the way'. Sommer, AU 120.
KAS.GÍD; read DANNA.
ᴅKAS.KUR; read ᴅILLAT.

kāsma 'ecce'. Sommer, ZA 33.86 and fn. 2. Cf. *kasa*.
KAS.BU; read DANNA.
KASPU 'silver'.
kåssas 'substitute', i.e. an animal slain in place of a sinner? Hrozný, CH 148.4, 150.21; Zimmern-Friedrich, AO 23.2.31.82; Götze, Hatt. 90.
ᴳᴵˢGA.ŠU 'comb'. Meissner, Beitr. 1.54 f.
ᴸᵁQA.ŠU.GAB; read QA.ŠU.DUₛ.
ᴸᵁQA.ŠU.DUₛ.(A), ᴸᵁQA.ŠU.DUₛ.LIŠ.A 'cup-bearer'.
kasza (acc. *kastan, gastan*) 'hunger'. Weidner, AOF 1.60; Götze, Madd. 78; HG 118, 149.
GAD = *kattanipū*? 'flax, linen cloth'; also as a determinative.
QATAMMA = *apenessan* 'just so'. Weidner, BoSt. 8.92 fn. 3. Götze, ZA NF 2.13.
ᴷᵁˢKA.TAB.ANŠU; read KUŠ.KA.TAB.ANŠU.
QĀTĒ, dual construct state of *QĀTU* 'hand'.
QATĪ = *tuhhusta* 'it is finished'.
katkattenu- 'pour water over, inundate, flood'. Götze, Hatt. 109.
katkattenuske/a- 'pour water over, inundate'. Hrozný, AOr. 3.446.49.
katral, a bronze part of the harness of horses and mules. 'Bell'?? Sayce, AOF 2.106.
ˢᴬᴸ*katras* 'bell-ringer'?? Sayce, AOF 2.106. 'Tambourine player'?? KBo. 5.1.3.48; cf. Sommer, BoSt. 10.69.
katta (sometimes written GAM) adv. 'afterwards'; preverb 'together; down'; postposition, rarely preposition, with dat., rarely w. gen., 'with; under; in, on'. Hrozný, MDOG 56.27, SH 181; Friedrich, ZA NF 1.173 f., Vert. 1.34; Sommer, BoSt. 10.8, 47; Sturtevant, Lang. 6.214, HG 105; Pedersen, AOr. 5.181. Cf. Götze, AOr. 5.18, 19, 21, 24, 26, 29 f.
ᴳᴵˢ*kattaluzzi* 'door'. Friedrich, ZA NF 5.48 f.; Sturtevant, JAOS 54.400.
ᵀᵁᴳGAD.DAM, a kind of clothing for the feet or ankles. 'Gaiters'?? Götze, NBr. 77 fn. 3.
kattan (often written GAM or GAM-*an*) adv. 'afterwards'; preverb 'together with, down'; postposition 'with, by way of, to'. See references s.v. *katta*.
kattanipū 'linen cloth'? Güterbock, KUB 25, preface.
kattanta (also *kattanda*, GAM-*anda*) 'down, in'. Hrozný, SH 227. Cf. s.v. *tarna-*.
ᵁᶻᵁ*kattapalan* (acc.), a part of a sacrificial victim. Friedrich, AO 25.2.6 fn. 7.
kattawanallis 'accomplice'? KUB 13.7.1.15 (G).

kattawatar 'function, business, concern'?   KUB 4.1.1.23 (G).
katte- (usually *katti-*, but *katte-* in KUB 20.83.3.9), a variant of *katta* (q.v.), which is used with enclitic possessives (e.g. *kattimi* 'with me').   Friedrich, ZA NF 3.183; HG 100, 105.
katterrahh- 'make lower, cause to be defeated'.   Götze, Hatt. 91; HG 242.
katter(r)as 'lower; worse, defeated'.   Götze, Hatt. 91, AM 205 fn.; Tenner, ZA NF 4.187 f.; HG 137.
katter(r)a, katterraz 'below, down'.
katti-; read *katte-*.
QADU 'with'; sign of the inst. or abl.
QĀTU = ŠU = *kessar, kessras* 'hand'.
QATŪ 'finish'.
KA × U = *ais* 'mouth'.   Hrozný, BoSt. 3.63 fn. 11.
KA × UD 'tooth'.   Hrozný, CH 6.19, 7 fn. 14, 80.18.   See also s.v. ALAN.
QA-UD-MA; read *QATAMMA*.
KAYAMĀNU 'fixed, regular' (of festivals).   Götze, AM 204 f.
ᴷᵁˢ*gazzimuel*, some part of a horse's harness.   Cf. Hrozný, CH 116.27.
QAZZU = *QAT-ŠU* 'his hand'.   HG 39, 40.
GE; read GI.
ke-; read *ki-*.
kē 'hi, haec', pl. of *kas*.
kĕl, gen. of *kas*.
keldi, a Hurrian word of unknown meaning.   Friedrich, AOF 10.294.   Cf. Ehelolf, KlF. 1.142 f.
GEMÉ; see GIM.
gemmanza; see *gimmanza*.
gemras, see *gimras*.
ᵁᶻᵁ*gĕnu* (*gēnu, ginu*, inst. *ganut*, pl. dat. *kinuwas*) 'knee'.   Friedrich, IF 41.372–6, ZA NF 5.37 fn. 4; HG 66, 89, 102.
ᵁᶻᵁ*gĕnus* (masc.; pl. acc. *gĕnussus*?) 'knee'.   Götze, AM 214 f.; Sturtevant, JAOS 54.401, Chrest. 171.   Cf. Götze, Lang. 11.269 f.
kenzan 'horum', pl. gen. of *kas*.
genzu (also *gimzu*), an abdominal organ or group of organs; 'love, affection, friendship; mercy'.   Friedrich, IF 41.374 fn. 1, Vert. 2.192; Götze, Madd. 132.
genzuwa(e)- (2 sg. *genzuwaisi*) 'attend to'.   Porzig, KlF 1.383.
genzuwalas 'friendly, merciful'.   Friedrich, ZA NF 1.42; Götze, KlF 1.186 fn. 8; Sommer, AU 50.

gebessar; read ᴳᴵ*pessar*.
GEŠPÚ 'strength, force, act of violence; fetter'. Sommer, AU 180–3 (S. transcribes ŠU.BULUG); Deimel, No. 354.63.
GEŠPÚ-*ahh*- 'compel, force'.
ˢᴵᴳ*kesris* 'glove'. Sommer, BoSt. 10.34.
kessar (inst. *kessarta, kissarta*) 'hand'. Hrozný, BoSt. 3.112 fn. 4; Zimmern, OLZ 25.297; Ehelolf, IF 43.317; HG 89, 167, 183; Götze-Pedersen, MS 67 f.; Kurylowicz, EI 8.
kes(s)ras (*kessiras*, acc. *kisseran, kissiran*, dat. *kissarĭ, kīsari, kissiri*, abl. *kissaraz*, pl. *kisserus*) 'hand'. See *kessar*.
kessran tuwaz dāi '(the sacrificer) reaches (his) hand (toward the sacrifice) from a distance'. Götze, Kulturg. 86 and fn. 3.
kesta- (*kistari*, pret. 2 sg. *kistati*, cf. *kestanu-*) 'go out, be quenched'. Friedrich, ZA NF 1.16; Sturtevant, Lang. 6.226, HG 122; Benveniste, BSL 33.138 fn. 3.
kestanu- (imper. 2 pl. *kestanuttin, kistanutten*) 'quench'. Ehelolf, IF 43.317. See *kesta-*.
GEŠTIN 'wine'
GIŠ G. 'grape vine'.
ᴳᴵˢGEŠTIN.È.A 'grape(s)'.
GEŠTIN.UD.DU.A; read GEŠTIN.È.A.
GEŠTU(G) = *istamanas* 'ear'.
GEŠTU(G) = *istammassuwar* 'obedience'.
kēt, inst. of *kas*.
kēdani, kēdaniya 'huic', dat. of *kas*.
kēdanta, inst. of *kas*. Sommer, AU 389.
kēdas, kētas 'his', pl. dat. of *kas*.
keti 'huic', dat. of *kas*.
GEDIM; read GIDIM.
kēz, kēza, abl. of *kas*. As adv. 'on this side; at this time'; *kēz* ... *kēzziya* 'on this side ... and on that side'. Friedrich Vert. 1.160; Götze, AM 260 f.
kezzi, kezziya = *kez* + *-a*, q.v.
GI 'reed, arrow'; also a determinative with the names of objects made of reeds.
KI = *pedan* 'place'. Sommer, AU 411.
KI = *QAQQARU* = *daganzipas* 'ground, floor'. Hrozný, BoSt. 3.72 fn. 5; Ehelolf, KlF 1.147 and fnn. 4, 6.
KI = *ERṢETU* = *tekan* 'earth'; also a post-determinative with names of countries.

-*KI* 'thy' (feminine).   Cf. -*ŠA* 'her'.
-*ki, -ka, -ku*; see -*kki*.
kī 'hoc', neut. of *kās*.
kī; read *kē* 'hi, haec'.
ki- (*kitta, kittari*, pl. *kiyanta, kiyantari*) 'lie, be placed'.   Hrozný, SH
   35, 164 f.; Sommer, BoSt. 10.52; Götze, Hatt. 75; HG 100.
   awan katta k. 'be dislocated'.   KBo. 1.42.2.32 f.
   kattan arha k. 'be excepted (from the oath)'.
KI.2; read KI.MIN.
GIG = *irmas, irmalas* 'ill'.
GIG = *irmaliya/e-* 'be ill'.
GIG = *irmas, irmatar* 'illness'.   Götze, AM 293.
^{uzu}GIG = ^{uzu}NÍG.GIG, q.v.   Sommer; AU 187 fn. 2.
KI.GAL = *salli pedan* 'throne'??   Sommer, AU 100.
KI.KAL.BAD; read KARAŠ.
^{giš}GIGIR 'chariot'.
?*kikki-* (imper. *kikkittaru?*) 'be'?   Friedrich, ZA NF 2.276; Chrest. 198.
kikkis(*s*)- (*kikkistāri*, pl. *kikkisanta*, sup. *kikkissuwwan*) 'become'.
   Friedrich, ZA NF 2.276; Götze, KlF 1.230 and fn. 2; HG 215.
KI.LAL 'weight'.
   KI.LAL.BI 'its weight'.
KI.LAM; read MALBA.
KILĪLU 'ring, wreath'.
^{dug}KIL.KIL = *KUKKUBU?* 'jug, pitcher'?   Sommer, BoSt. 10.57.
GIL.RA; read KUR$_4$.RA.
KIL × DI; read SI × DI.
KILŪLU; error for *KILĪLU* in KUB 9.31.2.48.
GIM (GIM-*an*) = *mahhan* 'as, when'.
GÌM, GEMÉ 'female slave'.
GÌM-*ahh-* 'make (a woman) a slave'.
KI.MIN = *dakki* 'ditto'.
gimmantariya/e- (also *gimmandariya/e-*) 'pass the winter'.   Götze, AM
   294.   See *gimmanza*.
gimmanza [kemants] 'winter'.   Sommer, BoSt. 4.18–23; HG 100.
gimmaras, variant of *gimras*, q.v.
gimras (acc. *gimran*, gen. *gimras, gimmaras*, dat. *gimri, gimra*) 'rus;
   campaign'.   Friedrich, ZA NF 1.180 f., AOF 10.294; Sommer,
   BoSt. 10.12 fn. 1; Sturtevant, Lang. 6.216, HG 170.
gimzu; see *genzu*.
GÍN 'shekel'.   In the Hittite texts, *ZU* 'half-shekel' has sometimes been
   misread as GÍN.   Sommer, BoSt. 10.35.

KIN = *aniya/e-* 'work, perform; care for'.
KIN = *anniyaz* 'performance, report; service, use'.
KIN; ERÍN.MEŠ KIN 'pioneers'? Götze, Kulturg. 117.
KI.NE; read GUNNI.
ᴸᵁ*kinirrilas* 'cithara player'??? Hrozný, SH 52 fn. 1.
ginu; read *genu.*
kinu- 'open, break open'. Ehelolf, KlF 1.141 fn. 2; Götze, NBr. 79.
kinu- 'cause to lie, place'? Hrozný, BoSt. 3.89 fn. 8.
kinun 'now, demum'. Hrozný, SH 37 fn. 2.
kinzan; read *kenzan.*
ᴳᴵˢKIB 'pear tree'? Hrozný, CH 102.15.
KI.BAL 'revolt, sedition'.
gipessar; see ᴳᴵ*pessar.*
QIBĪ (KI-BI), imper. of *QABŪ* 'say'.
   QIBĪ-MA 'just say' is an introductory formula in letters, the command being addressed to the tablet or its bearer.
GIBIL 'fresh, new'.
ᴸᵁ*kipliyalas*, a kind of servant in the royal kitchen. Friedrich, Altorient. Stud. 51.
QĪPTU 'commission'.
   LÚ *QĪPTU (KI-IP-DU)* 'commissioner, governor'? Friedrich, Vert. 1.72.
GÍR 'dagger, knife'.
GÍR 'girdle'.
GÌR 'foot'.
ᴰGÌR, a chthonic deity.
   halkiyas ᴰGÌR-*as* 'grain land'?? Friedrich, Vert. 2.31.
GIR₄ 'asphalt'. Ehelolf, BoSt. 10.56.
ᴰᵁᴳGÌR.KÁN, a vessel for wine. Cf. Götze, KlF 1.201.
ᴳᴵˢGÌR.GUB 'foot stool'.
ᴬᴺˢᵁGÌR.NUN.NA; read ANŠU.GÌR.NUN.NA.
ᵁᶻᵁGÌR.PAD.DU = *hastai* 'bone'. (The determinative occurs KUB 24.14.1.24.)
KÍR.RA; read KUR₄.RA.
ᴳᴵˢGÌR.DU; read ᴳᴵˢGÌR.GUB.
GIŠ = *taru* 'tree, wood'; also a determinative with words for kinds of trees, wooden objects, or utensils of any material.
kis-, kīsa- (kīsāri, 2 sg. *kistati*, pret. *kisat, kisati*, 1 sg. *kishat, kishahat)* 'happen, become'; with *-za* 'become'. Hrozný, MDOG 56.37, SH 17 f., 164-6; Götze, AM 294; HG 100, 228, 289 f.
   anda k. 'attach oneself to, conspire with'. Sommer, AU 58.

kisan; see *kissan*.
KIŠIB; ZA.KIŠIB 'seal, seal cylinder'. See s.v. É.
kiske/a- 'comb'? KUB 12.26.2.1 (X). See *kissa(e)-*.
GIŠ.KU; read ^{GIŠ}TUKUL.
KISLAḪ 'threshing floor'. Götze, AJSL 52.143-59.
GIŠ.PA; read ^{GIŠ}PA.
kisris; read *kesris*.
GIŠ.RU; read ^{GIŠ}ŠUB 'inventory'.
GIŠ.RU; read GIŠ-*ru* 'tree, wood'.
kis(s)a(e) = (*kissaizzi*, pret. pl. *kissir*) 'comb'. Götze, ap. Meissner, Beitr. 1.54 f., 55 fn. 1.
kis(s)an 'in this way, thus, as follows'. Hrozný, JSOR 6.69 fn. 1; Sommer, BoSt. 10.12 f.; Friedrich, Vert. 2.141 f.; Götze-Pedersen, MS 56.
GIŠ.ŠAR; see ^{GIŠ}ŠAR.
kissar; read *kessar*.
kissuwanza 'such'. Friedrich, Vert. 2.175.
kista-; read *kesta-*.
kistantit [kestantet] (inst.) 'with hunger'. Götze, Madd. 77 f.; HG 159. Cf. *kasza*, *kisduwanza*.
kistanu-; read *kestanu-*.
kistanziya/e- [kestantsiya-] (pret. *kistanziyattat*) 'be hungry'. Götze, Madd. 78 and fn. 3; HG 126, 225.
GIŠ.TUR.TÚG 'seat'? Ehelolf ap. Friedrich, ZA NF 5.62.
*kisduwanza [kestwants] (dat. *kisduwanti*, *kisduwanda*, pl. *kisduwantes*) 'hungry'. Götze, Madd. 77 f.; HG 160. Cf. *kasza*.
GÍD = *dalugi-* 'long'.
KID; read LÍL.
kidani; read *kedani*.
^{LÚ}*kītas*, a kind of priest. Götze ap. Friedrich, ZA NF 3.179; Sommer, BoSt. 10.69; AF 84.
GIDIM 'ghost, spirit of one dead'.
GIDIM.ḪI.A = *aggantes* 'Manes'.
kitpa(n)dalaz 'from now on'? Friedrich, ZA NF 2.282; Götze, NBr. 5.
GÍD.DA = *dalugi-* 'long'.
GÍD.DA = *dalugasti* 'length'. Cf. Sommer, AU 140 fn. 1.
KI.UD; read KISLAḪ.
GI.Ú.TAG.GA; read ^{GI}Ú.TAG.GA.
-k(k)i, *-k(k)a*, *-ku*, an enclitic appended to indefinite pronouns and adverbs. See *kwiski*.

ᵁᶻᵁGÚ 'neck'.
GU₄; read GUD.
KU; read DÙR.
ᴳᴵˢKU; read ᴳᴵˢTUKUL.
KÚ = et- 'eat, cause to eat'.
KÙ; read KU(G).
KU₆ 'fish'.
-ku . . .-ku; see -akku . . . -akku.
-ku; a rare variant for -kki, -kka (kwis-ku). HG 120; Hahn, Lang. 12. 110 and fn. 15.
kuaskuas-; read kwaskwas-.
kue-; for words beginning thus, see kwe-.
ᵀᵁᴳGÚ.Ê.A; read TÚG.GÚ.Ê.A.
ku-e-eš-šar = kuressar, q.v.
kuin-; read kwen-.
kuin, kuinki, kuinna; read kwin, kwinki, kwinna.
kuir-; read kwer-.
kuirwanas; read kwirwanas.
kuis, kuiski, kuis(s)a; read kwis, kwiski, kwis(s)a.
kuit, kuida, kuitki; read kwit, kwida, kwitki.
kuitman; read kwetman.
kuitta; read kwitta.
kuius; read kweyus.
ᶻᴬGUG, a precious stone.
KU(G) = suppis 'clean, pure, bright'.
GÚ.GAL 'bean, bean plant'.
    GÚ.GAL.GAL. Cf. Chrest. 124.
KÙ.GI; read GUŠKIN.
KU(G).GA = KU(G).
GUKKAL; read SÍG + SAL and see UDU.SÍG + SAL.
KU(G).GI; read GUŠKIN.
?kukkureske/a- (pret. pl. ku-uk-ku-ri-eš-ki-ir) 'cut off, mutilate'. HG 237 fn. 46; but one may read kukkursker.
kukkurske/a- (pl. kukkuraskanzi, kukkureskanzi) 'cut off, mutilate'. Hrozný, CH 74.43, 76.56; Ehelolf, KlF 1.397 and fn. 4; HG 119, 216, 237. Cf. kukursanza.
ᴸᵁKU(G).DÍM 'goldsmith'.
⁎kukupalatar 'offense'? KUB 26.1.4.52 (G).
ᴰᵁᴳKUKUBBU = KIL.KIL 'pitcher, jug'.
⁎kugurniyaman anda 'unter dem Siegel der Verschwiegenheit'??? Götze, KlF 1.410 f.

*kukursanza (pl. kukursantes) 'mutilated'.   Cf. kukkurske/a-.
KU(G).UD; read KUBABBAR.
GUL = walhh- 'strike, destroy; play (a musical instrument)'.
GUL = walhanna- 'strike, attack'.
GUL = walhanneske/a- 'strike, attack'.
GUL = walhheske/a- 'strike, destroy; play (a musical instrument)'.
?GUL (GUL-aszi, pl. GUL-askanzi) 'imprint, mark'?? Friedrich, OLZ 39.310; cf. Sommer ap. Fiesel, Etruskisch 79. Others read gulss-, gulske/a-, q.v.
KUL; read NUMUN.
kūlas, a costly object.   Götze, NBr. 58 fn. 1.
gulaske/a-; read gulske/a-.
gulas(s)-; read gulss-.
gulassas; read gulssas.
kulawanes; ERUM k. 'subordinate vassal'?? Sommer, AU 225, 348 fn. 1.
kulē (also kulī) 'by usurping'?? Walther, HC 255.46. Cf. Götze, NBr. 58 and fn. 1.
gullakuwan (neut.) 'soiled, defiled'?? Friedrich, Altorient. Stud. 50, 55.
?gulske/a- (gulaske/a-) 'protect'?? See gulss-. Others read GUL-aske/a-.
?guls(s)- (gulaszi, pl. gulsanzi, part. gulsanza, gulassan) 'see, perceive; observe, obey; protect'?? Götze, Madd. 121 fn. 2; Hrozný, ZA NF 4.180-4; Götze-Pedersen, MS 56. Others read GUL-as-.
ᴰgulssas (gulsas, pl. gulses, gulasses) 'protecting deity'. See gulss-.
GÙ.UN; read GUN.
GUN 'talent'.
GUN-an, see GUN.LIŠ-an.
KUN 'tail'.
kun-; see kwen-.
kūn 'hunc', acc. of kās.
*kunatar (gen. kunannas, dat. kunanna) 'a striking, slaying, execution'. Kretschmer, KlF 1. 301; Sommer, AU 412. See kwen-.
ᐊkunistayallis 'confidential'??   KUB 26.1.4.12 (G).
kunk- (1 pl. kunkuweni, part. neut. kungan) 'prepare, adorn'?? or 'toss, dandle'?? Götze, KlF 1.235 and fnn. 4, 5, 6; Carruthers, Lang. 9. 155.
kunkeske/a- 'prepare, adorn'?? or 'toss, dandle'?? Cf. Eheolf, OLZ 29.767.26. See kunk-.
ᶻᴬkunkunuzzi 'diorite'. Götze, KlF 1.201; Carruthers, Lang. 9.154 f.

GUN(.LIŠ)-*an*, a term in oracle texts, indicating the flight of birds; the contrasting term is TAR(.LIŠ)-*wan*, q.v. 'Uferwärts'?? Götze, Kulturg. 141.
kunnahh- 'make right, bring to success; succeed'. Sommer, AU 247; Ehelolf, KUB 27 preface p. V.
kunnahhiske/a- (ZAG-*nahhiske/a-*) 'make right, bring to success; succeed'.
kunnas 'dexter, favorable, good'. Ehelolf, KUB 27 preface p. V.
kunnatar (ZAG-*natar*, ZAG-*tar*) 'rightness, being on the right, favorableness'. Cf. Hrozný, BoSt. 3.35 fn. 7.
GUNNI = *hassas* 'hearth, stove'.
-KUNU = -*smes* 'vester'.
kunza-, kunzi- (acc. *kunzan*, neut. *kunzi*), probably a color word. Götze, KlF 1.404 and fn. 1.
GUB 'stand'.
GUB-(*as*) 'standing'. Sommer, AU 32.
GÙB (GÙB-*las*) 'left, unfavorable, bad'.
GÙB-*latar* 'leftness, being on the left, unfavorableness'.
kup- (pret. *kupta*) 'plan, make a plan; play (tricks)'? Friedrich, KlF 1.288 and fn. 3; Götze, AOr. 2.157.24.
*kŭpahis (acc. *kŭpahin*, pl. *kupahius*) 'hat, cap'? Sommer, BoSt. 10.37.
KUBABBAR 'silver'.
⁎*kupiyatis* 'plan, trick, secondary purpose'? See *kup-*.
KUR (pl. KUR.MEŠ, KUR.KUR.MEŠ) = *MĀTU* = *utne, utneyanza* 'country'; it may sometimes be interpreted as a determinative before names of countries.
ᴸᵁKÛR = *kururas* 'enemy'.
KÛR = *harra-* 'break, destroy'? Hrozný, BoSt. 3.238 fn. 7. Cf. Forrer, ZDMG 76.181; Friedrich, Vert. 2.105, 144. But this may not be the same sign as KÛR in other senses. Cf. Chrest. 41 near end.
KÛR; read PAB 'protect'.
kur-; see *kwer-*.
kurak-; read *kurk-*.
*kurakkis (acc. ᴳᴵˢ*kurakkin*, gen. ᴳᴵˢ*kurakkiyas*) a part of a house. Götze, NBr. 63 (read KBo. 4.1).
kuras; see *kweras*.
*kuratar (gen. *kurannas*) 'a cutting'; see *kwer-*.

kurawanas; see *kwirwanas*.
kuressar (also *ku-e-eš-šar*) 'a cutting'. HG 152; Ehelolf, ZA NF 9.172.
    ᵀᵁᴳ*kuressar* (inst. *kurisnit*), a strip of cloth used as a table cover or as an article of clothing. Sommer, AU 187 and fn. 3.
kurēwanas; see *kwirwanas*.
kurimpas (pl.) 'dregs'?? Sommer, BoSt. 10.67.
kurisnit; see *kuressar*.
kuriw(w)anas; see *kwirwanas*.
kurk- (pl. *kurkanzi*, imper. *kurakdu*) 'keep'. Chrest. 108.44.
    anda k. 'keep in'. Chrest. 121.
KUR.KUR; see KUR.
KUR₄.RA = *harsis* 'ordinary, usual'. Götze, KlF 1.199 f.
    NINDA KUR₄.RA 'ordinary bread'.
gursamassa; URU *g.* = URU *kursawansas*? q.v.
gursam[u?]- 'ruined'? Sommer, AU 272. Cf. Götze, AM 216 f.
ᴷᵁˢ*kursas* 'hide; shield (especially of an archer); leather table cover'. Sommer, AU 181 f., 381; HG 119.
⁑*gursawananza* 'ruined'? See *gursawara*.
kursawansas; URU *k.* 'ruined city'?? Sommer, AU 272 fn. 3.
⁑*gursawara* (pl. neut.?) 'ruined'? Sommer, AU 51 fn., 272. Cf. Götze, AM 216 f.
gurta- (acc. *gurtan*, dat. *gurti*) 'citadel'. Forrer, Forsch. 2.46; Götze, AM 248; Benveniste, BSL 33.139; HG 119.157.
kŭrur (gen. *kururas*) 'hostility; hostile'. Hrozný, BoSt. 3.137 fn. 7; Götze, Hatt. 79, 123; Friedrich, Vert. 1.88 f.; Sturtevant, Lang. 6.217, HG 97, 119, 148, 162.
kururahta; probably erroneous for *kururiahta*. See *kururiyahh-*. Cf. HG 73.
kŭruras 'hostile; enemy'. (Adj. developed from gen. of *kŭrur* 'hostility'? Cf. HG 166.)
*kururatar (dat. *kururanni*) 'hostility, war'. Sommer, AU 324.
kururihh-; read *kururiahh-*, and see *kururiyahh-*. HG 73.
kŭruriya/e- (pret. *kŭruriēt*) 'be hostile'. KUB 11.1.2.7.
kŭruriyahh- (also *kururiahh-*, *kŭrurriyahh-*) 'make war'. Hrozný, BoSt. 3.137 fn. 7; Götze, Hatt. 79. Cf. Sommer, AU 174.
kururiyahheske/a- 'make war'. See *kururiyahh-*.
kŭrurriyahh-, variant for *kururiyahh-*.
kŭrudawwanza 'silent'?? Götze, NBr. 34.
KUŠ = *MAŠKU* 'hide, leather'; also as a determinative before names of leather objects.

KUŠ (pl. KUŠ.MEŠ), a kind of omen. Cf. Hrozný, BoSt. 3.30.4, etc. (he writes SU).
kūs 'hi, hos', pl. of kās.
kus- (pret. 1 sg. kushahat) 'pay, repay'. Götze, Hatt. 91. NBr. 20.
kŭsăta (pl., gen. kūsadas) 'bride-price; marriage'. Hrozný, CH 24.11, etc.; Sturtevant, JAOS 54.402; HG 157.
GÚ.ŠEŠ 'bitter beans'. Sommer, AU 109.
KUŠ.E.SIR; read ^{KUŠ}E.SIR.
KUŠ.KA.TAB.ANŠU 'halter, bridle'.
ŠA KUŠ.KA.TAB.ANŠU 'groom', a functionary at court. Götze, Hatt. 56; Chrest. 87.
GUŠKIN 'gold'.
kuskuss- (kuskuszi, pl. kuskussanzi) 'mix'. Witzel, HKU 114.23, 116.41; HG 102, 123.
^{DUG}kuskussulli 'mixing bowl'. Witzel, HKU 114.22; HG 146, 159.
^{GIŠ}kuskussulli 'mixer'? Cf. Witzel, HKU 100.25.
KUŠ.LAL 'skin for carrying water'. Friedrich, Altorient. Stud. 50, 54.
LÚ.MEŠ A ŠA KUŠ.LAL 'water carriers'.
kusne/a- (kusnezzi) 'hire'. Hrozný, CH 122.34.
KUŠ.NÍG.BAR, ein ledernes Ding zum Ausbreiten? Götze, AOr. 5.22 fn. 3.
kŭs(s)an (dat. kussanī, kusni, abl. kusnaz) 'pay, fee, wages; price'. Hrozný, CH 8.28, etc.
^{LÚ}kussanattallas 'mercenary (soldier)'. Sayce, JRAS 1931.428; Götze, RHA 1.29.
kussane (neut., also kussani) 'pay, wages; price'. Hrozný, CH 122.32, etc.
kus(s)aniya/e- (kussaniyēzzi, kusaniizzi, kussaniyazi) 'hire'. Hrozný, CH 34.48, etc.; HG 225.
GUD 'cow, bull, ox'.
GUD.AM 'wild bull'.
GUD.ÁB = *LITTU* 'cow'.
GUD.APIN.LAL 'plow ox'.
KÙ.DÍM; read KU(G).DÍM.
GUD.LID; read GUD.ÁB.
GUD.MAḪ 'bull'.
kutruenes (pl.) '(divine) witnesses (to an oath)'? HT 1.1.57.
*kutrus (pl. kutruēs, acc. kutrūs) 'witness'. Sommer, BoSt. 7.14 fn. 2, 10.76; Götze, KlF 1.178; Carruthers, Lang. 9.151 f.; Pedersen, AOr. 5.177-9.

kŭtruwă(e)- 'provide a witness, act before a witness'. Hrozný, CH 94.7, 10; Friedrich, Vert. 2.101; HG 120, 227 (the meaning given there is wrong!). Cf. Götze, Madd. 82.

kutruwahh- (pret. 1 sg. *kutruwahhun*) 'make (one) a witness'. Friedrich, Vert. 2.101.

*kutruwatar (dat. *kutruwanni*) 'a witnessing, a being called to witness'. Götze, Madd. 95, KlF 1.178.

GUD.ŠE 'fat ox'.

kuttanalli 'necklace'. Friedrich, ZA NF 2.275; Sturtevant, Lang. 10. 267.

kŭt(t)ar (dat. *kuttani*) 'shoulder, neck; strength'. Friedrich, ZA NF 2.275. Rather 'neck; strength'. Mudge, Lang. 7.252.

**kut(t)as* (dat. *kutti*, abl. *kuddaz, kuttaz*, pl. acc. *kuddus, kudus*) 'wall, side'? Sommer, BoSt. 10.4 fn. 1, 53. Cf. Kretschmer, Glotta 15.158–60.

^{TÚG}GÚ.UD.DU.A; read TÚG.GÚ.È.A.

GÚ.TUR 'pea, pea plant'.

kuwāliu (neut.), an epithet of *hwnhwessar*; 'dark'??? Ehelolf, KlF 1.396.

kuwalutis (pl.?), something inlaid in gold. Ehelolf, KlF 1.396.

kuwapi [kwapi] (also *kuwapit*), indefinite, 'anywhere, ever' (especially in conditional or negative sentences); relative and interrogative, 'where, whither, when, while'; relative, 'as soon as; while, whereas'. Hrozný, MDOG 56.26, SH 146; Sommer, BoSt. 10.54, AU 159 f.; Friedrich, Vert. 2.141; HG 120, 203, Chrest. 76.73, 78.24. Cf. Götze, Hatt. 124, AM 296.

kuwapikki [kwapik·i] (rarely *kuwapiki*) 'anywhere, ever' (usually in conditional or negative sentences). Hrozný, SH 150; Götze, Hatt. 124; Sommer, AU 247 f., 341.

kuwapit; see *kuwapi*.

kuwapitta [kwapit·a] 'everywhere'. Sommer, BoSt. 10.54.

kuwapiya 'everywhere, always'. Sommer, AU 117.

kuwaske/a- [kwask·e-] 'strike, kill'. Tenner, HAT 23; Götze, Madd. 131 and fn. 5; HG 104, 134, 237. See *kwen-, kun-*.

kuwass- [*kuwaszi*, pl. *kuwassanzi*] 'kiss'. Ehelolf, OLZ 29.989 fn. 3; Sommer, OLZ 33.755; Benveniste, BSL 33.139.

kuwat [kwat] 'why' (interrogative). Hrozný, SH 146; Ungnad, ZA NF 3.287; HG 93, 203.

kuwatan; see *kuwattan*.

kuwaten (written *kuwatin*); see *kuwattan*.

kuwatka [kwatk·a] 'at all'? Hrozný, BoSt. 3.212.81. 'In any way, perhaps'? Friedrich, ZA NF 1.41. Götze (in conversation) holds that the word gives the verb a 'modal' force—'could, might' or the like.

kuwatta, dat. of *kwis* or of *kwissa*. HG 210. Cf. Friedrich, ZA NF 2.274; Sommer, AU 265.

kuwatta [kwat·a]; *kuwatta kuwatta* 'quot'?? Sturtevant, AJP 50.364. Cf. *kwitta*.

kuwat(t)a(n) [kwat·an], *kuwatin* 'whither, why'. Götze, Hatt. 124; Friedrich, ZA NF 2.274 and fn. 3; HG 83 (in line 16 from the bottom, for 'sometimes', read 'usually'), 203, 205, 206.

↟*kuwayami* (dat.) 'dangerous, of danger'?? Chrest. 66.51. Cf. Götze, Hatt. 74.

ᴳᴵˢGU.ZA 'throne'.

kwaskwas- (*kwaskwaszi*) 'pound, crush'? KUB 7.1.1.26. But cf. *kuskus-*.

kwĕ 'qui, quae', pl. of *kwis*.

kweka, *kwĕk(k)i* 'quaequam', neut. pl. of *kwiski*.

kwēl 'cuius', gen. of *kwis*.

kwĕlka 'cuiusquam', gen. of *kwiski*.

kwēlla 'cuiusque', gen. of *kwissa*.

kwemi; see *kwen-*.

kwen-, *kun-* (*kwenzi*, 1 sg. *kwemi*, 2 sg. *kwesi*, pl. *kunanzi*) 'strike; defeat; kill'. Hrozný, BoSt. 3.73 fn. 8; Friedrich, Vert. 1.152; Götze, Madd. 131 and fn. 5; Sturtevant, Lang. 6. 222 f., HG 123, 220.

?*kwenas* (SAL-*ú-i-na-as*) 'women'?? Götze-Pedersen, MS 65.

kwēne = *kwe* 'qui' + *ne* 'ea'?? Friedrich, ZA NF 2.292.

kwenna- (pl. *kwenanzi*, 1 pl. *kwennummeni*) 'strike; defeat; kill'. Friedrich, AOF 6.307; HG 245.

kwennes- (pret. *kwennesta*) 'strike; defeat; kill'. Friedrich, ZA NF 5.52; HG 230.

kwenneske/a- 'strike; defeat; kill'. Friedrich, ZA NF 5.55; HG 238.

kwenniya/e- 'strike; defeat; kill'. HG 225.

kwenu- 'cause to kill'. HG 235.

kwenzumnas 'cuias, of what country'. Friedrich, Vert. 2.152.

kwēr-, *kur-* (*kwirzi*, *kwērzi*, pl. *kuranzi*) 'cut, cut off'. Götze, OLZ 33.291 and fn. 6; Sturtevant, Lang. 6.225; Sommer, AU 187; Benveniste, BSL 33.138 fn. 3; HG 119, 220; Kurylowicz, EI 22.

istarna arha k. 'cut through'. Sommer, AU 187 fn. 3.

kweras (also *kuras*) 'country, territory; field, plain'. Hrozný, BoSt. 3.212 fn. 3; Sommer, BoSt. 7.30 and fn. 1; Friedrich, KlF 1.295; HG 59.

kwēs 'qui', pl. of *kwis*.

kwēsa 'quique', pl. of *kwissa*.

kwesi; see *kwen-*.

kweska 'quiquam', pl. of *kwiski*.

kwĕdăni 'cui', dat. of *kwis*.

kwēdaniya 'cuique', dat. of *kwissa*.

kwĕdan(n)ik(k)i 'cuiquam', dat. of *kwiski*.

kwetas (also *kwedas*) 'quibus', pl. dat. of *kwis*.

kwĕtman (*kwitman, kwētman*) in main clause 'in the meanwhile, for a while; immediately'. In subordinate clause 'while, as long as; until'. Hrozný, SH 146 and fn. 2; Sommer, BoSt. 4.14 fn. 1; Friedrich, Vert. 1.82; Ungnad, ZA NF 3.285-9; Götze-Pedersen, MS 56.

piran parā k. 'bis dahin, before'. Sommer, AU 277 fn. 1.

kweyus (*kwius, kweus*) 'quos', acc. pl. of *kwis*.

kweyussa (*kwiussa*) 'quosque', acc. pl. of *kwissa*.

kwez, abl. of *kwis*.

kwezka, abl. of *kwiski*.

kwezza, abl. of *kwissa*.

kwēzzi 'where'. Friedrich, AO 25.2.9.6.

kwin 'quem', acc. of *kwis*.

kwin-; read *kwen-*.

kwinki 'quemquam', acc. of *kwiski*.

kwinna 'quemque', acc. of *kwissa*.

kwir-; read *kwer-*.

$^{LÚ.MEŠ}$*kwirwanas* (pl., also *kurēwanes, kuriwanas, kuriwanus*) 'independent monarchs', honorific title of kings of Hittite protectorates. Sommer, AU 342-8; Meriggi, RHA 2.31-8. Cf. Götze, Kulturg. 91 f.

kwis 'quis, qui, aliquis' (interrogative, indefinite, relative). Hrozný, MDOG 56.26, SH 144-8, BoSt. 3.187 fn. 8; Friedrich, Vert. 1.87; Ungnad, ZA NF 3.288; Sturtevant, Lang. Monograph 7.141-9; Sommer, AU 133, 284; Götze, AM 295; HG 120, 202 f., 209 f.; Hahn, TAPA 64.28-30.

kwis . . . kwis 'one . . . another'. Ehelolf, OLZ 29.768, 769 fn. 7; Götze, Hatt. 123.

kwis imma kwis; see *imma*.

kwis kwis 'quisquis'.

kwisas; see *kwissas*.
kwiski (in negative sentences) 'quisquam'; (in conditional sentences) 'quis'. Hrozný, MDOG 56.36, SH 148-50; Marstrander, Car. 26; Sommer, BoSt. 10.13 fn. 1, AU 125; HG 202, 210; Götze-Pedersen, MS 56; Hahn, TAPA 64.29 f., 33, Lang. 12.110 fn. 14.
kwis(s)a 'quisque'. Sommer, BoSt. 10.16; HG 211.
kwis(s)as = *kwis* + *as*. Götze, ZA NF 2.267.
kwit 'quid, quod', neut. of *kwis*.
kwit 'because; that (with verbs of emotion, of saying, etc.); as to the fact that; at the time when, on the occasion when; since, after; if'. Friedrich, ZA NF 2.279 f., Vert. 1.30; Götze, OLZ 28.238 and fn. 1, KlF 1.220 f.; Sommer, AU 70. 186.
-*ma* . . . *kwit* 'whereas'. Sommer, AU 70.
kwida 'quidque', neut. of *kwissa*.
kwitki 'quicquam', neut. of *kwiski*.
kwitman; read *kwetman*.
kwitta 'several, respectively'. Sturtevant, TAPA 58.22; KUB 20.59.5. 13. Cf. *kuwatta*.

la-, see *lai-*.
lahha- (dat. *lahha*, *lahhi*, abl. *lahhaz*) 'campaign, war'. Hrozný, CH 34. 48; Götze, Hatt. 87.
lahheske/a-; and *lahhiyeske/a-*.
lahhilahheskinu- 'drive at a gallop'? Hrozný, AOr. 3.440.16, 456.42.
lahhiya/e- 'take the field, go on a campaign'. See *lahha-*.
lahhiyaiske/a-; read *lahhiyeske/a-*.
lahhiyanniske/a- 'take the field, go on a campaign'. Götze, Hatt. 87; HG 245.
lahhiyaske/a-; read *lahhiyeske/a-*.
lahhiyatar 'campaign'. Sommer, BoSt. 7.48; Götze, Hatt. 87; Friedrich, Vert. 2.95.
lahhiyeske/a- (2 sg. *lahhieskisi*, *lahhiyaiskisi*, imper. 2 sg. *lahhieski*, *lahhiyaiski*), 'take the field, go on a campaign'. Cf. Friedrich, Vert. 2.68 fnn. 1, 2, ZA NF 5.22.2.9. Cf. HG 54.
lahhu- lăhw- (*lăhwi*, *lăhuwi*, imper. 2 pl. *lahhutin*) 'pour'. Hrozný, SH 34, BoSt. 3.76 fn. 6; Sommer, BoSt. 10.74; HG 59, 60, 138; Couvreur, Hett. *h* 17. Cf. *lahhuwwa-*.
ser arha *l.* 'dip out'. KUB 13.4.1.62.
^{GIŠ}*lahhŭras*, a sacrificial implement. Sommer, AU 373, 413.
^{GIŠ}*lahhurnuz(z)i*, a kind of sacrificial table. Sturtevant, Lang. 4.2 fn. 11, TAPA 58.20; Götze, KlF 1.201; Sommer, AU 396.

lahhurnuzzius (pl.), a variant form of the preceding. HG 155.
lahhus 'basin, bowl'. Friedrich, ZA NF 1.11; Sturtevant, Lang. 4.162.
lăh(h)uw(w)ă- (*lăhhuwwăi, lăhuwwăi, lăhuwai,* imper. 2 pl. *lăhhuwatin*) 'pour'. See *lahhu, lahw-.*
lahlahheske/a- (1 pl. *lahlahhesgaweni*) 'fight repeatedly' or 'be anxious'? See *lahlahhiya/e-*; but cf. Hrozný, BoSt. 3.37 fn. 7.
lahlah(h)imas 'conflict; anxiety, grief, worry'. Götze, Hatt. 87, KlF 1. 185–7. Adj. (developed from the gen. of the substantive) 'terrifying' or the like.
lahlahhiya/e- 'fight repeatedly'? Götze, Hatt. 87. 'Be anxious' or the like? Götze, KlF 1.186.
?*lahlahhiyanu-* (pret. pl. *la-ah-la-ah-ḫi-nu-e-nu-e-ir*?) 'cause to fight repeatedly'?; 'cause to be anxious'? Cf. Götze, KlF 1.186.
lahuw(w)a-; see *lahhuwwa-.*
lahw-; see *lahhu-.*
lăi- (*lăi,* pl. *lānzi,* pret. 1 sg. *lāwun,* midd. *laittari*) 'loose, unharness'. Hrozný, BoSt. 3.59 fn. 5; HG 138, 248; Kurylowicz, EI 74. Cf. *laiske/a-.*
lăiske/a- 'unloose'. Friedrich, ZA NF 5.58. See *lai-.*
laittari; see *lai-.*
lăk- (*lāki,* midd. *lagāri*) act. 'cause to incline, cause to fall, overturn'; midd. 'incline, fall; lie'. Forrer, Forsch. 1.183–5; Sommer, AU 170 f.; Sturtevant, Lang. 6.216 f., HG 118. Cf. *salik-.*
laknu- 'cause to incline; tip (a table) over; win (an opponent) over'. HG 234. See *lak-.*
LÀL = *melit* 'honey'.
lāla (acc. *lālan*) 'virility'? Sommer, AF 85. Cf. *lalu.*
lalawwanzi (infin.) 'to fornicate'?? Götze, Kulturg. 149; cf. KUB 12. 62.1.12.
lalessar 'demand, request'?? Hrozný, AOr. 1.280.70. Cf. *ilaliya/e-.*
lālu 'penis erectus'. Friedrich, Glotta, 23.210–3.
lalukkimas 'rest, peace'?? Ehelolf, Berl. Mus. Ber. 49.34 fn. 3. 'Brilliance, joy'?? (G).
ᴰLAMA; see ᴰKAL.
lămăn (gen. *lamnas*) 'name, reputation'. Hrozný, BoSt. 5.27 fn. 5; Friedrich, Vert. 2.92 f., AOF 6.114; Hrozný, JA 218.316 f.; Kurylowicz, EI 75; Cuny, Mélanges offerts à M.O. Navarre 101.
lammar (gen. *lamnas*), an expression of time; perhaps 'hour'? or 'moment'?? Hrozný, BoSt. 5.27 fn. 5; Friedrich, Vert. 2.92 f.
  lammar 'on the hour(?), promptly'.
  lammar lammar 'every hour(?), repeatedly'.

lamniya/e- 'name, call; order, command'. Friedrich, Vert. 2.92 fn. 2. See *laman*.
ANA ^{GIŠ}DUBBIN *l.* 'indict, bring an action against'? Chrest. 89.
lamtati (midd. 3 sg.); *anku l., anda l.* 'is mingled, is combined'? Cf. Ehelolf, ZA NF 9.176 f.
LĀNU 'form, figure, body; self'.
lanzi; see *lai-*.
lap-; see *lapp-*.
lapanuwwani 'herd'?? Götze, KlF 1.109.
laparnas, a variant for *taparnas*, q.v.
LABKU (also *LABQU, LABGU*), an epithet of NINDA 'loaf'; possibly = SIG 'thin, flat'. (G).
lapnuske/a- 'make (red) hot'. See *lapp-*.
lapp- (*lapzi*, pl. **lappanzi*—cf. *lappas, lappiyas*) 'glow, be red-hot'. Friedrich, ZA NF 5.70–2, 80; Mudge, Lang. 7.252; Benveniste, BSL 33.140.
*lappas (abl. *lappaza*, pl. *lappus*) 'glowing, hot'. See *lapp-*.
lappiyas 'heat, fever'. See *lapp-*.
larpu- (*larputta*) 'be without obligations'?? Hrozný, CH 126.20. 'Be permitted'?? Walther, HC 267.162.
⁂*lawarr-* (pret. *lawarritta*, infin. *lawwarruna*) 'be broken, be destroyed'? Sommer, AU 108; Götze, AM 229.
lawun; see *lai-*.
lawwarr-; see *lawarr-*.
lazzais 'well being, favorable condition'. Götze, Madd. 98 and fn. 8.
*lazzis (acc. SIG$_5$-*in*) 'favorable, lucky; well, healthy; noble(?)'. Götze, KlF 184, Madd. 128; Friedrich, Vert. 2.138; Sturtevant, Lang. 10.270.
lazzin (SIG$_5$-*in*) 'favorably, well'.
lazziske/a- (midd. SIG$_5$-*iskittari*) midd. 'recover, be well'. See *lazziya/e-*.
lăzziya/e- (imper. SIG$_5$-*du*, midd. *lăzziatta*, SIG$_5$-*attari*) 'be favorable'; midd. 'recover, be well'. Zimmern, OLZ 25.298; Sommer, BoSt. 7.39.
lazziyahh- (SIG$_5$-*ahh-*) 'make favorable; give favorable omens'. Sturtevant, TAPA 58.21. Cf. Witzel, HKU 96.47.
lazziyahhiske/a- (SIG$_5$-*ahhiske/a-*) 'make favorable; give favorable omens'. KUB 14.8.2.39.
*lazziyatar (dat. SIG$_5$-*anni*) 'welfare'.
lē (w. pres.) 'ne'. Hrozný, SH 92 fn. 4, 184, JSOR 6.69 fn. 1; HG 251 and fn. 70.
^{GIŠ}*LEḪU* (properly *LĒ'U*) '(wooden) tablet'.

lēlaniyanza 'turned toward a *lelas* festival'?? KUB 17.10.2.33, 4.4. 'Hastening'?? Götze, Kulturg. 136.
lĕlas (also *lilas*), a kind of festival. Cf. Hrozný, BoSt. 3.10.43; KUB 9.15.2.24.
lĕliwanza (also *liliwanza*) 'quick, urgent' or the like? Cf. *liliwahh-*.
lenk- (*likzi, lingazi*, pret. *likta, linkatta, linikta*, 1 sg. *linkun*) 'swear'. Hrozný, SH 16; Friedrich, ZA NF 2.53, Vert. 1.173 f.; Sturtevant, Lang. 6.218, HG 118, 273 and fn. 114. Cf. *lenke/a-, lenkais.*
*lenkăis (acc. *lingain*, gen. *linkiyas, lenkias, lingayas*, dat. *linkiya, lenkiya, lingai*, pl. *lingăus, lengaus*) 'oath'. Sommer, AU 356 f.; Petersen, Lang. 9.18; HG 103, 147. See *lenk-*.
*lenkanas (inst. *linkanta*, pl. *linganus*) 'oath'. Ehelolf, IF 43.316; Götze, Madd. 114. See *lenk-*.
lenganu- (pret. *linganut, lenganut*) 'cause to swear, bind by an oath'. HG 235. See *lenk-*.
lenganuske/a- (pl. *linganuskanzi*) 'cause to swear'. KUB 21.42.1.9, 10.
lenke/a- (pret. 1 pl. *lengawen*, imper. 2 sg. *linki*). See *lenk-*.
lenkes- (pret. *linkesta*) 'swear'. HG 230. See *lenk-*.
lenkeske/a- (pret. *linkiskit*) 'swear', KBo. 6.34.3.14. See *lenk-*.
lenkiya/e- (part. *linkiyantes*) 'swear by'. Götze, KlF 1.182. Cf. Friedrich, Vert. 1.86. See *lenk-*.
^{LÚ}LI, an abbreviated writing for $^{LÚ}LIṬŪTU$, q.v. Sommer, AU 231.
^{GIŠ}LI.ḪU.SI; read ^{GIŠ}LI.U₅.
lik-; read *lenk-*.
LÍL = ṢERU = *gimras* 'country, rus'.
lilas; read *lelas*.
lilhuwai (infin.??) 'to offer'?? Cavaignac, RHA 1.103 and fn. 15.
liliwahh- 'go quickly, hasten'. Friedrich, ZA NF 1.20 f. Cf. *leliwanza*.
liliwahheske/a- 'go quickly, hasten'. See *liliwahh-*.
liliwanza; read *leliwanza*.
limma- (acc. *limman*, inst. *limmit*), a kind of drink. Cf. Ehelolf, KlF 1.138 and fn. 5.
$LĪMU$, (usually in the construct state, $LĪM$) 'thousand'.
linik-; read *lenk-*.
link-; read *lenk-*.
lingais; read *lengais*.
linkanas; read *lenkanas*.
linganu-; read *lenganu-*.
linkes-; read *lenkes-*.
linkiske/a-; read *lenkeske/a-*.

linkiya/e-; read *lenkiya/e-*.
LIBITTU 'sun-baked brick'.
lip(p)- (pl. *lipānzi, lippanzi*) 'spread, smear'? Sturtevant, Lang. 6.26 f. Cf. Götze, Madd. 73.
LIBBU = ŠA(G) = *karza* 'heart'.
    LIBBI, INA LIBBI = *istarna* 'within'.
    ANA LIBBI 'into'.
LIŠ 'fragment, bite (of food)'.
^{GIŠ}LIŠ 'tray, broad flat bowl'. Ehelolf, KlF 1.157.
^{DUG}LIŠ.GAL 'bowl'. Sommer, BoSt. 10.4 f.
LIṢṢURŪ-KA 'may they protect you'.
LID; see GUD.LID.
^{DUG}LID × A; read ^{DUG}DU$_{10}$ × A.
LI.TAR = *ŠA'ĀLU* = *punuss-* 'ask'. Weidner, Stud. 126; Ehelolf, ZA NF 9.192 and fn. 1.
^{LÚ}LI.DU 'singer'. Ehelolf ap. Sommer, AU 234 fn. 1.
$^{LÚ.MEŠ}$*LĪTŪTU* 'hostages'. Sommer, AU 234.
^{GIŠ}LI.U$_5$ = *LEḪU* 'wooden writing tablet'.
LU; read DIB 'take'.
LU; read UDU 'sheep'.
LÚ (gen. LÚ-*nas*, dat. LÚ-*ni*) = *AMĒLU* 'vir'; also a determinative before words indicating an occupation or a member of a class.
    LÚ ALAN.KA × UD 'worshiper of the statue'. Götze, ZA NF 6.70–3.
    LÚ É 'steward, major-domo'.
    LÚ É.GAL 'palace official'.
    LÚ É.DINGIR-LIM 'temple official'.
    LÚ GAL 'noble'.
    LÚ ^{GIŠ}PA; see s.v. ^{GIŠ}PA.
    LÚ SAG; read ^{LÚ}SAG.
    LÚ SAG.DU 'chief man'.
    LÚ SIG; read ^{LÚ}SIG.
    LÚ SIG$_5$ = LÚ *lazzis*? an official. Götze, Madd. 128.
    LÚ ŠU.GAL; read ^{LÚ}ŠU.GAL.
    LÚ ŠU.GI = *miyahu(wa)nza*? 'old man'.
    LÚ ŠU.GI-*es-* 'grow old'. KUB 8.35.1.9.
    LÚ ^{GIŠ}TUKUL; see s.v. ^{GIŠ}TUKUL.
    LÚ DUGUD 'vir gravis'.
    LÚ Ú.ḪUB 'deaf mute'.
LÚ-*natar* 'manliness, manly deed'.

LUḪ = arr-, arra- 'wash'.
^{LÚ}LUḪ; read ^{LÚ}SUKAL.
LÚ.ḪA.LA; see ḪA.LA.
luk-, luke/a-; see lukk-, lukke/a-.
LUGAL = ŠARRU = hassus 'king'.
LUGAL 'royal, of the king'. KBo. 6.3.3.63. But cf. Ehelolf, ZA NF 9.174.
LUGAL-(R)UT(T)U = ŠARRŪTU 'kingship, royalty'.
LUGAL-wet, LUGAL-weznatar, etc.; see hassuwe/a-, hassuweznatar, etc.
LÚ.KAL; read ^{LÚ}KAL.
LÚ.GÀL.LU = AMĒLU = antuhsas 'man'.
lukk- (lukzi, pret. pl. lukkēr, midd. lukta, pret. luktat) act. 'kindle; grow light'; midd. 'day dawns'. See lukke/a-.
lukkatta, lukkatti; read lukkitta, lukkitti, and see lukke/a-.
luk(k)e/a- (lukkizzi, midd. lukkitta, lukkitti, lukkitte, pret. lukkitti, lukit, lukkit, lukitte, lukittati) act. 'kindle; grow light'; midd. 'grow light, become day'. Zimmern, OLZ 25.300 f.; Sommer, BoSt. 7.22–32; Götze, AM 255–7; HG 102 and fn. 44, 263 f., 290 f.; Sturtevant, JAOS 54.405.

   lukitta, lukkitti, and lukkitte seem to have been stereotyped in narrative to mean 'next day'. Cf. the English cliché, *came the dawn*.

lukkes- (pret. lukkesta) 'become light'. Friedrich, ZA NF 5.49 f.; HG 232. See lukke/a-.
LUL 'be false, lie'.
LUL.A 'fox'.
lūli- (gen. luliyas, dat. lūli, lūliya), a storage place for water; 'cistern', or 'well', or 'pond'. Götze, NBr. 65 fn. 1; Walther, HC 251.25, 264.119.
lūlimis (lulimes, acc. lulimin, dat. lūlimi) 'effeminate'?? Chrest. 118.
⁑lūlū 'prosperity'. Friedrich, ZA NF 1.188, Vert. 1.79 f.
^{SAL}LUL.U.LAL; read ^{SAL}SUḪUR.LAL.
luluwā(e)- act. 'cause to prosper'; midd. 'prosper'. See lulu.
luluwiske/a- 'cause to prosper'. See luluwa(e)-.
⁑lumpastin (acc.) 'satisfaction'?? KUB 21.38.2.13.
lupastin (acc.) 'satisfaction'?? KUB 21.38.1.65; cf. Sommer, AU 29.
^{SAL}LUB.U.LAL; read ^{SAL}SUḪUR.LAL.
lūris (also lūres) 'misfortune, humiliation'. Weidner, Stud. 126; Chrest. 158.34.

luriyahh- 'humiliate'. Forrer, Forsch. 1.90.8; Chrest. 158.32.
lūriyahheske/a- 'humiliate'. KUB 21.37.1.15.
LÚ.URU.LU; read LÚ.GÀL.LU.
LU × UD.GAG; read PÍŠ.
ᴳᴵˢ*luttas*; read *luttais*. Correct HG 84, 126, 157, 178 f.
*luttāis (dat. ᴳᴵˢ*luttai*, ᴳᴵˢ*luttiya*, ᴳᴵˢAB-*ya*, acc. pl. *luttāus*) 'window'.
  Friedrich, ZA NF 3.297-9. Cf. Sturtevant, Lang. 6.30, HG 126.
Luwili 'in Luwian'. Forrer, ZDMG 76.190. Cf. Hrozný, BoSt. 5.27 f.
ᵁᴿᵁ*Luwis*, ᵁᴿᵁ*Luwiyas*, ᵁᴿᵁ*Lu(w)iumnas* 'Luwian'. Götze, Madd. 52
  f. Cf. Ungnad, ZA NF 1.1-8.
luzzi, goods and labor due the state from all who were not explicitly
  exempted. Götze, NBr. 54-63; Korošec, Vert. 55.

m, written by some for I as determinative before names of men.
ᴳᴵˢMA 'fig'.
ᴳᴵˢMÁ 'ship'.
-*MA*, an emphatic particle; in Hittite texts used especially before a
  direct quotation.
-*ma* (precedes other enclitics) 'aber, δέ'; English idiom sometimes requires 'but', sometimes 'and', and frequently no English translation
  is possible. Sommer, BoSt. 4.4 fn. 1; Ungnad, ZDMG 74.417-22;
  Friedrich, KlF 1.293 and fn. 3; Götze, AM 298; Götze-Pedersen,
  MS 57 f.; Sturtevant, Lang. 6.30 and fn. 19, JAOS 54.398, HG 87.
mā- before -*wa* sometimes stands for *mān* 'as, when, if'. Sommer, AU
  383 fn. 1.
mā-; see *māi-*.
ᴸᵁ́MA.É 'builder, mason'.
ᴸᵁ́·ᴹᴱˢMA.É-*ŪTU* 'work of building'. Götze, NBr. 56.
MAH 'strong, large, summus'.
MAḪAR, construct state of *MAḪRŪ*.
mǎhhan (often written GIM-*an*), after a gen. 'as'; conj. 'when, as';
  adv. in main clause 'in the meantime' or 'immediately'. Hrozný,
  MDOG 56.35, SH 185; Ungnad, ZA NF 3.286 f.; Sturtevant, RHA
  1.78; Götze, AM 246, 298 f.; Götze-Pedersen, MS. 58.
MAḪIṢ = *walhanza* 'bruised'.
ᴳᴵˢ*mǎhlas* 'vine branch'. Ehelolf, OLZ 36.5 f.
MAḪRŪ 'previous, of the first class; predecessor'.
MAḪAR = *piran*, *katta* 'before, with'.
mǎi- (*māi*, imper. *mǎu*) 'grow, ripen, be ripe; prosper'. Sommer ap.
  Zimmern, Streitberg Festgabe 438; Götze, KlF 1.240 f.; HG 135, 247.
  Cf. *meya-*, *meyeske-*.

makkēss- (*makkēszi*, pret. *makkesta*, part. *makkissan*) 'become great'. Götze, Hatt. 69; HG 98.

*maklanza (acc. *maklantan*, pl. *maklantes*) 'thin, lean'. Götze, NBr. 67; Benveniste, BSL 33.140; HG 97 f.

*maklatar (abl. *maklanaz*) 'leanness'. Sturtevant, JAOS 54.392.28.

mălă- (*malai*, 2 sg. *malăsi*, pret. *malāit*) 'approve, be favorable'. Sommer, AU 161 f; Friedrich, OLZ 39.308. Cf. *maleske-*.

malak- (*malakzi*) 'plait, twine' or the like?? KUB 7.1.2.14.

maleske/a- 'approve, be favorable'. KUB 24.3.1.42 (G). See *mala-*.

maleskunu- 'cause to approve, cause to be favorable'. KUB 21.42.2.8. See *maleske/a-*.

maliddus = meliddus 'sweet', q.v.

mălă- (*mallai*, *mallānzi*) 'grind, crush'. Sommer, ZA 33.98 fn. 2, AU 188; Friedrich, ZDMG 76.159; HG 145, 243 f.

malliske/a- 'grind, crush'. Sommer, AU 415.

MALBA 'market; price'. Götze, AM 204 fn. 1 (Götze writes KI.LAM).

MAL × ŠE; read ARÀḪ.

malt- (*malti*, *maldi*, verb. n. *malduwar*) 'pray (in some certain way)'. Götze, Madd. 63 and fn. 1; Mudge, Lang. 7.252; Sommer, AU 276.

mălta- (*maltai*, pret. *maltas*, 1 sg. *măldahhun*) 'pray (in some certain way)'. See *malt-*.

maltessar 'prayer (of some certain kind)'. Cf. Götze, Madd. 63. Cf. *malta-*.

*maltessnalas (acc. *maltessanalan*, *maltesnalan*) 'invoked by *maltessar*'. KUB 7.5.1.22; 7.8.3.13.

maldiya/e- 'pray (in some certain way)'. Cf. Götze, KlF 1.222. See *malt-*.

malzke/a- (1 sg. *malzakimi*) 'pray (in some certain way)'. KUB 14.4.2.18. See *malt-*

MĀMĒTU = *lenkais* 'oath'.

MA.MÚ 'dream'. Götze, AM 264.

-man 'meum', acc. of *-mes*.

măn (sometimes enclitic) 'ἄν'. It is used w. pret. in unreal clauses (including unreal conditions), and with the present in potential clauses (sometimes virtually equivalent to a wish). Ungnad ap. Sommer, BoSt. 7.52; Friedrich, KlF 1.286–96; Hrozný, JA 218.313; Sommer, AU 73 fn. 1; HG 88; Götze-Pedersen, MS 59.

măn 'as; when, if'. Hrozný, MDOG 56.38 and fn. 4; Friedrich, Vert. 1.32 f., 159; Götze, Madd. 167 f.; Sommer, AU 126 fn. 1; Ehelolf, OLZ 36.5; HG 88; Götze-Pedersen, MS 59; Hahn, Lang. 12.111 f.

mān . . . mān 'whether . . . or, if . . . or if'.
mān . . . -a 'although'.
MANA 'pound, mina'.
mānenkuwahhuwar 'a making short, a making contemptible, contempt'?
Forrer, RHA 1.150.8. Verb. n. from *maninkuwahh-*.
ᴸᵁ*maniahhatallas*; read *maniyahhatallas*.
maninkuess-; read *maninkwess-*.
maninkuwahh- (also *manninkuwahh-*) 'make short; approach'. Sommer, AU 257. Cf. Götze, Hatt. 58 and fn. 2. Cf. *manenkuwahhuwar*.
*maninkwanza (acc. *maninkuwwandan*, neut. *maninkuwan, manninkwan*) 'short; near'. Götze, Hatt. 57-9, 59 fn. 1; Sturtevant, Lang. 6. 217 f.
maninkwēss- (pl. *maninkwēssanzi*) 'become short'. Götze, Hatt. 59 fn. 1, 69 fn. 2.
manis 'bright red blood'? Sayce, RA 24.124; Friedrich, KlF 1.377.
măniyahh- 'assign, appoint; govern'. Götze, Hatt. 60-2; Mudge, Lang. 7.252.
ᴸᵁ*maniyahhatallas* (*ma-ni-aḫ-ḫa-tal-la-aš*) 'governor'. See *maniyahh-*.
*maniyahhatar (dat *maniyahhanni*) 'a being governed, government'. See *maniyahh-*.
ᴸᵁ*maniyahheskattallas* (*maniyahhiskattallas*) 'governor'. See *maniyahh-*.
maniyahheske/a- (also *maniyahhiske/a-*) 'assign, appoint; govern'. See *maniyahh-*.
*maniyahhiyaz (dat. *maniyahhiyatti*) 'assignment, share'? KUB 13.20.1. 34. Cf. Götze, Madd. 79 and fn. 7.
manka (*manga, manqa*) 'for oneself, selfishly'? Sommer, AU 125-7; Chrest. 95. Cf. Götze, AM 242-5 (*natta manka* 'nihil non'???).
manninkuwahh-; see *maninkuwahh-*.
manninkuw(w)anza; see *maninkwanza*.
MĀR, construct state of MĀRU.
ᴳᴵˢMAR, construct state of MARRU.
marah-; read *marh-*.
marak; read *mark-*.
⁎*marh-* (pret. *marhata, marahta*) 'succeed'? Götze, Hatt. 125.
ᴳᴵˢ*māri-* (acc. *māri, mărin*), a weapon of offense? Sommer, AU 381.
mark- (pl. *markanzi*, pret. *marakta*, midd. *markattari*) 'cut up, divide'. Sommer, BoSt. 10.20; Götze, Madd. 47; Benveniste, BSL 33.140; HG 117.
markiske/a- 'cut up'. Götze, Madd. 47.

markista- (gen. of verb. n. *markistawwas, markisdawwas*); *markisdawwas* UGU₆-*as* 'Krankheit des Dahinschwindens'? Götze, AM 239.

ᴳᴵˢMAR.GÍD(.DA) 'cart'.

markiya/e- 'disapprove, be unfavorable'. Forrer, Forsch, 1.179; Sommer, AU 161, 276; Friedrich, OLZ 39.308. Cf. Götze, Madd. 47.

marlatar 'cowardliness'. Sommer, AU 184.

marless- (part. *marlessanza*) 'become cowardly'. Sommer, AU 184.

marmaras 'murmur, lamentation'?? KUB 17.10.1.12 (W).

marnuwan; see *marnwanza*.

marnwanza; neut. (*marnwan, marnuwan*), a kind of drink. Zimmern, Streitberg Festgabe 432.16; Friedrich, Vert. 1.176; Götze, NBr. 65 fn. 1.

ᴳᴵˢMAR.BU.DA; read MAR.GÍD.DA.

*marranza (*marrantas*, case uncertain) 'broken, melted'? KBo. 3.13. 2.16. See *marriya/e-*.

marri 'of one's own accord; in one's own interest'. Sommer, AU 188 f.

marriya/e- (midd. *marriitta, marriētta, marriattari, marriyatari*) 'be broken, melt'. Götze, Madd. 73, 98 fn. 12; Sommer, AU 188 fn. 2; Benveniste, BSL 33.140; Sturtevant, RHA 1.82.

ᵁᴿᵁᴰ*MARRU* 'spade'? Thureau-Dangin, RA 24.147 f.

mars- (pret. pl. *marsēr*, part. *marsanza*) 'be bad'. Friedrich, Vert. 1.80 f.

marsahh- 'make bad, corrupt'. See *mars-*.

marsanu- 'make bad'. See *mars-*.

marsanza (pl. *marsantes*) 'bad, corrupt'. See *mars-*.

*marsas (*marsan* is probably acc. masc.) 'bad, corrupt'. Götze, Hatt. 88 and fn. 2. See *mars-*.

marsastaris (*marsastares*, acc. *marsastarin*), something in the nature of impurity that angers the gods. Friedrich, ZA NF 3.197, AOr. 6.361 fn. 9.

marsătar 'badness'. See *mars-*.

marsess- (pret. pl. *marsesser*) 'become bad'. See *mars-*.

MĀRTU 'daughter'.

MĀRU 'son'.

⁺*maruwāit* (pret.) 'decided (between two contestants)'? Götze, Hatt. 48.12.

MAŠ; read ½.

MAŠ; read BÁN, 'a dry measure'.

MAŠ, a careless writing for one form of I, determinative with men's names.

MÁŠ 'goat'.

MÁŠ = *hansatar* 'family, descendants'. Apparently a wider term than NUMUN, q.v.

MÁŠ LÚ 'on the father's side'. Friedrich, Vert. 2.72.33.

MÁŠ SAL; *IŠTU* MÁŠ SAL-*TI* 'on the mother's side'.

-*mas* 'mei', gen. of -*mes*.

-*ma-aš* is sometimes written for -*ma-aš-ma-aš* (haplography?). Friedrich, OLZ 39.309 fn. 1.

MÁŠ.ANŠU = *hwitar* 'animals'. Friedrich, ZA NF 5.41.

^{GIŠ}MA.SÁ.AB 'basket'.

MA.ŠAR; read MA.MÚ.

māsa- (acc. *māsan*) 'revolt'?? KUB 24.1.3.17 (G).

masasta; read *parsta*, and see *pars*-.

masē; see *masis*.

^{LÚ}MAŠ.EN.GAG; read MAŠDÁ.

*mashuil (Luwian?) 'mouse'. Götze, ZA NF 6.65-79.

masiēs; read *masēs*, and see *masis*.

*masis (neut. *masē*, pl. *masēs*) 'quantus'. Sturtevant, Lang. 10.267, 272 f.

măsiwanza 'quantus'. Friedrich, Vert. 2.92 fn. 2; Götze, NBr. 35; HG 161 and fn. 54.

masiyan, neut. of *masiyanza*.

masiyanki 'totiens'? Götze, NBr. 35.

*masiyanza (neut. *masiyan*, neut. pl. *masiyante*) 'quantus', 'tantus'?? Götze, NBr. 35; Sturtevant, Lang. 10.272.

MÁŠ.GAL 'full-grown goat'.

MÁŠ.GAL 'the royal family'. See MÁŠ.

MAŠKU 'skin, hide'.

MAŠLU; see *BAŠLU*.

massanas; read *parsanas*.

massiya/e-; read *parsiya/e-*.

^{LÚ}MAŠDÁ = *MUŠKĒNU*, a kind of palace retainer, whose social status is between that of a free man and that of a slave. Deimel, No. 74.235.

masta(e); read *parta(e)*-.

mastimastiske/a-; see *partipartiske/a-*.

MÁŠ.TUR 'kid'.

mat- (*mazzazzi* [matstsi], 2 sg. *mazatti* [matsti], pret. *mazzasta* [matst]) 'endure, withstand; stand one's ground, dare; refuse'. Hrozný, BoSt. 3.186 fn. 4; Götze, Madd. 125 f.; Sommer, AU 335; HG 129.

MADGALTU = *auris*, *awwaris* 'outpost, sentry'.

MĀTU = utne 'country'.
maunas; read kunnas.
ᴷᵁˢMÁ.URU.ÙRU, ᴳᴵˢMA.URU.ÙRU 'quiver'. Ehelolf, ZA NF 1.46 f.
mauske/a- 'fall'. Götze, Hatt. 95, NBr. 63 fn. 1.
mauss-, mus- (mauszi, part. maussanza, musān) 'fall'. Weidner, AOF 1.3, 66 f.; Friedrich, ZA NF 5.70; HG 103 f., 229 and fn. 27.
māw(w)a; mān-wa. KBo. 3.7.1.25; KUB 7.57.1.5, etc. (G).
MAYĀLU = sastas 'bed'. Götze, Madd. 143.
maza-, mazza-, mazzas-; see mat-.
ME = da- 'take'.
ME = ŠAKĀNU dai- 'place'.
MÈ = zahhais 'battle'.
MÈ = zahhiya/e- 'fight'.
MÈ = zahhiske/a- 'fight'.
MÈ = zahhiyanu- 'cause to fight'.
ME (for ME'AT?) 'hundred'.
MĒ, construct state of MŪ.
-me (-mi), Arzawan indeclinable possessive suffix, 'my'. HG 194.
-me 'meo', dat. of -mes.
mea/e-; read meya/e-.
MEḪRU = annawalis 'equal (in rank)'. Weidner, AOF 6.299 f.; Sommer, AU 322, 394 fn. 1.
ᴸᵁ·ᴹᴱˢMEḪRŪTI 'equals'.
mehunta(e)-, mēhwanda(e)- (imper. 2 sg. mihuntahhut, mēhuwandahhut) 'grow old'. See miyahwanta(e)-.
mehur (gen. mĕhunas, dat. mĕhūni, mēhweni) 'time; point of time, occasion'. Sommer, BoSt. 7.32-6; Sturtevant, RHA 1.78, Lang. 7.119, 12, No. 3.
mekkis (dat. mekki, abl. meqqayaz, pl. meggaēs) 'great; much, many'. Hrozný, SH 21, 232; Sommer, AU 145; HG 83, 179-81; Sturtevant, Lang. 10.266; Kurylowicz, EI 255.
  mekkayaz 'often'. Sommer, AU 228.
  mekki (adv.) 'much, very'.
melit (milit, LÀL-it) 'honey'. Ehelolf, OLZ 36.1-7; HG 89.
melitēs- (imper. militisdu, 2 sg. militēs) 'become sweet'. See melit.
meliddus (miliddus; also maliddus) 'sweet'. See melit.
MELQĪTU 'capacity, contents'.
  MELKIZU = MELKĪT-ŠU 'its contents'.

mĕmă- (*memăi*, 2 sg. *mĕmatti*, pl. *memanzi*, *memmanzi*, *mimmanzi*, pret. *memmas*, *memas*) 'say, speak; agree'. Hrozný, MDOG 56.37, SH 232; Friedrich, Vert. 1.86; Götze, OLZ 33.286 fn. 3; Sommer, AU 39–41; Sturtevant, Lang. 6.32 f., 7.117; Benveniste, BSL 33.140; HG 85; Götze-Pedersen, MS 59 f. Cf. *meme/a-*, *memes-*, *memiya/e-*.

 andan m. 'exorcise, bless' (G).
 appa m. 'answer'.
 awan katta m. 'confide secretly'.
 natta m., usually w. *-za*, 'say "no", refuse'. Friedrich, OLZ 39.308.
 piran m. 'recommend'.

memal 'meal; porridge'. Cf. Götze, KlF 1.228 fn. 4; Sturtevant, TAPA 58.22, Lang. 5.229, Chrest. 124.

ŠA ^{GIŠ}*INBI*-ḪI.A *m.* 'meal mixed with chopped fruit'?

ŠA LÀL *m.* 'meal mixed with honey'?

meme/a- (pret. 3 pl. *memir*, imper. 2 sg. *memi*) 'say, speak; agree'. See *mema-*. Cf. HG 218 f.

memes- (pret. *memista*, imper. 2 pl. *memestin*, *memistin*) 'say, speak; agree'. HG 230. See *mema-*.

memeske/a- (also *memiske/a-*) 'say, speak; agree'. Götze, AM 300.

memias; read *memiyas*.

memin-; see *memiyas*.

memis-; read *memes-*.

memiske/a- see *memeske/a-*.

memiya/e- 'say, speak; agree'. HG 224. Cf. *mema-*.

memiyas (acc. *memiyan*, dat. *memiyani*, *memiyanni*, *memini*) 'word, saying; thing, matter'. Hrozný, BoSt. 3.37 fn. 6; Schiele, ZA NF 2. 314; Friedrich, Vert. 1.43; HG 184.

memma-; variant for *mema*, q.v.

-men 'meum', acc. of *-mes*.

menahhanda (often written IGI-*anda*) 'opposite, against'. Sommer, BoSt. 10.47 f.; Götze, AOr. 5.20 fn. 1, AM 300.

mĕni (once *mene*) 'face'. Sommer, BoSt. 10.48. 'Side of the face, cheek'. Cf. Ehelolf, OLZ 36.6 fn. 3.

mēnu, a disease. KUB 17.12.2.12–4.

mēnu- 'cause the symptoms of *mēnu*'.

mēnus 'ill with *mēnu*'.

^{LÚ}MER; read ^{LÚ}NIMGIR.

^{TÚG}MER; read ^{TÚG}MIR.

mernu- (pret. 1 sg. *mernu*<*nu*>*un*) 'cause to die'? Cf. Friedrich, ZA NF 5.71 fn. 2.

merr- (pret. *merta*, imper. *merdu*, part. *merranda*) 'die'. Sturtevant, TAPA 58.23, Chrest. 123 f., HG 135, 221 and fn. 18a. Cf. Friedrich, ZA NF 5.71 fn. 2.

MEŠ, postpositive sign of the pl.; sometimes used with Akkadian words.

-mes (also *-mis*) 'my'. Hrozný, SH 123–5; Friedrich, ZA NF 2.295 fn. 1; HG 135, 190, 194.

-mĕs 'mei', pl. of *-mes*.

MEŠEL, construct state of *MEŠLU*.

MEŠEDI; LÚ *MEŠEDI* 'member of the king's body guard'. Götze, Kulturg. 83 and fn. 7.

GAL *M*., GAL LÚ(.MEŠ) *M*. 'chief of the guard'.

GAL *MEŠEDIUTTU* 'office of chief of the guard'.

MEŠLU 'half'? Götze, AM 300.

mĕs(s)ā (also *mīsā*, *missā*), a Hattic word designating a certain litany, whose first word it is. Sommer, BoSt. 10.69.

-met 'meum, mea', neut. sg. and pl. of *-mes*.

meya/e- (3 sg. *miyari*, imper. *miyyaru*, part. *miyanza*) 'grow, ripen, be ripe; prosper'. Sommer, ap. Zimmern, Streitberg Festgabe 438; Friedrich, ZA NF 3.200 f.; HG 111, 135, 224. Cf. *mai-*, *meyatar*.

mĕyani- (gen. *meyaniyas*, *mīyanas*, *mēanas*, dat. *mĕyani*) 'half'?? Ehelolf ap. Boissier, Mantique 22 f. But cf. *meyatar*.

meyantilis (dat. *miyantili*) 'ripe' (of a field). Cf. Tenner, ZA NF 4.189.

meyatar (*miyatar*, gen. *miyanas*, *miyannas*) 'a ripening; ripe crop, harvest; abundance, prosperity'. Götze, AM 300. Cf. Friedrich, ZA NF 2.53 f. Cf. *mai-*, *meya/e-*; *meyani-*.

meyĕske/a- (*miyēkizzi*, supine *miiskiwan*) 'grow, ripen, be ripe; prosper'. Friedrich, ZA NF 3.200. Cf. *mai-*, *meya/e-*.

MI = *dankus*, *dankwis* 'black'.

MI = *dankwes-* 'become dark'.

MI = *MŪŠU* = *ispant-* 'night'. Cf. MI.KAM.

-mi; read *-me*.

MI.AŠ; DUGUD is sometimes written in a way that may be mistaken for this.

mieske/a-; read *meyeske/a-*.

MIḪRU; read *MEḪRU*.

mihunta-; read *mehunta-*.

miiske/a-; read *meyeske/a-*.

MI.KAM = *ispant-* 'night'. Cf. MI.

MI.KAM-*za* 'by night'.

milit, militis-, miliddus; read *melit, melites-, meliddus*.
mimma- (*mimmai*, pret. *mimmas*) 'refuse, reject'. Hrozný, CH 22.10; Eheolf, KlF 1.139 fn. 4; Sommer, AU 40 and fn. 1; HG 133. Cf. Friedrich, IF 49.227.
MIMMŪ 'anything, everything; property'.
minu- (imper. 3 pl. *minuwandu*, verb. n. *minumar*) 'soften, smooth'. (W). Otherwise Hrozný, BoSt. 3.34 fn. 4. Cf. Friedrich, Vert. 2.95 f. See *miyumar*.
^{LÚ}MIR.; read ^{LÚ}NIMGIR.
^{TÚG}MIR 'headband'? Hrozný, CH 138.51. 'Dark garment'?? Walther, HC 270.182.
^{LÚ}MIR.UŠ; read ^{LÚ}UKUŠ.
-mis; read *-mes* 'my'.
misaris, an injurious insect? Friedrich, ZA NF 3.200.
MIŠĪ (*MI-I-ŠI*) imper. 'wash'. Friedrich, Vert. 2.148.
misriwanza 'brilliant, splendid, impressive'. Friedrich, ZA NF 3.203.
  misriwanda 'brilliantly, splendidly'. Götze, AOr. 5.20 and fn. 3.
misriwēs- (*misriwēszi*) 'become brilliant'. Götze, KlF 1.220.
missa; see *messa*.
MIT; read BE 'master'.
MIT; read BE 'if'.
MIT; read UG$_6$ 'die, death'.
MIT; read TIL 'complete'.
-mit; read *-be*, particle of identity.
-mit (*-mi-it*); read *-met* 'meum'.
mitā(e)- (*mitaizzi*, pret. 1 sg. *mitānun*) 'fix, determine' or the like. Götze, Madd. 84 and fn. 17. Cf. Sturtevant, Lang. 5.10 f.
mītis, *mitas (*mītis*, acc. *mitin, mitān*, pl. *mītes*) 'red' or 'blue'?? Chrest. 118 f. 'String'?? Götze ap. Pedersen, Hirt Festschrift 2.581.
miumar; read *miyumar*.
miya/e-; read *meya/e-*.
miyahua-; read *miyahwa-*.
miyahunza; see *miyahwa-*.
miyahuwa-; see *miyahwa-*.
miyahuwanta(e)-; see *miyahwanta(e)-*.
miyahwa- (imper. 2 sg. *miyahuwahhut*, part. *miyahunza* [miyahwnts]) 'grow old'. Friedrich, Vert. 1.94, 2.168.
miyahwanta(e)- imper. 2 sg. *miyahuwantahhut*) 'grow old'. Friedrich, Vert. 1.44 f., 94, 2.168; Götze, KlF 1.240. Cf. *mehunta(e)-*.
miyahwandanassas 'zum Alter gehörig'?? Götze, KlF 1.240.
miyantilis; read *meyantilis*.

miyanza; see *meya/e-*.
miyatar; read *meyatar*.
miyēs- (imper. *miyēstu*, *miēsu*, 2 sg. *miyēs*) 'become soft, smooth, pleasant'. Ehelolf, OLZ 36.3 and fn. 2; Chrest. 125.
miyeske/a-; read *meyeske/a-*.
miyumar (*miumar*) 'softness, smoothness, pleasantness'. Cf. Götze, NBr. 32 and fn. 1. Cf. *miyus*.
miyus (acc. ⁎*miyun*, neut. *miu*) 'soft, smooth, pleasant' or the like. Ehelolf, OLZ 36.3 and fn. 2.
MU = ŠUMU = *laman* 'name'.
MU = ŠATTU = *wett-*, *wettanza* 'year'. Cf. MU.KAM.
MU-*anni* = *wettantanne* 'within a year'.
ᴸᵁMU, ˢᴬᴸMU; read MUḪALDIM.
MŪ (construct state MĒ) = *watar* 'water'.
-*mu* 'mihi, me'. Hrozný, MDOG 56.36, SH 121; HG 194, 196.
MUḪ; read UGU.
ᴸᵁMUḪALDIM; ˢᴬᴸMUḪALDIM 'cook'.
MUIRTŪTU 'governorship'? Götze, Hatt. 60 f., NBr. 28.
LÚ.MEŠ MUIRTŪTI 'people of the governorship, subjects'?
mŭgă(ĕ)- (*mugāi*, pret. *mūgait*, 2 pl. *mukaēten*) 'lament, cry, implore'. Zimmern, Streitberg Festgabe 438; Götze, Hatt. 100; Friedrich, Vert. 2.24; Mudge, Lang. 7.253; Benveniste, BSL 33.140.
MU.KAM = ŠATTU = *wett-*, *wettanza* 'year, time'. Cf. MU.
MU.KAM GÍD.DA 'long life'.
MU.KAM-*tili* 'annually'.
mukeske/a- 'lament, cry, implore'. 2 BoTU 4A 3.13.
mukessar 'lamentation'; things used in a ritual of lamentation. Götze, Madd. 63 fn. 1; Chrest. 126. Cf. *galaktar*.
mukiske/a-; read *mukeske/a-*.
MUL = *astiras* 'star'.
MULTARRIḪU 'almighty'.
MULŪ = *sarizziyatar* (?) 'height, peak'. Götze, AM 301.
mummiya/e- (*mummiyētta*) 'fall off, be broken off' or the like. Götze, NBr. 63 and fn. 1; HG 216.
MUN 'salt'.
munna(e)- (*munnaizzi*) 'hide, cover'. Götze, ZA NF 2.16, Madd. 85 and fn. 2; Ehelolf, KlF 1.148 f.
arha m. 'hide away (from one)'.
munnanda 'secretly'. Friedrich, ZA NF 2.277.
ᴸᵁMUN(N)ABTU = *pitteyanza* 'fugitive'.

MUN(N)ABTU(TU) 'the state of a fugitive'; LÚ.MEŠ *MUNABTI* 'fugitives'. Sommer, AU 416.

MUR; NINDA MUR 'Aschenbrot'?? Hrozný, Wiener Sitzungsberichte 173.130–5; Sommer, BoSt. 10.64.

MUR$_7$; read SIGA.

*mŭris (pl. *mures*, acc. *mūrius*) 'cluster of grapes'. Ehelolf, OLZ 36.5.

*mūriyalas (acc. *mūriyalan*) 'made of grapes'?? Ehelolf, OLZ 36.5 fn. 3.

MÙRUB 'middle, mid'.

MUŠ = ṢĪRU 'serpent'; also a determinative.

mus-; see *mauss-*.

MUŠEN = *wattais*(?) 'bird'; also a post-determinative.

MUŠEN ḪURRI, a kind of partridge, 'alectoris Graeca'. Sommer, BoSt. 10.59–61.

^{LÚ}MUŠEN.DÙ 'bird-breeder; bird-maker; augur'. Chrest. 118.

MŪŠU = MI = *ispant-* 'night'.

MUD = *eshar*.

mŭtă(e)- (*mŭtaizzi, mudăizzi*) 'avoid'? Sturtevant, JAOS 54.404.

^{LÚ}*MUTU* = *antiyanza* 'husband'.

muwas 'strength'?? Forrer, Forsch. 1.63. 'Körpersaft' or 'Mana, Seelenstoff'?? Friedrich, KlF 1.375–8.

*muwattalas (pl. *muwattalus*), an adjective derived from *muwas*. Friedrich, KlF 1.376 fn. 3.

^{GIŠ}NÁ; see ^{GIŠ}NA(D).

NA$_4$; see ZÁ.

naes-; see *nais-*.

năh(h)- (1 sg. *nahmi*, pret. *nahta*, 1 sg. *nāhun, nahhun*), usually intransitive w. dat. (the part. is never passive), sometimes w. acc. of the person, 'fear, respect, revere'. Friedrich, ZA NF 1.17 f.; Sommer, AU 94; Götze, AOr. 5.30 and fn. 3; Götze-Pedersen, MS 61. See *nahsarriya/e-*.

nahhăn 'fear, reverence'. Götze, Hatt. 55; HG 149.

nahheske/a- 'fear, respect, revere'. KUB 14.3.2.29. See *nahh-*.

nahhut; see *nai-, ne-*.

nahsaraz; see *nahsarraz*.

nahsariske/a- 'fear, respect, revere'. Sommer, BoSt. 7.59. See *nahsarriya/e-*.

nahsariya/e-; see *nahsarriya/e-*.

nahsariyawanza 'having fear'. HG 160 f. See *nahh-*.

nahsarnu- 'cause to fear'. See *nahh-*.

nahsar(r)az (acc. *nahsarattan*, dat. *nahsarratti*) 'fear, reverence'. Götze, Madd. 79 and fn. 8, KlF 1.185 f.; HG 149. See *nahh-, nahsarnu-*.

nahsar(r)iya/e- (*nahsariyazzi*, midd. 3 pl. *nahsarriyandari*, pret. *nahsariyatati*) 'fear, respect, revere'. Hrozný, MDOG 56.35, SH 75 f.; Friedrich, ZA NF 1.18. See *nahh-*.

năĭ-, ne- (*nāi*, 1 sg. *nehhi*, pret. *năĭts*, midd. imper. 2 sg. *nāhut*) 'lead, send, conduct; turn'; midd. 'turn (intransitive), turn (one's eyes)'. Hrozný, SH 29 and fn. 3; Weidner, AOF 1.61–3; Friedrich, Vert. 1.36, 2.99 f.; Sommer, AU 58 and fn. 3; Sturtevant, Lang. 6.33 f., 7.115–7, HG 230, 231, 247, 249 and fn. 67; Götze-Pedersen, MS 61. Cf. *nais-, neya/e-*.

anda n. 'turn toward'.

arha n., midd., 'turn away, sich abwenden'. Sommer, AU 336 and fn. 1.

appan arha n. 'alienate'.

kattan n., midd., 'turn away, sich abwenden'? Sommer, AU 348.

parā n. 'send forth, deliver; draw (a weapon); continue(?)'. Friedrich, ZA NF 3.199; Ehelolf, ZA NF 9.175 fn. 2.

piran n. 'deliver'. Götze, NBr. 16.21.

năis-, naes- (pret. *naista, naesta*, midd. 2 sg. *naistati*, imper. 2 sg. *năishut, naeshut*, 2 pl. *naisdumat*) 'lead, send, conduct'; midd. 'turn, sich wenden'. See *nai-, ne-*.

naiske/a- 'lead, send, conduct, turn'. KUB 21.42.2.6.

NAG = *eku-* 'drink, cause to drink'.

NAG 'drink, beverage'.

ᵁᴿᵁᴰNAG 'copper drinking cup'.

NA.GAG; read NA.KAD.

ᴸᵁNAGAR 'joiner, carpenter'.

NA.KAD 'shepherd'.

GAL.NA.KAD 'chief of the shepherds'.

NA.KÍD (Hrozný, CH 98.4); read NA.KAD.

NAGGA 'lead' (i.e. the metal).

nakkeske/a- 'become heavy'. KBo. 4.14.2.27. See *nakkess-*.

nakkĕss- (*nakkĕszi*, pret. *nakkĕsta, nakkista*, part. *nakkĕssan*) 'become heavy, become important, become burdensome'. Sturtevant, Lang. 8.125. See *nakkis*.

nakkis 'heavy; important, revered; burdensome, difficult'. Götze, Hatt. 93 f., KlF 1.130, 181, Kulturg. 80; Sturtevant, Lang. 10.267.

nakkiyahh- 'make heavy'. Götze, Hatt. 94; HG 242.

nakkiyas- (*nakkiyaszi*) 'become heavy, become burdensome'? Götze, KlF 1.181.

nakkiyatar 'heaviness, weight; importance, respect; difficulty'. See *nakkis*.

nakkus = *nakkis* 'heavy, guilty'??? Götze, Hatt. 94 fn. 5. Rather for *nu + kus* 'et hos'? Goetze ap. Hahn, Lang. 12.117 fn. 61; Hahn, Lang. 12.117 f.

nakkussahiti (dat.) 'for substitution'?? KBo. 5.2.3.30; KUB 17.18.2.24 (G).

nakkussis 'substitute', something used to represent a person in sympathetic magic. KBo. 2.3.2.47, 50 (G).

NAKTAMU 'cover, lid'.

NAM 'insurrection'. Friedrich, AO 25.2.28.3.

$^{DUG}NAMANDU$; see *NAMMANDU*.

NAM.Á.DAḪ = *sardiyatar* 'help, succor'. Sommer, AU 180 fn. 3.

NAM.LÚ.GÀL.LU = *antuhsatar* 'mankind'.

NAM.LÚ.URU.LU; read NAM.LÚ.GÀL.LU.

namma 'next, besides, furthermore; again'; especially with *nu* 'therefore'; with a negative 'no more'. Hrozný, SH 135; Sommer, BoSt. 10.6 f. Cf. Götze, AM 260.

$^{DUG}NAM(M)ANDU$, $^{DUG}NAMMATU$, a small vessel for liquids. Götze, KlF 1.202 fn. 4.

NAM.RA (usually pl. NAM.RA.ḪI.A or NAM.RA.MEŠ) 'captured non-combatants carried off by a victorious army, captives'. Götze, AM 217-20, Kulturg. 99 and fn. 1; Sommer, OLZ 38.280 f.

NAMZĪTU 'fermenting vat'. Friedrich, ZA NF 5.22.

nan = *nu + an*; see *nas*.

nannă- (*nannăi*, pret. 1 sg. *nannahhun*) 'drive; march'. HG 215; Götze-Pedersen, MS 14-16, 62. Cf. *nanne/a-, nannes-, nanniya/e-*. *arha n.* 'drive away'.

?*nanne/a-* (pret. pl. *nannir* or *nanniir*) 'drive; march'. Cf. HG 218 f. See *nanniya/e-*.

nannes- (pret. *nannista*) 'drive; march'. See *nanna-*.

nanneske/a- 'drive; march'. See *nanna-*.

nannis-; read *nannes-*.

nanniya/e- (pl. *nanniyanzi*, pret. pl. *nanniēr*) 'drive; march'. See *nanna-*.

napa = *nu + apa*. Ungnad, ZA NF 3.283.

NAB. AN; read MUL.

SAL*NAPŠAḪ*; read SAL*NAPTER<TA>*. Friedrich, Vert. 2.172; Götze, AOr. 2.155 fn. 1.

SAL*NAPṬARTU*, SAL*NAPTERTU* 'secondary wife' or the like. Friedrich, Vert. 2.128.64, 172; Götze, AOr. 2.153–5.

SAL*NAPTIGA*; read SAL*NAPṬARTU*. Götze, AOr. 2.154 fn. 1.

LÚNAR 'singer, musician'.

NĀR, construct state of *NĀRU* = ÍD 'river'.

NARĀMU 'favorite'.

NARĀRU 'help'.

LÚ.MEŠ *NARĀRI*, ERÍN.MEŠ *NARĀRU* = *sardiyes*(?) 'auxiliary forces'. Cf. Chrest. 227 on *sardiyas*.

ANA *NARĀRI* LÚKÚR 'for aid against the enemy'.

-*nas* 'nos, nobis'. Hrozný, SH 129 f.; Sommer, BoSt. 7.52 fn. 10; HG 194.

nas = *nu* + *as* 'et is'. Ungnad, ZDMG 74.420 f.; Sturtevant, JAOS 47.174, HG 199.

Nāsili = *Nesumnili* 'in the language of Nēsas, in Nesite'? Hrozný, AOr. 1.294 f.; JA 218.317–20. (By this Hrozný means what others call 'in Hittite'.)

nasma 'or'. Hrozný, SH 135; Marstrander, Car. 19; Sommer, AU 24 f., 61 fn. 1.

nassu 'either; or'. Hrozný, SH 135; Marstrander, Car. 19; Sommer, AU 100.

nassuma = *nasma* 'or'? Sommer, AU 100.

nasta = *nu* + *asta* 'then, thereupon; and finally'. Hrozný, SH 185.

GIŠNA(D) 'bed'.

nat = *nu* + *at*; see *nas*.

natta (usually written Ú-UL or UL) 'not; no'. Zimmern, OLZ 25.297; Götze, AM 255, 315; Sommer, AU 41, 88, 98, 384; HG 39, 99.

năwi (also *nawwi*) 'not yet'. Sommer, BoSt. 4.12–8, 10.5.

NE; read IZI 'fire'.

NE; read BIL 'burn'.

ne = *nu* + *e*. Friedrich, ZA NF 2.291–3; HG 198 fn. 21.

nehhi, 1 sg. of *nai-*, q.v.

neku- (*nekuzi*, midd. pret. *nekuttat*) act. 'go to bed'? Sturtevant, JAOS 52.10, Chrest. 119. Midd. (impersonal) 'people go to bed(?); night falls'. Cf. Sommer, BoSt. 7.36.

nekumanza (also *nikumanza*) 'naked'. Götze, Madd. 120; Sturtevant, JAOS 52.10, HG 122 f.

nekuz (gen. *nekuz*) 'bed-time(?), night-fall, evening'. Sommer, BoSt. 7.32–6; Sturtevant, JAOS 52.10 f.

NĚLU; read *NĪLU*.

nenenk- (*ninikzi*, pl. *nininkanzi*, pret. *ninikta*, 1 sg. *nininkun*) 'raise, lift up, take; gather, mobilize'; midd. 'be exalted, get drunk; be mobilized'. Sommer, BoSt. 7.38 f., 39 fn. 1; Götze, Madd. 115–8; Sturtevant, Lang. 6.215, HG 233 f., Chrest. 7.52, 169.

nenk- (*nikzi*, pl. *ninkanzi*, pret. pl. *ninkēr?*, *ninkir*, imper. 2 sg. *nik, ninga*) 'rise, be exalted; satisfy oneself with drink, get drunk'. Ehelolf, KlF 1.137–42; Götze, Madd. 116–8; HG 117.

nenganu- (*ninganu-*) 'cause to be exalted, strengthen'. Götze, KlF 1.188 and fn. 10.

?*nenke/a-* (imper. 2 sg. *ninkihhutti* or *ninkiahhutti?*) 'be exalted'? See *nenkiya/e-*.

?*nenkiya/e-* (pret. pl. *ninkiēr?*; imper. 2 sg. *ninkiahhutti* or *ninkihhutti?*) 'be exalted'. KUB 17.5.1.12; KUB 1.16.3.31. See *nenk-*.

nepis (nom.-acc. *nepis* [*nepes*], gen. *nepisas, nepias*, abl. *nepisaz, nepisanza, nepisz-*) 'sky'. Hrozný, BoSt. 3.72 fn. 5; HG 89. Cf. Friedrich, ZA NF 2.273; but see Hrozný, AOr. 1.280.

nepisanza 'the heavens'. Götze, AOr. 5.10.

NEŠ; see *NĪŠU*.

neshut (midd. imper. 2 sg.) 'turn'. KBo. 4.6.1.16. See *nai-, nais-*. Cf. *pennes-, unnes-*.

Nesumnili 'in the language of the people of Nesas'. See *Nasili*.

netta = *nu* + *e* + *tta* 'et ea tibi, et ei tibi'. Friedrich, ZA NF 2.292 f.; HG 198 fn. 21.

newahh- (also *newwahh-*) 'renew'. Forrer, ZDMG 76.181 f.; Sommer, BoSt. 10.5, KlF 1.347; HG 241; Kurylowicz, EI 73.

*newas (inst. *newit*) 'new'. Sommer, KlF 1.347; HG 89.

něya/e- (pl. *něyanzi*, pret. *neit*, pl. *neyēr*, imper. 2 pl. *neyattin*, midd. *něari, neyari, neyya*) 'lead, send, conduct; turn'; midd. 'turn oneself, turn (one's eyes)'. See *nai-*.

nezzan = *nu* + *e-zan*. Friedrich, ZA NF 2.292 f.; HG 198 fn. 21.

NI; read YÀ.

-NI 'our'.

NI.E.DÉ.A; NINDA NI.E.DÉ.A 'pap, porridge, mush'.

NI.ḪI.GA; read YÀ DÚG.GA.

nik-; read *nenk-*.

NI.GAB; read NI.DU$_8$.

NÍG.HAR; read NINDA MUR and see s.v. MUR.

^{uzu}NÍG.GIG 'entrails, intestines'? Deimel, No. 597.366. Cf. Sommer, AU 187.

nikku [nek·u] 'neque'? Hahn, Lang. 12.110 fn. 14.

ᴳᴵˢNÍG.GUL 'hammer'. Deimel, No. 597.352.
ᵀᵁᴳNÍG.LÁM, a fine garment.
NÍG.BA 'gift'.
ᴷᵁˢNÍG.BÁR 'bag' or the like.
NÍG.SI.DI 'right, just'.
NÍG.SI.DI-*tar* 'right, justice'.
NÍG.TUKU 'wealth; enrich oneself'.
nikumanza; read *nekumanza*.
NĪLU 'semen virile'.
ᴸᵁNÍ.ME; read ᴸᵁIM.ME.
ᴸᵁNIMGIR, an official. Deimel, No. 347.11.
NIM.LÁL 'bee'.
NĪMUR = *aumen* 'we saw'.
NIN (perhaps better SAL + TÚG; the classical Assyrian sign is SAL + KU) 'sister'. Chrest. 229.
ᴰNÍN; read ᴰINANNA.
ninink-; read *nenenk-*.
nink-; read *nenk-*. HG 273 fn. 114.
ninganu-; read *nenganu-*.
ᴰ*ningas*; see *anningas*.
ninke; read *nenke/a-*.
ninkiya/e-; read *nenkiya/e-*.
NINDA 'bread, loaf'.
    N. GIBIL 'fresh bread'.
    N. GÚ.GAL 'bean bread'.
    N. KUR₄.RA 'ordinary bread'.
    N. MUR(.RA) 'Aschenbrot'?? See s.v. MUR.
    N. NI.E.DÉ.A 'porridge'.
    N. SIG 'thin bread, flat bread'.
    N. U + DAR.RA 'dry bread, Zwieback'?? Deimel, No. 597.339.
ᴸᵁNINDA.DÙ.DÙ 'baker'.
NIN.DINGIR, a kind of priestess.
NI.NUN; read YÁ.NUN.
NIR.IG; read NIR.GÁL.
NIR.GÁL = *MUṬALLU* 'mighty, proud'. Hrozný, BoSt. 3.178.4; Götze, Hatt. 56.
NĪŠ; see NĪŠU.
NISABA, a vegetable substance, used to cleanse the body, etc. Ehelolf, KlF 1.157.
NISABA = *warp-* 'bathe, wash'. Ehelolf, KlF 1.158–60.

NĪŠŪ 'elevation, lifting up'.

NĪŠ (often written *NI-EŠ*) DINGIR-*LIM* = *lenkais* 'oath'.

NĪŠU (pl. *NĪŠĒ*) 'people'.

LÚ.MEŠ*NI-ŠU-U-ŠU* 'his people, his relatives'. Hrozný, CH 46.4.

NITA 'male'.

LÚNITA-*tar* 'manhood'.

NITÁ 'male'.

NITAḪ; read NITÁ.

NIDABA; read NISABA.

NÍ.TE = *twekkas* 'body, self'.

ANA NÍ.TE-*ŠU* 'apud se, in his house'. Chrest. 170.

IŠTU NÍ.TE-*YA* 'by myself, with my own resources'. Götze, Hatt. 18.39, 20.67.

ZA*nitri* 'niter'?? Hrozný, BoSt. 3.87 fn. 7.

LÚNI.DU8 'porter, doorkeeper'.

**niwallas* (acc. *niwallan*) 'innocent'? Friedrich, Vert. 1.176.

**niwallis* (acc. *niwallin*) 'innocent'? Friedrich, ZA NF 5.50.

LÚNÍ.ZU (1) 'thief'. Zimmern, ZA NF 2.319 f. (2) 'Helper'??? Zimmern, ib. p. 320. Rather 'spy, sentry' or the like. KUB 13.2.1.4, 5, 11, etc.

NU = *natta* 'not'.

nu 'then, and; however, but'; the most common sentence connective; always the first word in its clause. (The other sentence connectives are *-ma* and *-a*; one of these is normally required with every clause, except (1) an initial clause, (2) a tautological or explanatory clause, (3) a subordinate clause following its main clause, (4) between a verb of saying, commanding, etc. and the dependent 'that'-clause, (5) after an introductory verb of motion: *ehu, i-, pai-, we/a-*.) Hrozný, MDOG 56.34; Ungnad, ZDMG 74.417–22; Friedrich, KlF 1.293; Sommer, AU 95, 99 fn. 2, 453; Götze-Pedersen, MS 62.

NU.IG; read NU.GÁL.

NU.GÁL 'non-existent, does not exist, is not'.

LÚNU.GIŠ.ŠAR 'gardener, cultivator of an orchard'.

NUKURTU 'hostile; enemy'.

nūmăn 'no longer, never'? Friedrich, Vert. 2.86, 201; Götze, AM 247.

NUMUN 'seed; descendants, legitimate descendants of a king'. Götze, AOr. 2.159f.; Sommer, AU 136–8. Cf. MÁŠ.

**nuntar* (gen. *nuntaras*) 'haste, speed'? Friedrich, AOr. 6.372 f.

nu(n)taras 'hastily, speedily'? Cf. *nuttariyas*.

nuntariyashas; EZEN *n*., a festival in which the king visits the principal cult cities. Götze, Kulturg. 154; Friedrich, AOr. 6.372 f.

nuntarnu- 'hasten'. Friedrich, AOr. 6.368–73.
ᶻᴬNUNUZ 'pearl'.
NU.BE; read NU.TIL.
ᴰᵁᴳ*NŪRU* = ᴰᵁᴳ*sasannas* 'lamp'.
nus = *nu* + *us*; see *nas*.
nūs (or *nuwus* ?), occurs in lists of blessings. Götze, NBr. 32 fn. 2.
nussan = *nu* + *san*.
NU.TIL 'incomplete'.
nutta = *nu* + *ta* 'et tibi, et te'.
*nuttariyas (acc. *nuttariyan*) 'quick, swift'?? Friedrich, AOr. 6.372.
    Cf. *nuntar*, *nuntarnu-*.
NU.TUG 'not abundant'.
nūwa; read *nuwwa*.
nuwus; see *nūs*.
nuwwa 'still, yet'. Götze, Hatt. 56 and fn. 1.
nuwwān 'no longer, never'?? Friedrich, Vert. 2.86.

PA, a dry measure, twice the size of a BÁN.
PA; read UGULA 'foreman'.
ᴳᴵˢPA 'staff, scepter, verge'.
    LÚ ᴳᴵˢPA 'scepter-bearer', a kind of herald.
PA₄; read PAB, PAP 'protect.'
PA₄; read KÚR 'destroy'.
ᴸᵁ́PA₄; read ᴸᵁ́KÚR.
PA₅ = *amiyar-*. 'canal'.
-pa; see *-apa*.
PA₄.E; read PA₅.
pahhar; read *pahhur*.
pahhas-; read *pahhss-*.
pahhasnu-; read *pahhssnu-*.
pahhassanu-; read *pahhssnu-*.
?ᴳᴵˢ*pah(h)isa-* (or ᴳᴵˢPA-*ah(h)isa-*?) 'stick, switch'? Ehelolf, OLZ 32.
    322 and fn. 2.
pahhss- (1 sg. *pahhashi*, 2 sg. *pahhasti*, pl. *pahsanzi*, midd. *pahsari*, pl.
    pahhassantari, pret. 1 sg. *pahhashat*, *pahhashahat*) act. and midd.
    'protect, keep (an oath)'; midd. w. dat. 'be true to'. Hrozný,
    BoSt. 5.28 fn. 5; Götze, ZA 34.185, NBr. 12.6; Friedrich, Vert. 1.26
    f.; Kurylowicz, Symb. Gramm. 102, EI 73, 254 f.; Sturtevant,
    Lang. 7, 120, HG 85.

pahhssnu- (2 pl. *pahhasnutteni*, pret. pl. *pahsanwir, pahhassanwir*) 'cause to endure, make (a building) firm'. Friedrich, ZA NF 1.16, Vert. 2.24 f.; Sommer, AU 229. See *pahhss-*.

pahhuen-; read *pahhwen-*.

pahhun-; see *pahhur*.

ᴰᵁᴳ*pahhunali* (abl. *pahhunaliyaza, pahhunaliaz, pahhwinaliaz*) 'brazier'. Sayce, JRAS 1924.645; Sturtevant, Lang. 10.267. Cf. *pahhur*.

ᶻᴬ*pahhunali* 'heating stone'? KUB 7.18.3,7 (W).

pahhur (nom.-acc. *pahhur, pahhuwar*, gen. *pahhwenas*, dat. *pahhweni, pahhuni*) 'fire'. Hrozný, SH 68 f.; Friedrich, ZA NF 1.188; Ehelolf, KlF 1.159; Kurylowicz, Symb. Gramm. 102, EI 73; Sturtevant, Lang. 6.152 f., RHA 1.80 f., HG 130 and fn. 93, 138.

pah(h)ursis, pahhurzis 'bastard'? Götze, KlF 1.132, AOr. 2.156 and fn. 1.

*pahhurul (abl. ᴳᴵᴾ*pahhurulaz*) something connected with fire, perhaps 'ashes' or 'soot'?? Cf. Ehelolf, KlF 1.159.

pahhuwar; see *pahhur*.

pahhwen-; see *pahhur*.

*pahhwenali (abl. ᴰᵁᴳ*pahhwinaliaz*); see *pahhunali*.

pahs-; see *pahhss-*.

pahsanu-; see *pahhssnu-*.

pahsnu-; see *pahhssnu-*.

pāi- (*păizzi*, pl. *pănzi*, pret. *păit*, 1 sg. *păŭn*) 'go, pass'; sometimes a mere introduction to the following verb; in which case there is no sentence connective between them, and the subject follows *pai-*. Sommer, BoSt. 4.1 f., 10.42; Friedrich, Vert. 1.153, 162 f., 2.146; Sturtevant, Lang. 7.9–13, HG 221, JAOS 54.403; Götze-Pedersen, MS 62 f.

anda p. 'enter; go to (a person)'.

andan p. 'go to (a place), arrive at'. Götze, AOr. 5.19 f.

appan p. 'go behind, follow; support'.

appanda p. 'follow, pursue'.

arha p. 'go away'.

istarna p. 'pass' (of time).

kattan p. 'descend'.

paranda p. 'take refuge in (a place)'.

tapūsa p. 'go to one side, be distorted'? Friedrich, ZA NF 2.288, OLZ 39.305.

păi-, pe- (*pāi*, 1 sg. *pihhi* [peh˙i], pret. *păis*, 1 sg. *pihhun, pēhhun*) 'give,

send'. Hrozný, MDOG 56.38, JSOR 6.69 fn. 1; Sturtevant, Lang. 8.121, HG 223 and fn. 22, 247; Petersen, Lang. 9.32; Pedersen, AOr. 5.183 fn. 1; Götze-Pedersen, MS 63. Cf. *pais-, pes-, peya/e-*.
 anda p. 'pay at the same time'.
 appa p. 'surrender, extradite'.
 kattan p. 'betray, slander; desert'. Götze, AM 265 f.
pais- (2 sg. *paisti*, pret. 2 sg. *paista*) 'give, send'. HG 229. Cf. *pai-*.
paiske/a- (*paiskitta*, supine *paisgawan*) 'go'. Götze, Hatt. 68.
paknu- 'praise'?? Sturtevant, AJP 50.364.
BAL = *wakkariya/e-* 'revolt'. But cf. Sommer, AU 218.
BAL = *wakkariyawwar?* 'revolt, insurrection'. Götze, AM 304.
BAL = *wakkariyanu-* 'cause to revolt'. Sommer, AU 218 fn. 1.
BAL = *sippant-* 'pour a libation, sacrifice'.
BAL (dat. BAL-*hi*, pl. BAL-*has*) 'libation'.
BAL (dat. BAL-*si*) 'time, occasion'.
palahsa- (acc. *palahsan*) 'protection' or the like. Götze, Hatt. 75; Chrest. 90.
ᴳᴵˢBALAG, a musical instrument, perhaps 'tambourine'. Sommer, BoSt. 10.69.
ᵁᴿᵁ*Palaumnili* 'in Palaic, in Palaumnian'. Götze, Madd. 53.
*palhas; DUG *palhan* (pl. DUG *palha*) = DUG *palhi*; see s.v. *palhis*.
palhāsti, palhastis 'breadth'. Forrer, ZDMG 76.262; Sturtevant, Lang. 4.231, HG 155 f. See *palhis*.
palhatar 'breadth'. Forrer, ZDMG 76.262; HG 151. See *palhis*.
*palhessar (dat. *palhesni*) 'breadth'. Ehelolf ap. Friedrich, ZA NF 5.77; HG 152.
palhis (acc. *palhīn*) 'broad'. Friedrich, ZA NF 5.35 f., 77; Sturtevant, RHA 1.82, HG 106 f.; Kurylowicz, EI 73; Couvreur, Hett. h 19. Cf. *palhas*.
 DUG *palhi*, a kind of vessel.
pallassurimis 'commoner, common man'. Meissner, Beitr. 2.18.
paltanus (pl.) 'arms (of the body)'. Götze, Madd. 135 fn. 14.
ᴸᵁPA.LU; read ᴸᵁSIPAD.
palueske/a-, paluiske/a-; see *palweske/a-*.
palwă(e)- (*palwăizzi*), perform a certain ceremony in the ritual, probably 'recite (in a certain way)'. Sommer ap. Friedrich, ZA NF 3.179.
ᴸᵁ*palwat(t)allas*, ˢᴬᴸ*palwatallas*, agent noun from the preceding.
palwĕske/a- (pl. *palwĭskanzi, palwēskanzi*); see *palwa(e)-*.
palzah(h)as 'basis (for metal figures of animals)'? Götze, AOr. 5.32 (his word is 'Platte').

BA.MIT; read BA.UG₆.
ᴳᴵˢBAN (or ᴳᴵˢPAN) 'bow'.
BÁN, a dry measure, one half a PA.
PĀNĪ; see PĀNŪ.
pangarit (inst.) 'in force, in great numbers'. Friedrich, ZA NF 2.274; Götze, Madd. 114 f. Cf. *pankus*.
pangariya/e- (pret. *pangariyattati*) 'be common, be prevalent'. Götze, Madd. 115.
pankur (gen. *pankunas*) 'relationship, relatives'? Götze, AOr. 2.161 and fn. 1; HG 185.
pankus (gen. *pangawas, pankus*, dat. *pangawi, pangawe*) 'all, whole; every; general, wide-spread'; as a substantive 'totality; (the nobles as a) whole, senate'. Sommer, BoSt. 7.17 fn. 1; Götze, AM 239 f., Kulturg. 80 f.; Sturtevant, JAOS 50.125 f., HG 118.
ᴳᴵˢBANŠUR = ᴳᴵˢ*papus*?? '(sacrificial) table'. Sommer, BoSt. 10.88, KlF 1.344; Deimel, Nachträge, No. 187.
LÚ ᴳᴵˢBANŠUR 'table man', a palace official.
pandu, panzi; see *pai-* 'go'.
PĀNŪ 'face'.
PĀNĪ, ANA PĀNĪ = *piran* 'before'.
panza; see *pai-* 'go'.
PAB, PAP = *pahhss-* 'protect; be loyal'.
PAB, PAP = *pahhssnu-* 'cause to endure'.
PAB, PAP; read KÚR 'destroy'.
ᴸᵁPAB, ᴸᵁPAP; read ᴸᵁKÚR.
paparas-; see *pappars-*.
BA.BAD; read BA.UG₆.
BA.BA.ZA 'flour' or 'gruel'. Sommer, BoSt. 10.68.
UTÚL BA.BA.ZA 'gruel'. Chrest. 124.
BA.BE; read BA.UG₆.
PAB.E, PAP.E; read PA₅.
ᵁᴿᵁ*Papilili* 'in Babylonian', i.e. 'in Akkadian'. Friedrich, Vert. 2.148.
BABBAR = *harkis* 'white'.
pappars- (*papparaszi*, pl. *papparsanzi*, pret. 1 sg. *paparashun*) 'sprinkle, pour' (the object may denote the liquid or that upon which the liquid is poured). Friedrich, ZA NF 1.188, AOF 2.122 fn. 2; Götze, Madd. 44; HG 130. See *pappassanta*.
papparsiske/a- (pl. *papparsiskanzi*) 'sprinkle, pour'. Götze, Madd. 44 and fn. 3.

papparske/a- 'sprinkle, pour'. Hrozný, BoSt. 3.66 fn. 4; Götze, Madd. 44 fn. 3; HG 106.
pappassanta = papparsanta? KUB 17.10.2.29.
BAPPIR 'malt cakes'. Götze, Madd. 64–77.
papra (acc.) 'uncleanness' or the like. KUB 7.53.3.10. See *papre/a-*.
paprahh- 'make unclean'. Götze, Hatt. 96.
paprahhiske/a- 'make unclean'. See *paprahh-*.
paprannanza 'unclean, guilty'. KUB 12.58.4.2. Cf. *papre/a-*.
papras-; read *paprs-*.
paprătar 'uncleanness'. See *papre/a-*.
papre/a- (*paprizzi*, pret. *papritta*) 'be unclean; make unclean'; w. dat. 'put filth into'. Cf. Götze, Hatt. 95; Friedrich, AOr. 6.259 fn. 4; HG 255.
papreske/a- 'be unclean, be guilty'. See *papre/a-*.
papris-; read *paprs-*.
paprs- (*papraszi*, *papriszi*) 'be found guilty'. Sturtevant, Lang. 8.123, HG 70 (delete *pa-ap-pár-as-zi*). Cf. *papre/a-*.
*papūs (acc. ᴳᴵˢ*papūn*) 'table'?? Sommer, KlF 1.344.
BAR; read ½.
BAR; read BÁN, a dry measure.
BAR, a careless writing for one form of I, determinative with men's names.
parā 'before; forth, forward; thenceforth, henceforth, furthermore'. Hrozný, MDOG 56.27, SH 181; Sommer, BoSt. 4.15 fn. 2, 10.8; Götze, Hatt. 81; Tenner, HAT 17 f., 23 f. Cf. Götze, AM 305.
  parā w. a noun denoting a period of time: 'next'?? Sommer, AU 272 fn. 1, end.
para handandatar; see *handandatar*.
para handatar; see *handatar*.
parahh-; read *parhh-*.
parăi- (*parāi*, pret. *parais*) 'send forth; offer; blow, kindle'. Friedrich, ZA NF 2.164 fn. 1, 3.199, 5.49 f., Vert. 2.32; Götze, AM 255; Sturtevant, Lang. 8.121, HG 247. Cf. *parais-*, *pariya/e-*.
parais- (2 pl. *paraisteni*) 'send forth; offer; blow, kindle'. See *parai-*.
paranda; see *parranda*.
paras-; read *pars-*.
parāsessir (pret. pl.) 'they mutinied' or the like. Tenner, HAT 20; Götze, AM 254 f.; HG 214.
parasna(e)-; read *parssna(e)-*.
parasnawwanti; see *parssnawwanza*.

parassana(e)-; read *parssna(e)*-.
**parassis* (acc. *parassin*) 'patron deity'?? Chrest. 97.
parasdus; read *parsdus*.
parasza (*pár-aš-za*) 'on the back'?? Götze, AOr. 5.6.
ᴸᵁBAR.EN.DÚ; read MAŠDÁ.
parh-; see *parhh*-.
parhh- (*parahzi, parhizi, parhazi*, pl. *parhanzi*) 'drive; drive (horses) at a gallop; drive, ride'. Forrer, ZDMG 76.252; Friedrich, Vert. 1.164 f.; Götze, Madd. 44; Hrozný, AOr. 3.434; Sturtevant, Lang. 4.161, HG 90, 130, 243; Kurylowicz, EI 73. Cf. *parhha*-, *parhheske/a*-.
   arha p. 'drive out, banish'.
parhhă- (*parhăi, parahhăi*) = *parhh*-, q.v.
parhhanna- (*parhannai*) 'drive; drive at a gallop'. Sommer, BoSt. 10.22; HG 245 and fn. 58.
parhhanu- (*parhanuzi*) 'drive; drive at a gallop'. Friedrich, ZA NF 1.16. See *parhh*-.
parhhanuske/a- (*parahhanuskizzi, parhanuskizzi*). KBo. 3.5.1.32, 2.6.
parhheske/a- (pl. *parheskanzi, parahhiskanzi*) 'drive; drive at a gallop'. See *parhh*-.
parhhessar (*parhessar*, dat. *parhesni*) 'the act of driving; haste'. Friedrich, ZA NF 2.277. See *parhh*-.
parian; read *pariyan*.
pariya/e- (pl. *pariyanzi*, pret. pl. *pariir*, mid. pret. 1 pl. *pariyawwastati*) 'send forth; offer; blow, kindle'. See *parai*-.
pariya(n), w. acc., 'beyond, across'; adv. 'besides'. Friedrich, Vert. 1.161, ZA NF 5.55 and fn. 5.
pariyan, pariyawan, of the flight of birds, 'to that side'? Götze, Kulturg. 141. Cf. *pariyan* 'beyond, across'.
pariyas (gen. ?) 'of a pair'?? Hrozný, CH 65 fn. 28, 68.18.
pargamus (acc. pl.) 'high'. Götze, Madd. 120 fn. 4. Cf. *parkus*.
parkan 'atonement' or the like. Götze, KlF 1.190-2.
parganu- 'cleanse'. KUB 24.7.2.11. Cf. *parkunu*-, *parkus* 'pure'.
parganu- (imper. 1 pl.? *parganula*) 'make high'? Götze, Madd. 145 Cf. Hrozný, Congr. 1.163 fn. 1. Cf. *parkus* 'high'.
parkasti (*parqasti*) 'height'. Ehelolf, ZA NF 5.77. Cf. *parkus* 'high'.
pargatar 'height'. Friedrich, ZA NF 5.35 and fn. 4. Cf. *parkuwatar*.
**parkessar* (dat. *parkesni*) 'height'. Ehelolf, ZA NF 5.77. Cf. *parkus* 'high'.

parkiyanu- (pl. *parkiyanuwanzi*) 'make clean, acquit'? Friedrich, ZA NF 5.51.
parkiyas 'pure'??
parkues-; read *parkwess-*.
parkuis; read *parkwis*.
parkuis-; read *parkwess-*.
parkuiya/e-; read *parkwiya/e-*.
parkunu- 'purify; acquit'. Sommer, BoSt. 7.3 and fn. 1. 'Deprive (an animal) of marks of ownership'? Götze ap. Chrest. 222.37, 228. Cf. *parkus* 'pure'.
parkunuske/a- 'purify; acquit'. KUB 7.53.3.14.
*parkus (acc. *parkun*—KUB 24.7.2.10) 'pure'. Sturtevant, HG 122, Lang. 10.268. See *parkwis*, *parkunu-*.
parkus 'high'. Friedrich, ZA NF 2.278 f.; Marstrander, Car. 148 f.; Meillet, MSL 23.328; Sturtevant, Lang. 6.216, HG 106; Rosenkranz, IF 53.115.
parkuszi; see *parkwess-*.
parkuwa(e)- 'make pure; quash (an indictment)'. Götze, Madd. 82; KUB 13.9.3.20.
parkuwatar 'height'. Friedrich, ZA NF 5.35 fn. 4; Götze, Madd. 95. Cf. *parkus* 'high'.
parkuyatar; read *parkwiyatar*.
parkuwess-; read *parkwess-*.
parkuway-; read *parkway-*, strong stem of *parkwis*, q.v.
parkwĕss- (*parkwēszi, parkwiszi, parkuszi* — HG 60 —, pret. 1 sg. *parkwēssun, parkuwēssun*) 'become pure; be acquitted'. Götze, Hatt. 69.
parkwis (acc. *parkwin*, neut. *parkwi*, dat. *parkuwaya*, pl. *parkuwais*, dat. *parkuwayas, parkwiyas*) 'pure, guiltless; acquitted'. Hrozný, BoSt. 3.66 fn.5; Sommer, BoSt. 10.32; Sturtevant, Lang. 6.228, 10.268. See *parkus* 'pure'.
parkwiya/e- (midd. pret. *parkwiyatat*) 'be pure'. KUB 24.8.1.31. See *parkwis*.
parkwiyătar (*pár-ku-ya-a-tar*, gen. *pár-ku-ya-an-na-aš*) 'purification'. HG 56. See *parkwiya/e-*.
parnallis 'of the house'? Sturtevant, Lang. 10.267. See *parnan*.
*parnan (pl. *parna*) 'farm buildings, house; court; palace'. Sommer, BoSt. 10.62; Götze, ZA NF 2.17, 261 f.; Friedrich, ZA NF 2.45; HG 177 and fn. 88; Pedersen, AOr. 5.179 f.; Eheloff, ZA NF 9.185 and fn. 1.

parna adv. 'home'? Forrer, Altorient. Stud. 33; Götze, NBr. 71. 'Foras'?? Sommer, BoSt. 10.62; Götze, NBr. 71.

parnanza 'all the houses'? Cf. Friedrich, ZA NF 3.299 and fn. 2.

**parnawa(e)-* 'intend for the palace, use for the palace'. Götze, NBr. 34 f. Cf. *parnawaiske/a-*.

parnawaiske/a- 'intend for the palace, use for the palace'. Chrest. 98.

parnawiske/a-, variant of the prec.

par(r)anda (also *parranta*, rarely *paranda*), adv. or postposition w. dat. or acc., 'beyond, across, out; besides'. Friedrich, Vert. 1.156 f., 181, ZA NF 5.55 and fnn. 4, 5.

parriyanta (*parrianta*), w. dat., 'in addition to, besides'. Friedrich, AOr. 6.361 and fn. 1; cf. Friedrich, Vert. 1.161.

pars- (pl. *parsānzi*, pret. *parasta*, pl. *parser*) 'flee'. Götze, Hatt. 109, Madd. 45; HG 90, 229.

pars- (*parsi*, pl. *parsānzi*, part. *parsān*) 'break, divide'. HG 258. See *parsiya/e-*.

parsanas 'leopard'. Friedrich ap. Landsberger, Die Fauna des alten Mesopotamiens 76 fn. 4.

parse/a- (*parsizi*, midd. *parsittari*) 'break, divide'. See *parsiya/e-*.

ᵀᵁᴳBAR.SI 'head band'. Ehelolf. KlF 1.153.

parsiya/e- (*parsiyazzi*, *parsiyazi*, pl. *parsiyanzi*, midd. *parsiya*, pl. *parsiyanda*) 'break, divide'. Sommer, BoSt. 10.21–5, 65 f.; Mudge, Lang. 7.252; HG 131, 258.

parsiyannă- (*parsiyannăi*, 1 sg. *parsiyannahhi*) 'break, divide'. Götze, Madd. 130; HG 245. See *parsiya/e-*.

parsiyanniske/a- 'break, divide'. See *parsiyanna-*.

parsiyaniya/e- (pl. *parsiyannianzi*) 'break, divide'. HG 225.

parsna(e)-; see *parssna(e)-*.

parssnă(e)- (*parasnăizzi*, *parsanāizzi*, pl. *parasnānzi*, part. *parasnăntes*, *parassanantes*) 'crouch down, kneel'. Friedrich, AOF 7.200.

*parssnawwanza (dat. *parasnawwanti*) 'crouching'? KUB 25.1.6.3. See *parssna(e)-*.

parssul (pl. *parsulli*, *parassulli*); NINDA *p.* 'broken bread'?? Cf. Götze, Madd. 45 fn. 1.

parsdus (*pár-aš-du-uš*) sprout, shoot'. Götze, Madd. 143 and fn. 2.

parsūr 'bread crumbs' or the like? Sommer, BoSt. 10.41 and fn. 2.

partā(e)- (*partāizzi*) 'fly'??? Holma, JSFO 33.23; KBo. 3.8.3.6, 24. 'Pick to pieces'?? Friedrich, ZA NF 5.52 fn. 1.

partăwwar (inst. *partāunit*) 'nest'? 'swing'??? Götze, Madd. 93 and fn. 2.

pās- (*pāszi, pāsi*) 'swallow'? Friedrich, AOr. 6.374. Cf. Sturtevant, Lang. 4.126, HG 130.

^{LÚ}*pasandalas*, a kind of servant in the royal kitchen. Friedrich, Altorient. Stud. 51.

⁎*pasihā-* (*pasihāti*, pret. *pasihāitta*?) 'rub; bruise, crush, trample'. Sommer, AU 107–9.

pasiha(e)- (*pasihaizzi*) 'rub; bruise, crush, trample'. Sommer, AU 109.

pasga- (pret. pl. *paskir*, verb. n. *pasgawwar*) 'set upright'. Hrozný, SH 79; Friedrich, ZA NF 5.78 f.

paskuwa(e)- (pret. 1 sg. *paskuwanun*, midd. *paskuwaitta* [*paskwaet a*]) 'drive out of one's mind, forget'? midd. 'forget (another's) admonitions, be disloyal'? Götze-Pedersen, MS 20, 63; Friedrich, OLZ 39.305.

paskwe/a- (midd. *paskwītta* [*paskwet˙a*]), variant of the prec.

BAŠLU (also written *PAŠLU, MAŠLU*) 'purified', of gold. Ehelolf ap. Sommer, AU 244.

^{ZA}*passilas* (acc. *passilan*, pl. acc. *passilus*) 'gravel, bits of gravel'. Witzel, HKU 102.56; Sturtevant, TAPA 58.22, JAOS 50.126, HG 131, 164 and fn. 62.

PĀŠU 'ax'.

BAD; read BE 'master'.

BAD; read BE 'if'.

BAD; read UG$_6$ 'die; death'.

BAD; read TIL 'complete'.

BÀD = *ḪALṢU* = *sahessar*? 'wall, fortress'.

BÀD KARAŠ 'fortified camp'.

BÀD-*anza* 'fortified'.

BÀD-*esna(e)-* 'fortify'.

-*pat*; see -*be*.

patalliya/e- (imper. pl. *patalliyandu*) 'make lame'??? Friedrich, ZA NF 1.162.24. Rather 'fetter'?

BA.TIL; read BA.UG$_6$.

^{LÚ}*patilis*, a kind of priest. Ehelolf, OLZ 32.322 f.

^{GIŠ}*patiyallēs* (pl.) 'bed posts'? Chrest. 106.13, 119.

BA.UG$_6$ = *akk-* 'die'.

paun; see *pai-* 'go'.

pawaritta (pret.?) 'bivouacked'?? Götze, AM 266.

pawwanza 'baked under hot ashes'??? 'thoroughly baked'?? Sommer, BoSt. 10.64.

BE = *BĒLU* = *eshas* 'master, lord'.

BE = *takku, man* 'if'.
BE; read TIL 'complete'.
BE; read UG₆ 'die; death'.
-*be* (the sign with which this word is always written may be interpreted instead as -*pit* or as -*pat*; it was formerly interpreted as -*mit*), the particle of identity, 'ipse, idem, itidem'; to be translated variously in English, and sometimes to be omitted in translation. Götze, Madd. 55–7, AM 207–9; Hrozný, OLZ 35.258; Sturtevant, JAOS, 50.127, HG 44 fn. 26, 131; Götze-Pedersen, MS 64; Güterbock, ZA NF 8.225–32; Pedersen, AOr. 7.80–5.

pĕ-, pē, a preverb, usually inseparable, 'secum', with an implication of motion, usually of motion away. Sometimes verbs containing the inseparable prefix stand in opposition to verbs containing the preverb *u-* 'hither'. Friedrich, ZA NF 2.53, Vert. 2.146; Sturtevant, Lang. 7.5–13, JAOS 54.403, 406, HG 131, 213; Götze, AOr. 5.16 fn. 1.

pe-; see *pai-* 'give'.

pē har(k)-; see s.v. *har(k)-*.

pehhi, pehhun, see *pai-* 'give'.

pĕhute/a- (*pēhutezzi, pihutezzi,* pl. *pēhudanzi, pihudanzi*) 'lead, conduct'. Götze, Hatt. 128, AOr. 5.22 fn. 3; Sturtevant, Lang. 7.7, OLZ 35.471, HG 222, 275 f.

pēhuteske/a- 'lead, conduct'. Friedrich, ZA NF 5.8.4.

BĒLU = EN = *eshas* 'master, lord'; ᴸᵁ̌·ᴹᴱˢBĒLU-ḪI.A, BĒLU-MEŠ 'nobles'.

BĒLĪ (gen. BĒLI-YA) 'my lord'.

BĒLI-NI 'our lord'.

BĒL QĀTI, etc.; see s.v. EN.

BĒLTU = GAŠAN = *parassis*?? 'mistress, lady'.

BĒLŪTU = *eshatar* 'mastery, lordship'.

pennă- (*pennăi,* 1 sg. *pennahhi, pinnahhi,* pl. *pennanzi, pinnanzi,* pret. *pennis,* infin. *pennummanzi*) 'lead with one; drive; drive (horses), ride'. Forrer, ZDMG 76.252; Friedrich, ZA NF 2.52 f., Vert. 2.146; Götze, Hatt. 101. AOr. 5.22 fn. 3; Ehelolf, KlF 1.140 fn.; Hrozný, AOr. 3.434–6; Sturtevant, Lang. 7.6 f., HG 213, 244; Götze-Pedersen, MS 63 f. Cf. *pennes-, penniya/e-*.

arha p. 'drive away'.

pennes- (pret. *pennesta, pennista*) 'lead with one; drive; drive (horses), ride'. See *penna-*.

penneske/a- 'lead with one; drive; drive (horses), ride'. Hrozný, AOr. 3.456.42.

penniya/e- (pl. *penniyanzi*, part. *penniyan*) 'lead with one; drive; drive (horses), ride'. See *penna-*.

pennummanzi, infin. of *penna-*, q.v.

per; see *pir*.

peran; see *piran*.

ᶻᴬ*pĕrunanza* (*pirunanza*) 'rocky'. See *perunas*.

*pĕrunas (dat. ᶻᴬ*pēruni, piruni*, pl. *pērunus*) 'stone, rock, mountain; rocky'. Forrer, Forsch. 1.61; Friedrich, Altorient. Stud. 51. Cf. *pirwa*.

pĕs- (*peszi*, 2 sg. *pesti*, 2 pl. *pĕstēni, pisteni*, pret. *pĕsta, pista*) 'give, send'. HG 229. See *pai-* 'give'.

peske/a- (*peskizzi, piskizzi*) 'give, send'. See *pai-* 'give'.

    kattan p. 'traduce' or the like. KUB 21.17.1.7 f. Cf. Hrozný, BoSt. 3.240.16 f.

ᴳᴵ*pessar* (or *gipessar*), a measure of length and of surface. Friedrich, ZA NF 2.284 f., 5.56, 79.

pesseske/a- 'throw'; *arha p.* 'reject'. Götze, Madd. 118.

pesseya/e- (*pessiyazi, pessiyazzi, pesseyazi, pesseyazzi*) 'throw, throw away; repudiate, surrender; give forth (an oracle)'. Sommer, BoSt. 4.15 fn. 1, 10.64 f., 65 fn. 1; Götze, AOr. 5.22 fn. 3, 34 fn. 1; Chrest. 225.40.

    arha p. 'throw away; give forth (an oracle)'.

pĕdă (*pēddăi, piddăi*, pl. *pēdanzi, bedănzi*, 1 pl. *pitummeni*, pret. *pēdas*, pl. *pēter, bedāir*) 'carry, bring, take away; carry off booty; pass (days, years, etc.)'. Sommer, BoSt. 7.45; Friedrich, ZA NF 2.52 f.; Götze, AOr. 5.22 fn. 3; Sturtevant, Lang. 7.1-9, JAOS 54.406; Güterbock, ZA NF 8.225-32; Pedersen, AOr. 7.85, 86. Cf. Götze-Pedersen, MS 17.

    anda p. 'bring (words), declare, depose'.

    arha p. 'take away'.

    kattan arha p., w. dat., 'carry away to'. Götze, AM 146.7.

    kattanta p., w. dat., 'carry (down) into'. Götze, AM 306.

    parā p. 'take forth, out, away'.

bedă- or *piddă-* (*bedăi* or *piddăi*, pl. *bedănzi* or *piddănzi*) 'dig'. Götze, Kulturg. 146 and fn. 10; Güterbock, ZA NF 8.227 f.; Pedersen, AOr. 7.87.

beda(e)-; read *pidda(e)-* 'furnish, pay'.

pĕdan (*pĕdan, pĕtan*, dat. *pēdi, pēti, pēte, pidi*) 'place'. Sommer, BoSt. 7.36–45, AU 61 fn. 7; Ehelolf, KlF 1.146 fn. 6; HG 89; Götze-Pedersen, MS 64.
 salli p. 'lofty place, throne'. Friedrich, Vert. 2.40 fn. 2; Götze, NBr. 34 and fn. 1.
 tān pēdas (gen. sg. becoming an adj.; hence acc. *tān pēdan*) 'of second rank'. Sommer, BoSt. 7.44; Götze, Madd. 125.
 tān pēdassahh- 'make of second rank'.
 pedessi (also *pidessi, pidisi*) 'in its (his) place, on the spot'.
bedanna-; read *piddanna-*.
betessar or *pittessar* 'hole (in the ground)'. Güterbock, ZA NF 8.227 f.
pedda(e)-, peddai-; see *pidda(e)-, piddai-* 'flee'.
pettar; see *pittar*.
pĕya/e- (*peyazi*, 1 sg. *piyemi*, 2 sg. *piyesi*, pl. *pianzi, piyanzi, pēanzi*, pret. *piyēt*) 'give, send'. HG 223 and fn. 22. See *pai-* 'give'.
pĕyana(e)- (*piyanaizzi*, infin. *pĕyanawwanzi*) 'reward'? Friedrich, Vert. 2.23 and fn. 2; Walther, HC 255.45.
pēyaniske/a- (pret. 1 sg. *pīyaniskinun*) 'reward'.
BI; read KAŠ.
PI; read GEŠTU(G).
PĪ; see PŪ.
pian, a variant for *piran* occurring chiefly in omen texts. Sommer, AU 141, 178.
pihaimis, epithet of the storm god. Sommer, AU 355.
pihhi; see *pai-* 'give'.
pihute/a-; read *pehute/a-*.
BIL = *warnu-* 'cause to burn'.
BÍL; read GIBIL.
pinna-; read *penna-*.
↟*pintanza* 'rudders'??? Sommer, ap. Friedrich, ZA NF 5.57.
pipessar 'a sending, gift'. See *pippa-*.
pippa- (*pippai*, pret. *pippas*) 'place, put, put on'. Götze, KlF 1.222 f., 223 fn. 1, AOr. 5.22 fn. 3.
 arha p. 'remove'.
 sarā p. 'remove'. KUB 7.2.4.7 f.; 24.14.1.25 (G).
pippit (Arzawan for *kwit kwit*?) 'whatever'. Forrer, Forsch. 2.60–4; HG 119 fn. 73.
 pippitmi 'whatever I have'?
 pippitti 'whatever you have'?

BIBRU, a kind of cup.   Cf. Chrest. 164.52.

BIR; read KALÁM.

pir [per] (nom.-acc. É-*ir*, *pí-ir*, dat. É-*ri*, abl. É-*ir-za*) 'house'. Hrozný, SH 59-61; Friedrich, ZA NF 5.54 f.; Forrer, JA 217.242; Sturtevant, ap. Welles, Royal Correspondence in the Hellenistic Period 320; Götze-Pedersen, MS 77.

   piran [peran] 'forth, before; on account of', w. dat. Sommer, BoSt. 4.7 f., 10.8; Götze, Madd. 79, AOr. 5.32 and fn. 2; HG 212 f.

   piranset 'before him'; *pirantit* 'before you', etc. Friedrich, ZA NF 3.183.

   piran appa(n) 'back and forth'.   Götze, KlF 1.223 f.

   piran parā 'previously; first of all'. Friedrich, Vert. 1.75; Ehelolf, KlF 1.153.   See s.v. *kwetman*.

   piran sarā 'previously'?   Friedrich, Vert. 2.204; Sommer, AU 208.

BĪRTU 'fortress'.

ᶻᴬ*pirunanza*; read *perunanza*.

ᶻᴬ*pirunas*; read *perunas*.

pirwa, a kind of rock.   Sommer, AU 318 and fn. 1.   Cf. *perunas*.

PÍŠ 'mouse'.   Götze, ZA NF 6.65-70.

   PÍŠ.TUR = *mashuil* 'little mouse'.

PÍ-IŠ; read ŠIM.

pis-; read *pes-*.

ᴳᴵᠦPISÁN, a vessel for water.   'Water trough'?   Walther, HC 265.125.

piske/a-; read *peske/a-*.

BÍT; read BE 'master'.

BÍT; read BE 'if'.

BÍT; read UG₆ 'die; death'.

BÍT; read TIL 'complete'.

-pit; see *-be*.

pida-; read *peda-*.

pitala-; see *pittala-*.

pitea/e-; see *pitteya/e-*.

PITḪALLU 'saddle horse'.

   LÚ *PITḪALLI* 'horseman'.

pitta (nom.-acc.), some kind of penalty.   Güterbock, ZA NF 8.230 f.

piddă- or *bedă-*, q.v.

piddă(e)- (*piddāizzi*, *pí-it-ta-iz-zi* — KBo. 3.34.2.35, pret. *piddāit*) 'furnish, pay'.   Güterbock, ZA NF 8.228 f.; Pedersen, AOr. 7.86.

piddă(e)- (*piddaizzi* [p'et'aetsi], pl. *piddănzi*, pret. *piddāit*) 'fly, flee, hasten'. Götze, Hatt. 85; Friedrich, Vert. 1.81, 156; HG 89, 124; Güterbock, ZA NF 8.229 f.   Cf. *piddai-*, *pitteya/e-*.

kattan p. 'fall; be current (of rumors)'.
piddāi- (*piddāi* [pˈetˈai], pret. *piddāis*) 'fly, flee, hasten'. See *pidda(e)-*, *pitteya/e-*.
pittaiske/a- 'fly, flee, hasten'. Güterbock, ZA NF 8.230.
pittala- (2 sg. *piddalasi*, pl. *pittalanzi, piddalanzi*, pret. pl. *pittalair*) 'abandon, neglect' (sometimes intransitive). Güterbock, ZA NF 8.230 f. (G).
piddănna- (pret. *piddannis*, supine *piddānniwan*) 'furnish, pay'. Güterbock, ZA NF 8.228.
⁎*pittanu-*, doubtful variant of *pittenu-*. Friedrich, ZA NF 5.55.
pittar 'wing'? Hrozný, MDOG 56.28, SH 70 f.; Friedrich, ZA NF 5.36.
ᴳᴵ*pittar* (dat. *piddanĭ, pittāni*) 'basket' or the like. Friedrich, ZA NF 3.190 f.; Götze, AOr. 5.34.
pittarpalhis 'broad of wing'?, name of the oracle bird. Friedrich, ZA NF 5.36; HG 145.
pittenu- 'cause to fly, scatter; cause to flee, seduce, elope with; carry away'. Friedrich, ZA NF 5.55, 78; Walther, HC 251.28; Götze, Kulturg. 109 fn. 3; Güterbock, ZA NF 8.230.
pittessar or *betessar*, q.v.
pitteya/e- (1 sg. *pittiyami*, pl. *pittiyanzi*, part. *pittiyanza, pitteyantes, pitean*[) 'fly, flee, hasten'. See *pitta(e)-, pittai-*.
ᴸᵁ́*pit(t)eyanza* 'fugitive'. Götze, Hatt. 85; Friedrich, Vert. 1.47.
pitteyantili 'in the manner of a fugitive'. Hrozný, SH 180.
pittiyalis 'runner'?? KUB 15.39.2.25 (G).
ˢᴵᴳ*pittălas* 'noose, loop, knot' or the like. See *pittuliya/e-*.
pittuliya/e- 'fasten together, lace up, squeeze' or the like. Götze, KlF 1.187–90.
pittuliyas (acc. *piddulian*) 'noose; anxiety'? Götze, KlF 1.187–90, 402, AM 262. Cf. *pittulas*. Probably an *i*-stem with heteroclitic nom.; see Sturtevant, Lang. 10.272.
BĪTU = *pir* 'house'.
pitummeni 'we carry'; see *peda-*.
piya/e-; read *peya/e-*.
piyana(e)-; read *peyana(e)-*.
piyaniske/a-; read *peyaniske/a-*.
BU; read ŠER.
PÚ; read TÚL.
PŪ (gen. *PĪ*) = *ais* 'mouth'.
PŪḪU 'substitution, substitute'.
pŭhugaris, an epithet of sacrificial animals; 'for atonement, expiatory'?? Götze-Pedersen, MS 27, 64 f.

puk-, pugga- (imper. *puktaru, puggaru, puggataru*, part. *pukkanza*) 'be hated' or the like? Friedrich, ZA NF 3.186.
pukkanu- 'cause to be hated'?? KUB 24.7.1.49.
pukkunumar 'quarrel'?? Forrer, RHA 1.151.4.
ᴰᵁᴳ*pulla-*, a kind of vessel. Sommer, BoSt. 10.56.
ᴰᵁᴳ*pulluriya* (pl.), vessels into which honey is put, and whose openings are closed with figs. Sommer, BoSt. 10.8*.38 f., 56.
✴*pulpuli*, a kind of tree?? Friedrich, ZA NF 5.47. 'Trunk (of a tree)'?? Götze, ap. Friedrich, ZA NF 5.77.
BULÜG 'sugar malt'. Götze, Madd. 64–77.
BULÜG.AL.GAZ 'crushed malt'. Hrozný, AOr. 3.446.27.
pŭnus(s)- (punuszi, pl. *punussanzi*, pret. *punusta*, 1 sg. *pŭnussun, punusun*) 'ask, question'. Hrozný, SH 79; Sturtevant, JAOS 50.126, HG 229, 274 f.
punuske/a- 'ask, question'. Hrozný, SH 79; Götze, ZA 34.184.
*pupullis (neut. *pupulli*) 'ruined'?? Cf. Walther, HC 269.173.
*pupus; ᴸᵁ́*pupun* or LÛ *pupun* (acc.) 'adulterer'?? Hrozný, CH 148.12. 'Paramour'?? Friedrich, OLZ 26.47. Carruthers, Lang. 9.155 f.
ᴳᴵˢ*BUBUTU*, part of a wheel. Götze, NBr. 60.
pūramimma, a kind of omen. Sommer, AU 421.
*pūris (acc. ᴳᴵˢ*pūrin*, dat. *pūriya*) an implement used in connection with libations. Sommer, BoSt. 10.48. Cf. Hrozný, AOr. 3.440.23.
*pŭrpuras (acc. *pūrpuran*, pl. *pūrpurēs*, acc. *pŭrpurus*) 'lump'? Friedrich, ZA NF 3.190 and fn. 5.
BÛRU 'hole'.
    BÛRU-*uzziya* (dat.) 'in the sacrificial trench'? Sommer, BoSt. 10.18f.
ᴳᴵˢBURU₇ 'fruit'.
purul(l)i-; EZEN × ŠE *purulliyas*, a winter festival whose cult legend is the Iluyankas myth. Götze, AM 264 f., Kulturg. 131 f.
pŭrut (abl. *puruddaza*, inst. *puruttit*—Ehelolf, OLZ 36.7 fn. 2), some part of a house; hence by a figure 'house'. Friedrich, ZA NF 2.281 f.; Sommer, AU 196. 'Earth, dirt'?? Forrer, RHA 1.147.34, 148.36. 'Mortar'?? Götze-Pedersen, MS 65.
ᴰᵁᴳBUR. ZI = *waksur*, a vessel for relatively valuable foods. (G).
ᴰᵁᴳ*BURZITU* (i.e. *PURSITU*) = preceding word.
BU.DA; read GÍD.DA.
putalliya/e- 'lead (an army) in light order'. Sommer, AU 63 f., 388; Götze, AM 250.
    putalliyanda, adv., 'in light order'.

putkiya/e- (midd. *putkiyētta*) 'ferment'? Friedrich, ZA NF 1.163 fn. 8; Chrest. 122.
PŪTU 'madder' or 'madder berries'. Walther, HC 263.110.
puwattis 'color, paint; mark (of slavery)'. Weidner, Stud. 126; Delaporte, Voc. 63.
RA = *MAḪĀṢU* = *walh-* 'strike'.
RA-*IṢ* = *MAḪIṢ* = *walhanza* 'bruised'. Sommer, AU 216.
RAMĀNU = *twekkas* 'self'.
RABŪ = *sallis* 'great, noble'.
RIKELTU, RIKSU 'treaty'.
RIMMU 'womb'? Sommer, BoSt. 7.8.
ᴳᴵˢRU; read ŠUB 'inventory' or GIŠ-*ru* = *taru*.

ᵁᶻᵁSA 'sinew, muscle'.
SA₅ 'red'.
ŠÀ; read ŠA(G).
-ŠA = -*ses* 'her'. The Akkadian possessive suffixes of the second and third person indicate the sex of the possessor. HG 40.
ŠA 'of, concerning', a sign of the gen. Sommer, AU 60; HG 40.
-*sa*, a particle occurring only after -*nza*, and apparently equivalent to -*a*. Possibly -*n-za-sa* is a way of writing -*nz* + *a*. Friedrich, Vert. 1.32 f.
sā(e)- (pret. *sātt*, midd. pret. pl. *sāntati*, part. *sānza*, verb. n. *sāwwar*) 'be angry'. Weidner, Stud. 129; Friedrich, ZA NF 5.71 fn. 2; Götze, NBr. 80; Chrest. 125.
sawwar 'anger' or the like.
ŠAḪ 'pig'.
ŠAḪ is often written for TIR, especially in omen texts. Eheolf and Götze, ap. Friedrich, Vert. 2.172.
sah-; see *sanh-*.
sāh; see *sanhh-*.
SAḪAR 'dust, dirt'.
sahessar 'fortress'? Forrer, Altorient. Stud. 31.8.
sahh-; see *sanhh-*.
sahhan (pl. *sahhana*), goods and services rendered to an overlord for the use of lands, 'ground-rent'. Götze, NBr. 54–63; Korošec, Vert. 55.
ŠAḪ-*IZ-ZI*; read ŠAḪ.GIŠ.GI.
ŠAḪ.GIŠ.GI 'wild boar'. Cf. Hrozný, AOr. 1.278.60, 284.
ŠAḪ.ŠE 'fat pig'.

ŠAḪ.TUR 'sucking pig'.
sahuwihwissuwalis 'legitimate (son)'? Götze, NBr. 24 f.
sāi- (*sāi*, imper. *sāi*) 'press down, crush; oppress; pitch (a tent); set (a stone); put in, put on; seal; thrust in (a weapon), sting (of a bee)'. Götze, NBr. 76–80. See *siya/e-*.
ᴸᵁŠÁ'IDU (written ZA-A-I-DU) 'hunter'. Götze, Madd. 140.
SAG = *harssan* 'head'. Cf. SAG.DU.
ᴸᵁSAG 'chief, captain', or the like.
ᵁᶻᵁŠA(G) = LIBBU = *karza, kardi-* 'heart'.
ŠA(G), ŠA(G)-BA, ŠA(G)-*na*, INA ŠA(G)-BI = (INA)LIBBI = *istarna* 'within' or *anda* 'in'.
sak-, sek-; read *sakk-, sekk-*.
sagāis 'sign, omen'. Götze, KlF 1.402; HG 120, 147.
SAG.AMAT.ÎR.MEŠ; read SAG.GÎM.ERUM.MEŠ.
ᴳᴵˢŠA(G).A.TAR, a musical instrument. Götze, Hatt. 101 f.
ᴸᵁSA.GAZ = HABIRU 'robber; Bedouin', q.v.
ŠAKIN, construct state of ŠAKNU.
sākiske/a- 'give an omen; signify, declare'. Götze, KlF 1.412.
sakiya/e- 'signify, declare'. Götze, KlF 1.408–13; Milewski, L'Indo-Hittite et l'Indo-Européen 42 f.
sakiyahh- 'give an omen; signify'. Götze, KlF 1.401–13.
*sakiyassar (dat. *sakiasni*) 'sign, omen'. Götze, KlF 1.411; HG 152.
sakiyawanza 'giving omens'?? Cf. Götze, KlF 1.412, NBr. 34. Cf. HG 160 f.
sāk(k)-, sekk- (*sakki*, 1 sg. *sāggahhi*, pl. *sakanzi*, 1 pl. *sekkweni*, pret. *sakkis* [sak˙s], pl. *sekkir*, 1 pl. *sekkwen*) 'know'. Weidner, Stud. 38; Hrozný, JSOR 6.69 fn. 1; Götze, ZA 34.184; Tenner, HAT 18; Sturtevant, Lang. 3.161–4, HG 120, 239 f., 283, JAOS 54.406, Lang. 11.182 f.; Benveniste, BSL 33.140 f.; Milewski, RO 8.110 fn. 22.
ŠA(G).GAL 'forage, fodder'.
ᴳᴵˢŠA(G).KAL, some part of a wagon.
ᴰᵁᴳ*sakkān* (acc. *saqqān*), a kind of vessel. KBo. 3.34.1.10. Cf. *sakkar*.
ŠA(G).GAR = *kasza*? 'hunger, famine'.
sakkar (gen. *saknas*) 'dung'. Götze-Pedersen, MS 35 fn. 1; Sturtevant, JAOS 54.405, Lang. 12, No. 3; Benveniste, Origines de la Formation des Noms 9. Cf. *saknwanza* 'unclean', *zakkar*.
ᴸᵁŠA(G).GA.DÙ 'maker of undergarments'.
TÚG ŠA(G).GA.DÙ 'undergarment'? Witzel, HKU 100.33.
SAG.KI = *hanza* 'front, face'.
SAG.GÎM.ERUM.MEŠ 'slaves, servants'.
SAG.GÎM.ÎR.MEŠ; read SAG.GÎM.ERUM.MEŠ.

sakkis; see *sakk*.
ᴳᴵˢSAG.KUL = *hattalu* 'bolt (of a door)'.
săklăis (dat. *sakliya*, *saklāi*) 'rite; custom, law'. Hrozný, BoSt. 3.88.11; Friedrich, ZA NF 3.193; HG 87.
saknas; see *sakkar*.
ŠAKNU 'governor'.
saknwanza (acc. *saknuwandan*) 'full of excrement, unclean'. Friedrich, AOr. 6.365–8; Götze-Pedersen, MS 35 fn. 1; Sturtevant, JAOS 54. 405, Lang. 12, No. 3. Cf. *sakkar*.
ŠA(G).BAL(.LAL), ŠA(G).BAL.BAL 'descendant, posterity'.
sakruwanzi (3 pl.) 'they clean (horses)'?? Forrer, ZDMG 76.252.7. 'They water (horses)'?? Hrozný, AOr. 3.440.7.
ŠA(G).ŠAḪ; read ŠA(G).TIR.
sāktā(e)- (*sāktāizzi*) 'make unfit for work'??? Zimmern-Friedrich, AO 23.2.7.10. 'Care for'? Walther, HC 249.10.
ᴸᵁŠA(G).TAM 'treasurer'.
ŠA(G).TIR (also written ŠA(G).ŠAḪ, ŠA(G).DIR) = TĒRANU 'convolution of the intestines'. Götze, Lang. 11.187 and fn. 5; Boissier, Mantique 23 f.
SAG.DU = *harssan* 'head; person, self; chief'.
ᴸᵁSAG.DU; read LÚ SAG.DU, and see s.v. LÚ.
sakuis; read *sakwis*.
sakuneske/a- 'flow, gush'? Forrer, RHA 1.148.37; HG 123.
sakuni- (gen. *sakuniyas*, dat. *sakuniya*) 'spring, pool'? Forrer, RHA 1.147.33 f.; HG 123.
sakuntarriyanu- 'cause to rest, neglect'. Sommer, OLZ 33.758. See *sakuwantariya/e-*.
SAG.UŠ = KAYAMĀNU 'fixed, regular' (of festivals). Götze, AM 204 f.
ᴸᵁŠA(G).UD; read ŠA(G).TAM.
sakuwa; read *sakwa*.
săkuwa(e)- (pret. *sakuwa[it]*, midd. imper. *sakuwaru*, part. *săkuwanza*) 'allow to rest; cause to rest, arrest'. Götze, AM 202 f.
  săkuwanza 'still unused, not burnt' (of a torch); 'not changed, not heated, cool' (of water). Cf. Ehelolf, OLZ 36.3 fn. 2.
**sakuwanna-* (part. IGI-*wannanza*); part. 'dilatory'? Sturtevant, JAOS 54.398.
sakuwandareske/a- 'rest'. Götze, AM 308.
**sakuwantarinuske/a-* (pl. IGI-*wantarinuskanzi*) 'cause to rest, neglect'. Cf. Tenner, HAT 21.
săkuwantariya/e- 'rest'. Götze, AM 201–3.

sakuwantariyanu- 'cause to rest, neglect'. Götze, AM 201 f.
sakuwanza; see *sakuwa(e)-*.
sakuwas(s)ar, verb. n. from *sakuwa(e)-*; adv. 'without change'. KUB 14.3.1.66 = Friedrich, Vert. 1.91.63.
sakuwassar(r)as (adj. developed from the gen. of the preceding word?) 'unchanged, complete, of full value, fully equivalent; legal, loyal'. Friedrich, Vert. 1.90 f.; Sommer, AU 67 f.; Götze, AM 223 and fn. 1.
sakuweske/a- 'allow to rest; cause to rest'. Götze, AM 203.
săkwa (nom.-acc. *săkuwa*, gen. IGI.ḪI.A-*was*, inst. *săkwit*) 'eyes'. Friedrich, Vert. 1.35 f.; Ehelolf, KlF 1.397 and fn. 3; Sturtevant, Lang. 3.163, HG 93, 120, 165 f.; Benveniste, BSL 33.140 f.
sakwis 'spring, well'? Forrer, RHA 1.148.36; HG 105, 123.
SAL = *SINNIŠTU* (nom. SAL-*za*, gen. SAL-*nas*, pl. SAL-*winas*?) 'woman'; also a determinative before names of women and before words indicating a woman's occupation or class. Götze-Pedersen, MS 65.
SAL ŠU.GI 'old woman', especially a priestess or sorceress.
SAL-*annatar* 'conception'? KUB 24.13.2.15.
SAL-*nili* 'in the manner of women'. Hrozný, SH 180; Sommer, ZA 33.90.
*salhiantis (acc. *salhianten*) 'Wachstum'?? Götze, Kulturg. 135.
sălĭk- (*salikzi*, pl. *salikanzi*, midd. *salĭga*, *sālika*, pret. 1 pl. *salikuwastati*, imper. *salikaru*) 'lie together, be contaminated'; w. dat. 'lie with, contaminate, defile'. Hrozný, CH 146.51, 53, BoSt. 3.47 fn. 6; Sommer, BoSt. 10.66, AU 276; Friedrich, AOr. 6.358-65; Sturtevant, Lang. 6.216 f., HG 89, 105, 118, Lang. 12, No. 3. Cf. *lak-*.
   anda s. 'lie among'.
   parā s. = simplex.
saliga- (*saligai*) = *salik-*. KUB 26.12.4.37.
salikeske/a- 'be impure'; w. dat. 'defile'. Friedrich, AOr. 6.363 f.
ṢALITTU (for ṢALIMTU), fem., = *dankus, dankwis* 'black'.
salke/a- or *salka(e)-* (1 sg. *salgami*, pl. *salkanzi*) 'prepare (gruel)' or the like. Friedrich, AOr. 6.365.
SAL + KU; see NIN.
salla- (midd. imper. *sallattaru*) 'melt'. KUB 7.53.2.20. See *salliya/e-*.
salla- (verb. n. *sallawwar*) 'oppose'? Götze, Hatt. 87.
sallalitahh- (pret. *sallalitahta*) 'make angry'?? KUB 21.19.1.17.
sallannāi- (*sallannāi*, pl. *sallanniyanzi*) 'lay low' or the like?? Götze, AM 262 and fn. 7.
sallanniske/a- 'lay low' or the like?? See *sallanai-*.

sallanu- 'make great; think well of'. Friedrich, ZA NF 5.43. Cf. *sallis*.

sallanu-; *arha s.*, destroy in some way. Friedrich, ZA NF 5.43 fn. 3. 'Cause to melt'? Cf. *salliya/e-*.

sallanuske/a- 'make great; think well of'. Friedrich, ZA NF 5.47, 77.

*sallatar (dat. *sallanni*) 'greatness'? KBo. 3.21.3.3. Cf. *sallanu-*, *sallis*.

salles- 'become great'. Götze, Hatt. 69. See *sallis*.

salleske/a- 'become great'. Friedrich, ZA NF 5.74.

sallis 'great, important, glorious'. Götze, NBr. 34 and fn. 1; HG 138; Sturtevant, Lang. 10.267; Götze-Pedersen, MS 53.

salliya/e- (midd. *salliyaitta*, imper. *salliittaru*) 'melt'. Götze, Madd. 98 fn. 12 Cf. *salla-*, *sallanu-* 'cause to melt'?

SAL.LUGAL (dat. SAL.LUGAL-*ri*, unless we should read SAL.LUGAL-*RI* = *AŠŠAT ŠARRI*) 'queen'. Ehelolf, ZA NF 9.186.

salpis 'stench'. Weidner, Stud. 129.

SAL.SUḪUR.LAL 'female temple-slave'. Friedrich, Vert. 2.155 f., 170 f.

SAL.SUḪUR.LÁL, variant of the preceding word. Friedrich, Vert. 2.155 fn. 4.

SAL.TIN.NA; read ^{SAL}TIN.NA.

ŠÁM = *was-* 'buy'.

ŠÁM = *ŠĪMU* 'price'.

ŠAM, construct state of *ŠAMMU* = Ú, q.v.

SAMAG; read SIG$_7$.

samanas 'foundation'. Hrozný, CH 116.22; KBo. 4.1.2.31.

*samanatar (dat. *samananni*) 'fixation' or the like. KBo. 4.1.1.41.

*samankurwanza (pl. *samankurwantes*, acc. *samankurwandus*), an epithet of serpents. KBo. 3.8.3.25 (cf. l. 7).

-samas; read *-smas*.

ŠAMÉ, gen. of *ŠAMÛ* 'sky'.

samen- (*samenzi*, imper. *samendu*) 'disappear'; w. abl. expressed or implied, 'withdraw from, renounce, desist from'. Hrozný, CH 24. 15; Friedrich, Vert. 2.146. Cf. *samenu-*.

samenu- 'cause to disappear, remove'? Friedrich, Vert. 2.146, 162 f.; Walther, HC 269.176A.

appan s. 'cause to reappear, restore'. KUB 9.15.3.15 f.

parā s. 'cause to disappear; rescue (from a person)'.

-samet, -samit; read *-smet*.

samna(e)- (pret. *samnait*, part. *samnan*) 'cause to grow, create', or the like. Friedrich, ZA NF 5.32, 76 f. Cf. *samniya/e-*.

samnaiske/a- 'cause to grow, create', or the like. See *samna(e)-*.
samniya/e- (pret. pl. *samniir* [samniyer], part. *samniyantan*) 'cause to grow, create', or the like. See *samna(e)-*.
sampukki, a kind of gruel. Sommer, BoSt. 10.89.
ᴰŠAMŠU 'sun' = ᴰUTU, q.v.
ŠAMŪ = *nepis* 'sky'.
ŠAMŪ = *istamass-* 'hear'.
-san (*-ssan* after a vowel), a particle of unknown meaning, appended to the first word (or phrase) of a sentence, always in the final position. It is never used with *-kan*. It is used chiefly with verbs of placing, setting, pouring, arriving, and the like, and these are often combined with *ser*. Ungnad, ZDMG 74.417–22; Götze, AOr. 5.30–8, AM 308; Götze-Pedersen, MS 66.
-san 'suum', acc. of *-ses*.
san 'eum, et eum', acc. of *sas*.
sana-; see *sanna-*.
sanahh-; read *sanhh-*.
sanas (nom. 1-*as*, gen. 1-*ēl*, dat. 1-*edani*, *sanē*, *sanī*, *saniya*) 'one'. Götze, Lang. 11.185–90; Hahn, Lang. 12.119 fn. 76. Cf. *sanetta*, *sannapilis*.
ŠANE; read *sane* and see *sanas*.
sānĕt(t)a (1-*ētta*, *sānita*) 'altogether'. Götze, Lang. 11.190.
sanezzis 'first (?), best, excellent'. Ehelolf, OLZ 36.4, 6; Lohmann, IF 51.325 f.; Sturtevant, Lang. 10.268–72, JAOS 56. 282 fn. 3. Cf. *sanas*.
sanezziyah (imper. 2 sg.) 'sate yourself'. Ehelolf, OLZ 36.5. Cf. *sanezzis*.
sanh- (*sanhazi*, pl. *sanhanzi*, pret. *sahta*, *sanahta*, imper. *sahdu*, 2 sg. *sanha*), clean in some way; 'sweep'? Ehelolf, KlF 1.146–9.
sănhh- (*sanhazi*, *sanahzi*, pret. *sanahta*, 1 sg. *sanhun*, *sanahhun*, *sahhun*, imper. 2 sg. *sāh*, *sanha*) 'approach; attack; ask for, inquire for; try'. Sommer, BoSt. 7.45–56; Friedrich, Vert. 2.22; Götze, NBr. 28–32; Kurylowicz, Symb. Gramm. 102, EI 73; Sturtevant, Lang. 6.153; Couvreur, Hett. *h* 19.
    anda s., w. acc. of the fault, dat. of the person, 'punish'. KUB 14.14.1.34.
    appan s. 'care for (a person)'.
sanhheske/a- (*sahiskizzi*, 1 sg. *sahhiskimi*, 2 sg. *sanheskisi*, *sanahheskisi*, *sanhiskisi*, pl. *sanheskanzi*) 'approach; attack; ask for, inquire for; try'. See *sanhh-*.

sănhu- (pl. sanhuwanzi, sanhunzi, midd. sanhuta, pl. sānhuwwanta, part. sanhunda) 'roast'. Friedrich, ZA NF 3.188.
ŠANI; read sani and see sanas.
ᴸᵁSANGA, ᴸᵁSANGU = sankunnis 'priest'.
　ᴸᵁSANGA-anza 'acting as priest'.
　ᴸᵁSANGA-UTTU 'priesthood'.
ᴸᵁSANGA GIBIL 'new priest'.
ᴸᵁsankun(n)is 'priest'. Götze, Hatt. 59 f.
ᴸᵁsankunniyanza 'acting as priest'.
săn(n)ă- (sannāi, 2 sg. sannatti, pl. sannanzi, 2 p. sānattēni) 'keep still about, conceal'. Hrozný, SH 122; Friedrich, Vert. 1.43; HG 214. Cf. sannes-.
sannapi 'in one place'. Götze, Lang. 11.185-90. See sanas.
　sannapi sannapi 'here and there'.
sannapiles- (pret. sannapilesta, imper. sannapilesdu) 'become single, become uniform; become formless, be destroyed'. Cf. Götze, Lang. 11.188.
sannapilis 'single, alone, only'. See sannapi.
　sannapili 'solely, only'.
sannaske/a- 'keep still about, conceal'. Götze, Madd. 170. See sanna-.
sannes- (pret. sannesta) 'keep still about, conceal'. Forrer, Forsch. 2.3.36. See sanna-.
sanza; see sa(e)-.
sap- (sapzi) 'cleanse'. KUB 25.36.1.13, 5.13, 25. See sapiya/e-, sappeske/a-.
ŠAPAL, the construct state of ŠAPLU.
ŠÀ.BAL(.LAL), ŠÀ.BAL.BAL; read ŠA(G).BAL(.LAL), ŠA(G).BAL.BAL.
SABAR; read ŠEG₉.BAR.
ᴸᵁsapasāllis 'watchman, sentry', or the like. Götze, Madd. 134.
sapĭya/e- (imper. 2 sg. sapiyai; part. sapīyanza, sapianza) 'cleanse'. Forrer, RHA 1.147.32; Chrest. 174. Cf. sap-, sappatta, sappeske/a-.
ŠAPLU; ŠAPAL, ANA ŠAPAL = kattan 'under'.
ŠAPLŪ, fem. SAPLĪTU = katteras 'lower'.
　KUR ŠAPLĪTU = udne katteran(?) 'the Lower Country', i.e. the part of the central plateau of Asia Minor that lies immediately south of the Halys.
⁺sappatta (pret.) 'he trimmed (poles)'? Friedrich, ZA NF 5.56. Cf. sap-, sapiya/e-, sappeske/a-.
sappeske/a- 'cleanse'. See sap-, sapiya/e-.

ᴸᵁ*ṢABTU* (pl. ᴸᵁ·ᴹᴱˢ*ṢABTŪTU*) = ŠU.DIB = *appanza* 'captive'.
SAR = *ŠAṬĀRU* = *hatra(e)*- 'write'.
ŠAR 'vegetable'; also a post-determinative with names of vegetables.
ŠAR; read SAR 'write'.
ᴳᴵˢŠAR or GIŠ ŠAR 'garden, orchard, vineyard'.
ᴸᵁŠAR or LÚ ŠAR 'gardener, cultivator of fruit trees, vinegrower'.
sarā 'up'. Hrozný, SH 183; Götze, Hatt. 70 f.; Pedersen, AOr. 5.180–2. W. gen. 'above'. Chrest. 110.36.
sarā- (pl. *sarānzi*, infin. *sarāwanzi*) 'lift up, hold up'?? 'pluck, unravel'??? 'weave'?? Sommer, BoSt. 10.70 f.; Sturtevant, AJP 50.362, Lang. 10.271; Götze, AM 262 and fn. 3. Cf. *sariya/e-*.
sarăman- (gen. *sarāmanas*, abl. *sarămnaz*) 'receptacle; place of refuge'? Götze, AM 220.
sarappuwas; read *sarppuwas*.
sarăz(z)is 'upper, highest; superior, best; successful (in a law suit)'. Götze, Hatt. 91 and fn. 2; Lohmann, IF 51.319–26; Sturtevant, Lang. 10.268–73.
sarazzēs DINGIR.MEŠ 'di superi'. Tenner, ZA NF 4.187.
sarăz(z)iyahh- (pret. *sarāzziyahta*, *sarāziyahta*, imper. pl. *sarazziyahhandu*, *sarazziahhandu*) 'make highest; cause to win (a law suit)'. Friedrich, ZA NF 1.16; Götze, Hatt. 91.
sarāzziyatar 'height, ridge, crest'. Götze, AM 263. Cf. *sarazzis*.
sarhiske/a- (pret. *sarhiskit*), treat in the manner of a lion. KUB 24.3.2. 45 (G).
sarhuw(w)anda (neut. pl.) = next word.
**sarhuw(w)anza* (acc. ᵁᶻᵁ*sarhuwwandan*, *sarhuwandan*, acc. pl. *sarhuwandus*) 'entrails; uterus, embryo; contents'. Zimmern, OLZ 25.298; Friedrich, ZA NF 1.185; Götze, Madd. 80 fn. 1.
sarikuwa(s); LÚ.MEŠ s., an inferior class of soldiers. Götze, AM 230–2.
saripuwas; read *sarppuwas*.
sariske/a- 'weave'? See *sariya/e-*.
sariya/e- 'weave'? Götze, AM 262 and fn. 3.
*sargawatar (dat. *sargawanni*) 'strength, glory', or the like. Sommer, AU 91. fn. 3.
ᴳᴵˢŠAR.GEŠTIN 'vineyard'.
sarku- (part. *sarkuwan*) 'put on (shoes, gaiters)'? Götze, NBr. 77 fn. 3.
sarkus 'mighty, illustrious', or the like. Sommer, AU 91 f.
sarlă(e)- (1 sg. *sarlāmi*, pl. *sarlanzi*, pret. *sarlāit*) 'lift; cause to win (a law suit); exalt, praise; remove'. Götze, KlF 1.226 f.

sarlaimmis 'high, exalted'?? Forrer, Forsch. 1.21. Cf. Götze, KlF 1.227.

*šarlattaš; *šarlattan* SISKUR 'praise offering'. Probably an adj. developed from the gen. of *sarlaz*. Cf. HG 157 and fn. 42.

*sarlaz (gen. *sarlattas*) 'praise'. Götze, Madd. 79 and fn. 9, KlF 1.227 and fn. 2.

sarleske/a- 'lift; exalt, praise'. Cf. Witzel, HKU 94.44.

*sarlis (acc. *sarlin*, dat. *sarliya*) 'lifter, spoon'? Chrest. 123.

sarnenk- (*sarnikzi*, pl. *sarninkanzi, sarnenkanzi,* 1 pl. *sarninkweni*, pret. *sarnikta*, 1 sg. *sarninkun*) 'restore, make restitution, give as indemnity'. Hrozný, SH 54; HG 233, 274 and fn. 116.

sarnenkeske/a- (1 sg. *sarninkiskimi, sarnenkiskimi, sarninkeskimi*) 'restore, make restitution, give as indemnity'. See *sarnenk-*.

sarnenkwas, sarnenkwes (*sarnink-*) 'of atonement'. HG 153. See *sarnenk-*.

sarnenkzěl (*sarnikzel, sarnikzīl*) 'indemnification, recompense'. Hrozný, CH 16.55; Zimmern-Friedrich, AO 23.2.8.21; Friedrich, Vert. 1.158; HG 156. See *sarnenk-*.

sarnenkzelēske/a- (1 sg. *sarnikzilēskimi*) 'make restitution'. Götze, KlF 1.198 and fn. 2.

sarnik-; read *sarnenk-*.

sarnink-; read *sarnenk-*.

ᴳᴵˢ*sarpas* 'brushwood, verbenae'? Chrest. 123 f.

ᴷᵁˢ*sarpas* 'strip of hide'?? KBo. 5.2.1.31.

sarp(p)uwas (*sarappuwas, saripuwas*), a kind of stew. Chrest. 124.

sarra- (*sarrai*, 2 sg. *sarratti*, pl. *sarranzi*, infin. *sarrumanzi*, midd. *sarratta, sarradda, sarrattari*) 'separate, divide, break; break (an oath); cross (a boundary); open (a door)'; midd. w. *-za* 'go apart, separate from one another'. Friedrich, ZA NF 2.50; Götze, AM 309; Sturtevant, JAOS 54.400. Cf. *sarre/a-*.

arha s., midd., 'part, take leave of one another'.

sarras 'a part' or the like. Götze, NBr. 21–3; Chrest. 169 f. Cf. *sarra-*.

sarras . . . sarras 'the one part . . . the other part'.

taksan s. 'half'.

taksan sarranza 'by halves'?

sarre/a- (*sarrizzi, sarrēzzi*, pret. *sarrit*) 'separate, divide, break; break (an oath); cross (a boundary); open (a door)'. HG 219. See *sarra-*.

sarreske/a- (*sarreskizzi*, pret. *sarriskit*) 'separate, divide, break', etc. See *sarra-, sarre/a-*.

ŠARRU = ḫassus 'king'.
sardiyas 'help, helper; rescuer'. Ungnad, OLZ 26.572 fn. 3; Friedrich, Vert. 1.167; Sommer, AU 180. fn. 3. Cf. Götze, ap. Chrest. 227.
sāru (dat. sāruwi) 'booty'. Sommer, BoSt. 7.12 and fn. 1; Götze, AM 309.
sarupa 'quarrel, discord'?? Friedrich, Vert. 1.83 f.
sărwă(e)- (pret. sarwait, săruwăit, pl. saruwāir) 'sack, plunder'. Götze, Hatt. 61, Madd. 83; HG 227.
sarwe/a- (pret. pl. saruwēr) 'sack, plunder'. HG 228.
-sas 'sui, eius', gen. of -ses.
sas 'is, et is', an archaic pronoun, usually initial in its clause. Hrozný, SH 137; Götze, Madd. 137; HG 200, 207.
sas-; see ses-.
*sasan(n)as (acc. ^{DUG}sasannan, pl. ^{DUG}sasannus) 'lamp'. Ehelolf, ZA NF 9.190–4.
săstas 'bed; lair'. Ehelolf, OLZ 29.988; Götze, KlF 1.134; Friedrich, ZA NF 5.73; HG 157.
^{GIŠ}ŠA.A.TAR; read ŠA(G).A.TAR.
ŠĀTU, a dry measure. Hrozný, AOr. 3.449 fn. 12.
sadupsāhi (probably a foreign word) 'on the throne'?? Götze-Pedersen, MS 43.
saw(w)ar 'anger'; verb. n. from sa(e)-, q.v.
săwitesza [sawet'ests] (săwitesza, săwitisza, gen sawitistas) 'of the same year, less than a year old'. Hrozný, SH 93 fn. 2; Sturtevant, Lang. 4.228, HG 90, 105, 149, 164.
ŠE = ŠE'U 'grain'.
ŠE 'be willing'.
ŠE = warkanza 'fat' (of animals).
ŠE$_{12}$ = gimmanza 'winter'. Sommer, BoSt. 4.22 f.
ŠE$_{12}$ = gimmandariya/e- 'pass the winter'.
ŠE$_{12}$ = warsiya/e- 'rest, be pleased, be propitious'. Götze, NBr. 61 fn. 1; Sommer, AU 134.
ŠE$_{12}$ = warsanu-, warsiyanu- 'cause to be well disposed, propitiate'.
-se (more often -si) 'sibi, ei'; sometimes equivalent to -ses 'suus, eius'. Hrozný, MDOG 56.38, SH 132; HG 194, 197; Götze, AM 310.
-sĕ 'sua', neut. pl. of -ses. HG 177 fn. 88, 198.
se 'ei, ea', pl. of sas.
*sehelliskis (acc. pl. sehelliskius—probably Hurrian) 'tray, bowl', or the like. Sommer, BoSt. 10.33 f., OLZ 38.29.
sehel(l)iya- (also sihilliya-, sehilla-, sihilya—probably Hurrian) 'spring, well'? Hrozný, SH 63; Sommer, BoSt. 10.34 and fn. 1.

sĕhur (gen. sēhunas, dat. sĕhuni) 'urination, urine'. Sturtevant, Lang. 12, No. 3.
ŠEG₉ 'goat'.
sēkan, a measure of length. Forrer, ZDMG 76.254.
sekk-; see sakk-.
ᵀᵁᴳseknu(š) (acc. sekunu, seknus, sekunus, seknun, abl. seknuaz, pl. dat. seknuš), a garment that may be put upon the head. (G). Cf. Hrozný, BoSt. 3.76 fn. 8.
ŠEG₉.BAR 'wild goat' or the like. Landsberger, Die Fauna des alten Mesopotamiens 96 and fn. 3.
sēl 'eius', gen. of sas.
*sĕliš (gen. sēliyaš, sēliya, sēli, pl. selias, selius) 'meadow'. Hrozný, CH 68.19; KUB 21.17.3.10, 14.
?*sĕlis (pl. sēlēs or waelēs) 'in love'? Hrozný, CH 24.16; Zimmern-Friedrich, AO 23.2.10.32.
sēliyaš (gen.); EZEN × ŠE sēliyaš, name of a festival. Sommer, AU 424.
ŠE + LUB; read NISABA.
-semet; read -smet.
sĕnahhaš (also sinahhaš) 'ambush, ambuscade'. Forrer, Forsch, 1.130; Götze, AM 250-2.
sēnaš 'lump (of clay, wax, tallow, dough); figure, model'. Sommer, BoSt. 10.55; Friedrich, ZA NF 5.43 fn. 3, KlF 1.155 and fn. 1, 160; Götze, NBr. 77 fn. 3.
ŠE.NUMUN 'seed grain'.
sēpa- (acc. sēpan) 'sheaf'? Walther, HC 267.158; KUB 11.33.3.19.
ᵁᴿᵁᴰsepikkustaš 'brooch'? Götze, KlF 1.234 f.; Friedrich, AOF 7.199.
SER (Forrer); read SÌR 'sing, singer, song'.
ŠER 'herd, flock'. Friedrich, ZA NF 3.184.
ser, postposition (except that an enclitic pronoun is appended to it), usually w. dat., rarely w. gen.; also an adv.; 'above, over, upon; for, for the sake of; besides'. Sommer, BoSt. 10.33 and fn. 1, 47; Götze, Hatt. 71, AM 309 f.
ᵁᴿᵁᴰŠERINNĀTU 'bit (of a bridle)'.
*Šĕriš; GUD Šĕrin (acc.), a divine bull. Götze, Kulturg. 133 and fn. 3.
ŠEŠ 'brother'.
ŠEŠ-UTTU = AḪŪTU = ŠEŠ-atar (dat. ŠEŠ-anni) 'brotherhood'.
ŠEŠ-ahh- 'make (one) a brother, treat as a brother'. Sommer, AU 213 f.
-ses (usually -sis) 'suus, eius'. Hrozný, SH 132 f.; HG 177 fn. 88, 194, 197 f.

sēs-, sas- (*seszi*, pl. *sēsanzi, sasanzi,* pret. *sesta,* 1 sg. *sēsun*) 'sleep, pass the night'; w. *-za* 'lie down, go to bed'. Sommer, BoSt. 7.25 fn. 1; Friedrich, ZA NF 2.277; Götze, AOr. 5.5 f.; HG 89 and fn. 18, 220. Cf. Ehelolf, OLZ 29.988; Götze, KlF 1.233 f.; Götze-Pedersen, MS 66 f.; Sturtevant, Lang. 11.41.

   katta(n) s. w. dat. 'sleep with'. Sommer, AU 383.

   sarā s. 'spend the night on the citadel'. Chrest. 156.6, 158.30.

   ser kattan s. w. dat. 'sleep on the citadel with'. KUB 16.42.1.33.

sesariske/a- 'strain, filter'. Friedrich, Altorient. Stud. 47.3.23,55.

*sesarul (inst. ᴳᴵˢ*sesarulit*) 'strainer, filter'. See *sesariske/a-*.

seshǎ- (*seshāi,* 1 sg. *seshahhi,* pl. *seshanzi*) 'assign, order, direct'? Friedrich, Vert. 1.45 f.

ŠEŠ.ḪI.GA; read ŠEŠ.DÙG.GA.

seske/a- (*seskizzi,* pl. *seskanzi,* imper. 2 sg. *seski*) 'lie down, sleep, pass the night'. See *ses-*.

seskeske/a- 'lie down, sleep, pass the night'. See *ses-*.

seskiya/e- 'lie down, sleep, pass the night'. HG 225.

sessar 'lair (of beasts)'?? KBo. 6.34.3.29; HG 152. But cf. Ehelolf, ZA NF 9.187.

sessiyan (acc.) 'debt'??? Forrer, Forsch, 2.2.26.

sesd- (*seszi,* verb. n. *sisduwar*) 'prosper, grow'. Götze, KlF 1.240 f.

ŠEŠ.DÙG.GA 'step-brother'?? Forrer, Forsch. 1.101 fn. 1.

ŠE'U 'grain'.

seunihta; read *siuniyahta*.

ŠE.ZIZ, a variety of wheat.

SI (nom.-acc. SI-*ar,* inst. SI.ḪI.A-*anda*) 'horn'. Ehelolf, IF 43.317.

ŠI; read IGI.

ṢI; read ZÍ.

-si; read *-se*.

SI.A; read SA₅.

sihilla-, sihilliya-, sihilya-; see *sehelliya-*.

ᴸᵁŠI.ḪU; read ᴸᵁIGI.MUŠEN.

SIG = *LABKU*?? 'thin, flat'. Sommer, BoSt. 10.38.

ᴸᵁSIG 'subaltern' or the like.

SÍG = *asaras*?? 'wool'; also a determinative.

SIG₄ = *LIBITTU* 'sun-dried brick'.

SIG₅ = *assus, lazzis* (also SIG₅-*ant-*) 'good; favorable, lucky; well, healthy; noble'.

SIG₅ = *lazzais* 'well being, favorable condition'.

SIG₅ = *lazziya/e-* 'be favorable; recover, be well'.

SIG₅ = *lazziyahh-*, *lazziyahhiske/a-* 'make favorable, give favorable omens'.
SIG₅ = *lazziyatar* 'welfare'.
SIG₅ = *assutar* 'welfare'.
SIG₇ 'yellow, green'.
SIGA; read SIG₄.
ᴳᴵˢŠI.GAG; read ᴳᴵˢŠUKUR.
ŠI.GAB.A; read IGI.DU₈.A.
ᴳᴵˢŠI.GAR 'neck brooch, neck band', also '(dog's) collar'? Sommer, BoSt. 10.59; Friedrich, ZA NF 5.72.
SIGIŠŠE; read SISKUR.
SIQQA; read ŠEG₉.
SIQQA.BAR; read ŠEG₉.BAR.
ᵀᵁᴳ*siknus*; read *seknus*.
SÍL; read SILÁ.
SILÁ 'lamb'.
SILIM = *assul*, *assulas* 'health; kindness, favor'. Sommer, AU 80.
SILIM.BI (adv.) 'well'.
ŠIM 'pleasant odor, sweet smelling plant'.
ṢIMDU = *turan*? (see *turammit*) 'team'.
ŠĪMTU 'fate'.
ŠĪMU = *wesiya-*? 'price'.
ᴸᵁSIMUG.A; read ᴸᵁE.DÉ.A.
ᴰSIN = *armas*? 'moon'.
sinahhas; read *senahhas*.
sinahila 'commander-in-chief'? Friedrich, ZA NF 2.282.
sinakkuriya/e- 'be abundant'? Weidner, Stud. 130.
ᴳᴵˢ*sinapsi*, a tree or an implement. Sommer, BoSt. 10.11 f.
  É *sinapsi*, a building to which a woman goes for child-birth under certain conditions.
ᴳᴵˢŠINIG = *suwaru*? 'tamarisk'. Götze, NBr. 64 and fn. 3.
sinūra- 'inclined to weep'?? Weidner, Stud. 130.
ᴸᵁSÍB, ᴸᵁSIBA; read ᴸᵁSIPAD.
sipant-; see *sippant-*.
sipanzake/a-; see *sippanzke/a-*.
ᴸᵁSIPAD = ᴸᵁ*westaras* 'shepherd'.
    ᴸᵁSIPAD.GUD 'cowherd'.
    ᴸᵁSIPAD.UDU 'shepherd'.
ŠIPAT, construct state of ŠIPTU, q.v.
ŠIBIR 'harvest'.

ṢIBITTU 'captivity'.
    BĪT ṢIBITTI 'house of captivity, captivity'.
    BĪT ZIMITTI, false writing for prec.
sip(p)ant- [sp·ant-] (*sipanti, sippanti,* pl. *sipandanzi, sippantanzi*) 'pour a libation to, sacrifice (an animal) to, dedicate (a place) to' (w. acc. of the god and inst. of the offering, or w. acc. of the offering and dat. of the god). Hrozný, MDOG 56.29, SH 4 and fn. 1; Sommer, BoST. 10.15 f., 23 f., 25 f.; Götze, AM 168. 17, 22; Sturtevant, Lang. 11.42, HG 94, 127.
sip(p)anzake/a- [sp·antsk·e-] (*sipanzakizzi, sippanzakizzi, sipanzakanzi, sippanzakanzi*) 'pour a libation to, sacrifice (an animal) to'. HG 71, 107.
ŠIPRU = *hatressar* 'message, announcement, report'.
*siptamas (dat. *siptamiya* [sep·t·amiya]) 'seventh'. Hrozný, SH 96; Sturtevant, Lang. 4.6 and fn. 1; Ehelolf, OLZ 32.322–8; HG 89, 98, 171.
ŠIPTU 'incantation, exorcism'.
ŠĪBU = *kutrus* 'witness'.
SIR; read SUD.
SÌR = ZAMĀRU = *ishamiya/e-* 'sing'.
    SÌR-*RU* = *IZAMARŪ* 'they sing'.
SÌR = *ishamais* 'song'.
^{LÚ}SÌR = ^{LÚ}*ishamatallas* 'singer'.
SIR₄; read ŠIR.
ŠIR 'testicle'.
sirais 'sole, unique'?? Weidner, Stud. 130.
^{GIŠ}*ṢIRTU*; read ^{GIŠ}*ZERTU*.
-sis; read *-ses*.
sīshau 'sweat'?? Hrozný, AOr. 3.444.21.
SISKUR (also SISKUR.SISKUR) = *anniur* 'rite, sacrifice'.
SI × DI = *handa(e)-* 'establish, determine, fix (especially by an oracle)'.
sit(t)ar (abl. *sittarza, sittaraza*) 'sun-disk'? Ehelolf, ZA NF 9.187 fn. 3; cf. Hrozný, BoSt. 3.4.9, 5 fn. 9; Sturtevant, Lang. 4.2.
sittaris 'sun-disk'? See *sittar*.
ŠI.DUB; read IZKIM.
^{LÚ}ŠI.DUB; read ^{LÚ}AGRIG.
siunas (nom. DINGIR-*LIM-as*, gen. *siunas,* dat. *siuni,* gen. pl. *siunan*) 'god'. Ehelolf, ZA NF 9.170–81.
    siunan antuhsas 'man of the gods, seer'.

siunis = *siunas*, q.v.
siuniyahh- (midd.) 'be made divine, be crazed'?? Cf. Ehelolf, ZA NF 9.179 f.
ᴸᵁ*siuniyanza* (ᴸᵁDINGIR-*LIM-niyanza*) 'man of god' or the like. Cf. Ehelolf, ZA NF 9.180.
siuniyatar (DINGIR-*LIM-niyatar*) 'divinity, godhead'. See *siunas*.
ŠI.UR; read ḪUL.
?*sius* (DINGIR-*LIM-us*) = *siunas*, q.v.
siwannis 'god'? Ehelolf, ZA NF 2.318; Hrozný, ZA NF 4.185; Götze-Pedersen, MS 72 f., 80.
??*siwanza* 'god'?? Sommer, KlF 1.341. See *siwannis*.
ˢᴬᴸ·ᴹᴱˢ*siwanzannis* 'mothers of god'(?), priestesses of a certain kind. See *siwannis*.
siwatili (UD-*tili*, UD.KAM-*tili*), adv., 'daily'. Sommer, ZA 33.90 and fn. 2, AU 432. See *siwaz*.
sīwaz (nom. UD-*az*, UD-*za*, dat. *siwatti*, *sīwat*, UD-*at*, UD-*ti*) 'day'. Hrozný, AOr. 1.283 f.; Götze-Pedersen, MS 72 f.; Ehelolf, ZA NF 9.181 fn. 3. Cf. Sommer, IF 53.88. Cf. *anisiwat*.
siyă/e- (*siyāri*, pl. *siyandari*, pret. *siyati*) 'appear, be seen'. Götze, Madd. 113; Sommer, AU 187 fn. 3; Götze-Pedersen, MS 73.
sĭya/e- (*sĭyaizzi*, *siyēzzi*, pret. *siyăit*) 'press down, crush; oppress; pitch (a tent); set (a stone); put in, put on; seal; thrust in (a weapon), sting (of a bee)'. See *sai-*.
siyanta (neut. pl.?) 'salt'??? Forrer, Forsch. 1.112.63, 164. A fermented drink?? Sommer, AU 132.
*siyatar (gen. *siyannas*) 'a pressing down, a sealing'.
É *siyannas* 'house of sealing; house of seals, treasury'. Ehelolf, OLZ 29.988.
ᴳᴵˢ*siyattal* 'missile, arrow'. Forrer, Forsch. 1.197.
siyattalliya/e- 'sow'? Forrer, Forsch. 1.197.
siyattariya/e-; read *siyettariya/e-*.
siyeske/a- 'press down', etc. See *sai-*, *siya/e-*.
siyĕssar, 'beer'. Ehelolf ap. Sommer, AU 132 fn. 3, ZA NF 9.183f.
siyettariya/e- (*siyattariyazi*, *siyattariyēzzi*, pret. *siittariit*, *sietta[riit]*).
  anda s. 'take possession of, take over'? Hrozný, CH 30.39, 32.45; Götze, NBr. 57; Walther, HC 253.40 and fn. 1; Chrest. 220.39. 'Interfere harshly'?? or 'make short work of it'?? Walther, HC 257.55.
siyya/e-; read *siya/e-*.

-*sman*, acc. of -*smes*.
-*smas* (also -*sumăs*, -*summas*) 'vos, vobis; eos, eis, se, sibi'. Hrozný, SH 116 f., 131 f., 133; HG 194 f.
-*smas*, dat. pl. of -*smes*.
-*smes* (acc. -*sman*? neut. -*smet*, -*summit*, dat. -*smi*, -*ssummi*, nom. pl. -*smes*, dat. pl. -*smas*) 'vester; eorum, suus'. Friedrich, Vert. 1.81 fn. 2; HG 194 f., 198.
-*smes*, nom. pl. of -*smes*.
-*smet* (also -*summit*) neut. of -*smes*.
-*smi* (also -*summi*), dat. of -*smes*.
-*sta*; see -*asta*.
ŠU; read KUŠ.
ŠU = QĀTU = *kessar, kessras* 'hand'.
ŠU-*an* 'memorial, trophy' or the like. Götze, NBr. 27.
^{ZA}ŠU.U = ^{ZA}*kunkunuzzi* 'diorite'.
-ŠU = -*ses* 'his, her'; also (in Hittite texts) = -*smes* 'their'.
-ŠU (after numerals) 'times'; 2-ŠU 'twice'. See p. 290.
su- (pl. *suwwanzi*?, part. *suwwanza*?, *suwanza*?, midd. pret. *suttati*, *suttaru*) 'press out, fill'. Cf. Sommer, BoSt. 10.55; Friedrich, ZA NF 1.166. 17, 184; HG 94 fn. 32. See KBo. 6.34.3.17, 21; KUB 25.22.3.10 f. Cf. *sunna*-, *suwa(e)*-.
^{GIŠ}ŠÚ.A (acc. ŠÚ.A-*an*, dat. ŠÚ.A-*hi*, ŠÚ.A-*he*) 'chair, throne'. Ehelolf, OLZ 29.768 fn. 3; Friedrich, Vert. 2.25–7.
suhhă- (*suhhăi*, pret. 1 sg. *suhhahhun*, pl. *suhhāir*) 'pour, sprinkle, scatter'. Sommer, BoSt. 10.53; Götze, KlF 1.228 fn. 5; Sturtevant, Lang. 7.120, HG 140.
*săhhas (dat. *săhhi*, *suhha*, abl. *suhhaz*, pl. *suhhus*) 'roof'. Ehelolf ap. Götze, KlF 1.199 fn. 3; Friedrich, Vert. 2.171; Sturtevant, Lang. 7.120, HG 140. Cf. *suhha*-.
SUḪUR 'be afflicted by something'?? Deimel, No. 403.3.
^{SAL}SUḪUR.LAL; read SAL.SUḪUR.LAL.
^{LÚ}ŠU.I = *GALLĀBU* 'barber'. The barbers perform various tasks in the ritual, including the sweeping of the temple. Ehelolf, KlF 1.147 and fn. 4.
^{LÚ}ŠU.GAL 'commander'?? Friedrich, Vert. 2.162.
^{LÚ}SUKAL (or ^{LÚ}SUKKAL) 'bailiff, steward; vizier'.
^{IM}ŠU.(GAR.)RIN.NA 'portable stove'. Friedrich, ZA NF 1.187.
^{LÚ}ŠU.GI; read LÚ ŠU.GI and see s.v. LÚ.
^{SAL}ŠU.GI; read SAL ŠU.GI and see s.v. SAL.
^{LÚ}SUKKAL; see ^{LÚ}SUKAL.

ŠU.GUR 'ring'.
ᴳᴵˢŠUKUR 'spear' or a similar weapon. Cf. Deimel, No. 449.123. Correct Chrest. 37.
sullă(e)- (sullaizzi, pret. sullāit, sulāit) 'be angry (with), quarrel (with); punish (a rebellious people)'. Sommer, BoSt. 7.42 fn. 1. Cf. sullatar, sulles-, sulliya/e-, sŭllis.
sullas 'anger, quarrel'? Götze, AM 310. Cf. sullis.
sullatar 'anger, quarrel'. Sommer, BoSt. 7.42 fn. 1, 63f.
sullĕs- (sullēszi, sulliszi) 'quarrel'? Friedrich, Vert. 2.28 fn. 4. See sulla(e)-.
*sullis (acc. sullin) 'anger, quarrel', or the like. Friedrich, Vert. 2.28 f. See sulla(e)-.
sulliya/e- 'be angry (with), quarrel (with); punish (a rebellious people)'. See sulla(e)-.
ŠULMU 'peace; salutation (at the beginning of a letter)'.
ŠULUM ŠA 'a letter to'. Götze, ZA NF 2.14 f.
SUM = pai- 'give'.
SUM = dai-, tiya/e- 'set, place'.
ŠUM, construct state of ŠUMU.
sumanza; see summanzan.
-sumas; see -smas.
sumăs, acc. of sumes, q.v.
sumāsila 'vobis ipsis'. See -el, -ela.
SUM.EL.ŠAR 'onion'.
sumel, gen. of sumes.
sumenzan, gen. of sumes.
sumĕs (also summĕs, acc. sumās, summas) 'vos'. Hrozný, MDOG 56.26, SH 114–9; HG 193, 194 f.
sumēdaz, abl. of sumes? HG 196 fn. 13.
ŠUMMA = takku, man 'if'.
sum(m)anza(n) 'cord, rope'? Weidner, Stud. 130; Sayce, JRAS 1930. 316; Carruthers, Lang. 6.161; HG 97; Milewski, L'Indo-Hittite et l'Indo-Européen 14.
summas, variant for sumas.
summes, variant for sumes.
-summi, variant for -smi.
-summit, variant for -smet.
summittantan (acc., also summittandan) 'axe'? Friedrich, ZA NF 5.41 f.
ŠUMU = laman 'name'.
sūnie-; see sunniya/e-.

sunnă- (*sunnăi*, pl. *sunnanzi*, pret. *sunnas*, verb. n. *sunnumar*) 'fill'.
Hrozný, SH 12, 211; Sommer, BoSt. 10.24 fn. 1, 46 f., 46 fn. 2, 55;
Götze, NBr. 20; Sturtevant, Lang. 7.120, 168 f., HG 96, 245. Cf.
sunnes-, sunniya/e-.
sŭn(n)es- (pret. *sunnes, sunnista*, imper. 2 pl. *sūnistin*) 'fill'. Friedrich,
AOF 2.122; Götze, Hatt. 130; HG 230. Cf. *sunna-, sunniya/e-*.
sunneske/a- 'fill'. KUB 25.22.3.11. See *sunna-*.
sŭn(n)iya/e- (*sŭniyazi, sŭniizzi*, pl. *sŭniyanzi, sunnianzi*, pret. *sūniit,
sūniēt*) 'fill; sow (seed), sow (a field)'. Hrozný, CH 128.34, 39, 44;
Friedrich, Vert. 1.31 fn. 1, 91 fn. 4; HG 225. Cf. *sunna-*.
sunnumar; see *sunna-*.
sunnummessar 'a filling'?? KUB 13.4.1.7. Cf. *sunna-, sunnumăr*.
-ŠUNU = *-smes* 'their'; also (in Hittite texts) = *-ses* 'his, her'.
ᴳᴵᴸŠUB 'inventory'.
ᴸᵁŠU.PIŠ 'fisher'. Ehelolf, OLZ 29.767.
supla-; read *suppla-*.
ᴳᴵᴸŠUBBA; read ŠUB.
ᵁᶻᵁ*suppa* (nom.-acc. *suppa*, gen.-dat. *suppayas, suppas*) '(consecrated?)
meat'. Sommer, BoSt. 10.20; Götze-Pedersen, MS 19 f. Cf.
suppis.
suppa, adv.; *s. warp-* 'wash clean'. Ehelolf, KlF 1.144 fn. 3, 154 f.;
Götze-Pedersen, MS 18.
suppai, dat. of *suppis*. HG 171.
suppala-; read *suppla-*.
suppariya/e- (part. *suppariyanza*) 'sleep'. Ehelolf, OLZ 36.5; Sturtevant, JAOS 56.282-4. Cf. *sups-*.
suppas, gen. of *suppis*. HG 170.
suppayahhiske/a- 'make clean'. Ehelolf, KlF. 1.147 fn. 3. Cf. *suppiyahh-*.
suppayas, gen. of *suppis*. HG 170.
suppessar (*suppessar-*ḪI.A) 'purity'. Götze, AM 223.
suppes(s)aras (*suppisaras*, acc. *suppessaran*); DUMU.SAL s. 'virgin'?
Götze ap. Chrest. 119 f. Cf. Ehelolf, ZA NF 9.186.
suppihh-; read *suppiahh-* and see *suppiyahh-*.
suppis '(ritually) clean; holy, sacrosanct'. Sommer, BoSt. 10.7 f.;
Götze, AM 233 f.; Götze-Pedersen, MS 68; HG 179-81.
suppisaras; read *suppessaras*.
suppiya- (midd.) 'become holy'. KBo. 3.16.2.8.
suppi(y)ahh- 'make holy, make taboo'. HG 242. See *suppis*. Cf.
suppayahhiske/a-.

suppla- (nom. *suppalas*—KBo. 3.60.2.1, nom.-acc. *suppala*, dat. *suple*) 'pig sty, herd of swine, swine'? Carruthers, Lang. 9.156–8.
sups- (midd. *supsari*) 'become tired'? Friedrich, Vert. 1.92; Sturtevant, JAOS 56.282 f. Cf. *suppariyanza*.
?*ŠUBTU* (gen. *ŠUPPATI*?) 'habitation'?? Walther, HC 257.52, who now prefers 'seat'.
ŠU.BULÙG; read GEŠPÙ.
ŠUPUR = *hatra(e)-* 'send word, write'.
ŠUR ENI; read *ŠUR ĪNI*.
ŠUR IGI = *ŠUR ĪNI*.
ŠUR ĪNI 'eyebrow'.
IMŠU.RIN.NA; see IMŠU.GAR.RIN.NA.
ŠURĪPU 'cold weather, the cold season'.
SIG*sŭrita* 'fillet' of wool, which is wrapped about a lamb's head when it is about to be sacrificed.
LÚ*surralas*, a kind of servant in the royal kitchen. Friedrich, Altorient. Stud. 51.
IM*ŠURUPPŪ* 'cold wind'.
ŠUŠ(Š)U (in Hittite texts *ŠU-ŠI*) 'sixty'.
SUD = *hwittiya/e-* 'draw, lead'.
ŠU.DIM₄; read GEŠPÙ.
LÚŠU.DIB (pl. LÚ.MEŠŠU.DIB.BI.ḪI.A) = *ṢABTU* = *appanza* 'captive'. Götze, KlF 1.227, AM 311.
suttaru, sutlati; see *su-*.
ERÍN.MEŠ*ŠUTŪ*, a kind of light-armed auxiliaries. Götze, Kulturg. 117.
GIŠŠUDUN (also read GIŠŠUDUL) = *yugan* 'yoke'.
GIŠŠU.DUN; read GIŠŠU.ŠUDUN.
GIŠŠU.ŠUDUN, a variant for GIŠŠUDUN.
suwă(e)- (*suwăizzi, suwaēzzi, suwwăizzi*, pl. *suwwanzi?*, pret. 2 pl. *suwatten*, imper. 2 pl. *suwwattin*) 'press out, fill; give as security'. Götze, ZA NF 2.16 f., 263–6; Friedrich, ZA NF 2.45 f.; HG 94. Cf. *su-*, *sunna-*, *suwe/a-*.
   arha s. 'drive away'.
   parā s. 'drive out'.
suwanza 'full'; see *su-*.
suwaru 'tamarisk'? Götze, NBr. 64 and fn. 3.
suwe/a- (*suwĭzzi*) 'press out, fill; give as security'. See *suwa(e)-*.
SIG*suwēl* (also *suwīl*) 'cord, string'. Friedrich, ZA NF 3.185, 202; Carruthers, Lang. 6.161.
suwwa(e)-; see *suwa(e)-*.

suwwanza 'full'; see *su-, suwa(e)-*.

suwwanzi 'they press out'; see *su-, suwa(e)-*.

D is customarily written for DINGIR when this is a determinative.

TA = *IŠTU* 'from'.

-*ta* (after vowels usually -*tta*) 'tibi, te'; sometimes where logic would require the third person. Hrozný, SH 125–8; Sturtevant, Lang. 6.28, HG 124, 194; Sommer, AU 89 f. Sometimes -*ta*, as ethical dat., is no more than an enclitic particle. HG 99. Cf. -*du-*.

tă 'then, and; however, but'; a sentence connective sometimes used in archaic documents instead of *nu*. Ungnad, ZA NF 2.104 fn. 1; Sturtevant, Lang. 9.4, HG 199 f.; Friedrich, RHA 3.157–62; Hahn, Lang. 12.108 f., 111–3.

tă = *ta* + *a* 'et ea'. HG 198 and fn. 21. Probably also 'et id, et eum, et eam, et eos, et eas'; 'et ei'?? Friedrich, RHA 3.158–62.

dă- (*dāi*, ME-*i*, 1 sg. *dahhi*, pl. *dănzi*, 1 pl. *tummeni*, 2 pl. *datteni, tattini*, pret. *dās*, ME-*as*, pl. *dāir*, ME-*ir*, part. neut. *dān, tān*) 'take; take off, trim (?hair or finger nails)'; w. -*za* 'take for onself, keep for oneself; get; marry (a woman); take (for a specified purpose)'. Hrozný, BoSt. 3.136 fn. 4; Sommer, ZA 33.90 fn. 1, BoSt. 7.55 f.; Friedrich, Vert. 1.84; Ehelolf, KlF 1.150; Sturtevant, Lang. 3.216 f., 6.32 f., HG 243, 286 f., Chrest. 168; Götze, AOr. 5.10–2; Götze-Pedersen, MS 68.

arha d. 'take away'.

katta d. 'make subject, subject'. Sommer, AU 211 fn. 4.

kururanni d. 'take for war, declare war upon'. Sommer, AU 324.

sarā d. 'take up'; often merely introductory to another verb.

taksuli d. 'take for peace, make peace with'. Sommer, AU 324.

dāēr, dătr 'they placed'; pret. 3 pl. of *dai-*.

TAḪAPŠU, a kind of girdle? Sommer, BoSt. 10.90; Götze, NBr. 77 fn. 3.

taharan 'noise'?? Götze, ap. Friedrich, ZA NF 5.42.

tahhuss-; read *tuhhss-*.

tahs-; read *tuhhss-*.

dahusiyahha (Luwian? pret. 1 sg.) 'I endured it submissively, I submitted'? Götze, Hatt. 94, 130.

dăi-, te- (*dāi*, 1 sg. *tehhi, tehi, tihhi*, 2 sg. *daitti, taitti*, pret. *dăis*, ME-*is*, pl. *dătr, dāēr*) 'place, put; bury'. Sommer, BoSt. 4.7 fn. 2; Friedrich, ZDMG 76.169 f.; Sturtevant, Lang. 3.219, 6.32 f., HG 223, 247, 249, 287 f., Chrest. 225; Götze-Pedersen, MS 68; Kurylowicz, EI 74. With the supine 'begin and continue to'. HG 153 and fn. 31. Cf. Götze, Hatt. 66 f.; Götze-Pedersen, MS 21. Cf. *dais-, tiya/e-* 'place'.

appa d. 'replace; set aside'. Chrest. 110.41.

katta d. 'put down; defeat, subject'. Sommer, AU 211 fn. 4.

kattan d. 'put down, establish'. Chrest. 70.21. W. dat. 'besiege'? Götze, NBr. 11; Sommer, AU 211.

parā d. 'postpone'. Sommer, AU 252.

piran katta d., w. acc. and dat., 'set (something) down before (one), investigate (a charge) against (one), establish (a crime) in (one)'? Sommer, AU 146; Chrest. 74. 18 f.

sarā d. 'set up, set out (a feast)'. Sturtevant, JAOS 54.399. Cf. *sarā tittanu-*.

ser d. (w. dat.) 'set upon'.

daigas; read *day*<*u*>*gas*.

dāir 'they took'; pret. 3 pl. of *da-*.

dāis (imper. 2 pl. *dāistin*) 'place, put'. See *dai-*.

tāistai 'conceals'?? Hrozný, CH 112.5. 'Loads'?? Walther, HC 265. 124.

taiszin (acc.) 'barn'? Hrozný, CH 76.59.

ᴳᴵˢDAG, ᴰDAG = *halmasswittis, halmasswittas* 'throne'. Ehelolf, ZA NF 2.312 f.; Friedrich, ZA NF 3.181 and fn. 5.

TÁK; read ZÁ.

DAGAL = *palhis* 'broad'.

DAGAL = *palhater* 'breadth'.

takăn (also *dagăn*) 'to the ground'. Sommer, BoSt. 10.67. Cf. *tekan*.

daganzipăs (also *dagazipas*) 'ground, floor'. Hrozný, BoSt. 3.72 fn. 5; Ehelolf, KlF 1.147 and fnn. 4, 6; HG 118; Sommer, AF 84.

takīya 'in another place' (originally 'in this place'??). Chrest. 224 f.; Hahn, Lang. 12.117–20.

takīya . . . takīya 'in one place . . . in another place'

takkan = ta + kan.

taggass-; read *takkss-*.

takkess-; read *takkss-*.

dākki 'ditto'. Ehelolf, OLZ 32.328 fn. 1.

takkiss-; read *takkss-*.

takks-; see *takkss-*.

takkske/a- (*takkiskizzi*) 'join; build; do'. Chrest. 190.65.

takkss- (*takkiszi, takkĕszi, takkizzi; taggassi,* pl. *tăkkissanzi, takkessanzi,* 2 pl. *takkesteni, taggasteni,* pret. *takkista, taggasta,* infin. *taksuwanzi, takswanzi*) 'join; build; do (harm); thrust (a dagger)'. Sommer, BoSt. 7.35 fn. 2; Friedrich, ZA NF 1.179; Götze, Hatt. 104; Sturtevant, Lang. 6.214, HG 81. Cf. *taksan, taksatar, taksul*.

takku 'if' (chiefly in the Code; cf. *man* 'if'). Hrozný, MDOG 56.38, SH 136, 240; Ungnad, ZA NF 2.105 and fn. 2, 3.285; Hahn, Lang. 12. 109–13. Cf. *ta* and *-akku*.

taknas, takna, taknai, takni, taknaz; see *tekan*.

TAQBĪ = **tes* 'you said'.

taks-; see *takkss-*.

taksalaniyantaru (midd. imper. 3 pl.) 'let (the mountains) be leveled, cut through', or the like. KUB 15.34.1.45 (G).

taksan 'joint; middle'. Sommer, BoSt. 7.33, 35 and fn. 2.
UD-*az taksan* 'midday'. Cf. *takkss-*.

taksan 'together; apart, in two'. Hrozný, BoSt. 3.63 fn. 9; Sommer, BoSt. 7.35 fn. 2; Ehelolf, SBPA 21.270 f.; Götze, NBr. 21–3. See s.v. *sarras*. Cf. *takkss-*.

*taksatar (gen. *taksannas*, dat. *taksanna*) 'a joining, union'. Friedrich, ZA NF 2.49. Cf. *takkss-*.

taksessar 'agreement (upon a price), price'. Friedrich, ZA NF 2.49. CF. *takkss-*.

taksul 'unity, peace, friendship; friendly'. Götze, Hatt. 86; Friedrich, ZA NF 2.49 f.; HG 148, 162. Cf. *takkss-*.

taksulă(e)- (*taksulăizzi*, pret. *taksulăit*, 2 sg. *taksulăes*) 'be friendly, be kind; make peace'. Hatt. 86; HG 227. Cf. *takkss-*.

*taksulatar (dat. *taksulanni*) 'peace, friendship, kindness'. HT 1.2.27. See *taksula(e)-*.

dălă- (*talăi*, pret. 1 sg. *dălahhun*) 'leave, let alone, let go'. Sommer, BoSt. 7.37 and fn. 2; Friedrich, Vert. 1.91; Tenner, HAT 24. Cf. *dales-, daliya/e-*.

arha d. 'leave alone, leave unmolested'. Götze, AM 312.

^{DUG}*dalaimi*, a vessel. Sommer, AU 355.

dăles- (pret. *dalesta, tălesta*, imper. *tălesdu*) 'leave, let alone, let go'. HG 230. See *dala-*.

dăliya/e- (*daliyazi*, pret. *dăliyat, taliyat*) 'leave, let alone, let go'. HG 225. See *dala-*.

tallēs (imper. 2 sg.) 'become propitious'? Götze ap. Chrest. 125 (correct the translation on p. 115).

talleske/a- 'propitiate'? See *talliya/e-*.

talliya/e- 'propitiate'? Götze, ap. Chrest. 125.

dalugasti 'length'. Hrozný, MDOG 56.28, SH 23; Friedrich, ZA NF 5.35 f.; HG 126, 155 f.

talukes- (*talukiszi*) 'become long'. Götze, Hatt. 69 fn. 2.

dalugi- (pl. *dalugaēs*) 'long'. Hrozný, SH 23; Marstrander, Car. 147 f.; HG 107; Götze-Pedersen, MS 19 and fn. 1.

dalugnu- (a form of unknown morphology is *dalugnula*) 'make long'. Götze, Madd. 145; Hrozný, Congr. 1.163 fn. 1.

DAM = *AŠŠATU* 'wife'.

DAM.*ZU* = *AŠŠAT-ŠU* 'his wife'.

DAM-*UTTU* = *AŠŠŪTU* = DAM-*atar* (gen. DAM-*annas*) 'marriage'.

tamăēs, nom. pl. of *tamais*.

tamăi, neut. of *tamais*.

tamăĭn, *damăĭn*, acc. of *tamais*.

tamăĭs (also *damăĭs*, *dammais*, *tamas*?, acc. *tamăĭn*, *damăĭn*, *dammain*) 'other, second'. Hrozný, SH 21, 150–2; Sommer, BoSt. 10.12; Friedrich, Vert. 1.87 and fn. 3; Sturtevant, AJP 48.249, Lang. 6.32, HG 202, 209; Götze-Pedersen, MS 68 f. Cf. Hahn, Lang. 12.113–6.

?*tamas*, rare nom. for *damais*. Hrozný, CH 132.16; but see Goetze ap. Hahn, Lang. 12.115 fn. 48.

tamaske/a- 'press, oppress; shut in'. See *damass-*.

damass- (*damaszi*, *tamaszi*, *damasti*, pret. *tamasta*, 1 sg. *damassun*, pl. *tamassir*) 'press, oppress; shut in'. Götze, Hatt. 62–4, KlF 1.178 f.; Friedrich, Vert. 1.40 f.; Sturtevant, Lang. 8.119 f., HG 107, 127. Cf. *tamess-*, *dammeshas*.

appanda t. 'shut off (one's road)'. Hrozný, BoSt. 3.195 fn. 6.

dămăus, nom. and acc. pl. of *tamais*.

tamel, *damel*, gen. of *tamais*.

tamenk- (*tamekti*, pret. pl. *damenkir*, midd. *tamektari*, *tammektari*) 'attach oneself to (someone)'? Sommer, AU 252.

anda t., midd., 'grow up (again); unite with (someone)'?

tamenkiske/a-, midd., 'be favorable toward'? Chrest. 148.26. See *tamenk-*.

tamess- (pret. 1 pl. *tamessuwen*) 'press, oppress; shut in'. See *tamass-*.

damessar 'oppression' or the like. Götze, Hatt. 64.

damĕda 'elsewhere, at another time'. Sturtevant, JAOS 52.7 fn. 16; HG 205.

dămēdani, *tamēdani*, *damētani*, *tamētani*, dat. of *tamais*.

tamēdas, gen. of *tamais*. Friedrich, Vert. 1.87 fn. 3.

tamēdas, dat. pl. of *tamais*.

tamĕdaz, *tamĕtaz*, *damedaza*, abl. of *tamais*.

ᴸᵁDAM.QAR = *unattallas* 'merchant'.

dammain, acc. of *tamais*.

dammais = *tamais*, q.v.

ᴸᵁ*dammaras*, ˢᴬᴸ*dammaras*, some kind of menial connected with a temple. Ehelolf, KlF 1.152; Sommer, KlF 1.344, AU 279 fn. 3.

ˢᴬᴸ·ᴹᴱˢ*dammaranza*, Luwian (?) pl. of ˢᴬᴸ*dammaras*. Sommer, AU 280 and fn. 4.

dammek-; see *tamenk-*.

dammeli, dat. of *tamais*.

dammenk-; see *tamenk-*.

dammenzan, gen. pl. of *tamais*.

dammeshă(e)- (pl. *dammishanzi*, pret. *dammeshāit*, pl. *dammeshăir*, part. *dammeshan, dammishan*) 'injure, attack; punish'. Götze, Hatt. 62–4, KlF 1.178 f.; Friedrich, Vert. 1.40 fn. 3. Cf. *dammeshas*.

dammeshanu- 'cause to injure, cause to punish'. HG 235.

dammeshas (dat. *dammesha*) 'injury; punishment'. Götze, Hatt. 63, KlF 1.179; HG 160. Cf. *damass-*.

dammeshiske/a- 'injure, attack; punish'. See *dammesha(e)-*.

tam(m)ĕta (also *dameda*) 'abundance'?? KUB 2.2.3.28; 4.4.1.14; 8.22.3.3 (W).

dammili; read *dammeli*.

dampŭpis (acc. *dampūpin, dampupen*) 'of little value; unskilled, uncultivated, barbarous'. Friedrich, Vert. 2.153.

tan = *ta* + *an*; see *tas*.

tān (also *dān*) 'iterum', before a substantive 'secundus'. Hrozný, BoSt. 3.116 fn. 5; Sommer, BoSt. 7.44, AU 272 and fn. 1; Sturtevant, AJP 48.249, HG 128, 144.

tān pēdas 'of second rank'.

tān pēdassahh- 'make of the second rank'. Götze, Madd. 125.

tăninu- (*taninuzi, daninuzzi*, 1 sg. *tăninumi*, pret. *daninut, taninut, taninutta*) 'set, fix; set in order, establish'. Götze, Hatt. 108. Cf. *titta-, tittanu-, tiya/e-* 'take one's stand'.

dankui, dankuiske/a-; read *dankwi, dankwiske/a-*.

dankuis; read *dankwis*.

dankuneske/a- 'make dark, make black'? HG 123 f.

dankunu- 'make dark, make black'. HG 123 f.

*dankus (abl. *dankuwaz*, neut. pl. *dankuwa, tankuwa*) 'dark, black; impure'. See *dankwis*.

dankw- (*dankwi*) 'be dark, be black; be impure'. Götze, Madd. 82.

dankwes- (MI-*iszi*) 'become dark, become black'. HG 232.

dankwis (nom. *dankwīs*, acc. *dankwin*, neut. *dankwi*, gen. *dankuyas* [dankwiyas], dat. *dankuwai*, pl. *tankwēs, tankuwaēs, dankuwaēs*)

'dark, black; impure'. Forrer, SBPA 1919.1039; Friedrich, ZA NF 1.141 fn. 1; Sturtevant, Lang. 6.223, 10.268. Cf. *dankus.*
dankwiske/a- 'be dark, be black; be impure'. See *dankw-.*
DANNA 'two hours march; mile'.
tanna- (*2-anna*) 'for the second time'. Sommer, AU 272 fn. 1.
*dannaranza (acc. *dannarandan,* neut. *dannaran*) 'empty'? HG 157 and fn. 43.
dannaras 'empty'. Weidner, Stud. 122; KBo. 2.4.2.7.
dannat(t)ahh- (pret. *dannatahta* 1 sg. *dannattahhun, dannatahhun*) 'make empty'. Friedrich, ZA NF 1.17; HG 242.
tannatta(e)- (infin. *tannattawwanzi*) 'be empty'? KUB 24.3.3.5.
*dannattas (neut. *dannattan, tannattan*) 'empty; harvested (of a field); plundered, ravaged'. Götze, Hatt. 79 f.; HG 157. Cf. *dannattis.*
dannat(t)ess- (*dannatteszi, tannatteszi,* pl. *dannatessanzi*) 'become empty'. Götze, Hatt. 69 fn. 2.
dannattessar 'emptying, drying up (of a river)'. Götze, Hatt. 79.
dannattis (nom. sg.) 'empty; devastated'. KUB 21.29.1.12. See *dannattas.*
tan pedas; see s.v. *tan.*
tan pedassahh-; see s.v. *tan.*
TAPAL, construct state of *TAPALU.*
TAPALU 'pair'; used for 'two' with pluralia tantum. Götze, ZA NF 6.79 f.
⁎*tapar-* (pret. *taparta,* 1 sg. *taparha*) 'govern, rule'. Hrozný, BoSt. 3.211 fn. 3; Sommer, BoSt. 7.15; Götze, Hatt. 62–4; Friedrich, Vert. 2.90 f.; HG 66. Cf. *taparri-, taparriya/e-.*
tapari-; see *taparri-.*
tapariya/e-; see *taparriya/e-.*
*tapariyallas (pl. ᴸᵁ*tapariyalles*) 'prince'. Götze, Madd. 138.
tapariyas; see *taparriyas.*
tabarnas (sometimes *labarnas* by confusion with *Labarnas,* the name of the founder of the first Hittite empire; in Akkadian passages *TABARNA* or, as a royal title, ᴵ*TABARNA*) 'ruler, king'. Sommer, OLZ 24.316 f.; Chrest. 84 f., 172, 194 f.
tapar(r)i- (gen. *tapariyas, taparriyas, taparyas,* dat. *taparriya, tapariya,* abl. *taparriyaz, tapariyaz*) 'regulation, order; domain'. Sommer, AU 58. Cf. Sturtevant, Lang. 10.272. See *taparriyas.*
tapar(r)iya/e- (2 sg. *taparriyasi,* 1 pl. *tapariyaweni*) 'determine, designate; order'. Götze, Madd. 138; Friedrich, Vert. 2.90 f., 169. Cf. *tapar-.*

ᴸᵁ̌tapar(r)iyas (usually without determinative, and with single r; originally LÚ taparriyas 'man of authority'?) 'ruler, prince'. Götze, Madd. 138; Friedrich, Vert. 2.90 f. Cf. Sturtevant, Lang. 10.272. See taparri-.

taparuna 'on terms of equality'?? Cf. Götze, AM 228 f.

⋆tapassas (acc. tapassan) 'fever'? Hrozný, BoSt. 3.30 fn. 3; Sommer, BoSt. 10.13 fn. 1.

tapesni (dat.) 'at a store house'??? Hrozný, CH 72.35 f. 'In the very act'??? Zimmern, AO 23.2.19 fn. 2. Rather 'in the fore-court'? Cf. tapusa 'near'.

dapianza; read dapiyanza.

*dapis (gen. dapias, abl. dapiza) 'all'. Friedrich, ZA NF 1.11 and fn. 2; Sturtevant, Lang. 10.266. Cf. dapiyanza.

ᴰᵁᴳtapisanas, a kind of vessel that may be made of asphalt or of gold. Sommer, BoSt. 10.56.

dapiyanza (nom. dapianza, neut. dapian, pl. dapiantis) 'all'. Hrozný, CH 38 fn. 5. See dapis.

ᴸᵁ̌tappālas, a kind of servant in the royal kitchen. Friedrich, Altorient. Stud. 51.

ᴸᵁ̌TAPPŪ = aras 'companion, friend, equal'.

ᴸᵁ̌TAPPŪTU, TAPPUTTU 'friendship, equality'.

ᴳᴵˢtaptappas 'nest'? Götze, KlF 1.230 f.

tapulli 'plate, dish'?? Hrozný, CH 122.4; Carruthers, Lang. 9.160.

ᵁᴿᵁᴰtapulliyammit (inst.) 'with a fetter'?? Hrozný, AOr. 1.85.13.

*tapŭs (dat. dapusa, tapŭsa, abl. tapusza); dat. 'beside, near; to one side, away'; abl. 'from the side of; away; beside'. Sommer, BoSt. 10.26 f., AU 86; Friedrich, OLZ 28.662; Götze, Hatt. 101 f.; Götze-Pedersen, MS 23–5, 69. Cf. tapuwwas.

tāpuw(w)as (heteroclitic dat. pl. of preceding word) 'to the sides'. Forrer, Forsch. 1.139; cf. Götze-Pedersen, MS 27 and fn. 1.

DAR 'many-colored'.

TAR; see TAR.LIŠ.

dara- (pl. daranzi, taranzi, part. daranza, taranza) 'explain, declare, promise'. Hrozný, JSOR 6.69 fn. 1, Götze, ZA 34.184.

tarahh-; read tarhh-.

taraske/a-; read tarske/a- or tarskke/a-.

tarassawala (neut. pl.) 'capable of being decided'??? Friedrich, Vert. 1.89. Cf. Sommer, AU 50 and fn. 5. Rather 'verbis exponenda'?

dareske/a-; read tarske/a- or tarskke/a-.

tarhh- (*tarahzi, taruhzi*, pl. *tarruhhanzi*, pret. *tarahta*, 1 sg. *tarhun*, pl. *tarahhir*) 'be powerful; control, conquer'; w. infin. 'can'. Götze, Hatt. 77, Madd. 46; Kurylowicz, Symb. Gramm. 102. Cf. *tarhu-*.

tarhheske/a- (pret. *tarahheskit*, 1 sg. *tarahhiskinun*) 'be powerful; control, conquer'; w. infin. 'can'. See *tarhh-*.

tarhu- (*tarhuzzi*, imper. *tarhudu*) = *tarhh-*. Sturtevant, Lang. 10.268.

tarhuilatar; see *tarhwilatar*.

tarhuilis; see *tarhwilis*.

tarhuwilis; see *tarhwilis*.

tarhwilătar (gen. *tarhwilannas*) 'strength'; gen. 'strong'. Ehelolf, SBPA 1925.268.

*tarhwilis (acc. *tarhuwilin*, acc. pl. *tarhwilius, tarhwilaus*) 'strong'. Götze, Madd. 138, NBr. 63; Sturtevant, Lang. 10.267 f. Cf. *tarhu-*.

tariashas; see *tarriyashas*.

dăriya/e- (pret. *dāriyat*, 1 sg. *dariyanun, dariyahhun*, part. *dăriyantes*) 'invoke, summon, claim'. Götze, Hatt. 100; HG 225. Cf. *dariyanu-*.

anda d. 'cure (by incantations)'. Götze, Hatt. 106.

tariya/e- (pret. *dariyat*, part. *tariyan*) 'take pains, grow weary'? KUB 21.27.4.39; 24.3.2.35, 36 (G).

tariyala; read *triyalla*.

dăriyanu- 'invoke'. Götze, Hatt. 100; Sommer, AU 128; HG 217. Cf. *dariya-*.

tariyashas; see *tarriyashas*.

tarkummă(e)- 'explain, announce'. Friedrich, ZA NF 3.183; Götze, Madd. 84 fn. 11; HG 38, 227. 'Ask'. KBo. 4.9.5.29.

tarkummiya/e- 'explain, announce'. See *tarkumma(e)-*.

*tarlān*ᴹᵁˢᴱᴺ (acc.), a kind of bird? Friedrich, ZA NF 5.62.

TAR(.LIŠ)-*wan*, a term in oracle texts, indicating the flight of birds; the contrasting term is GUN(.LIŠ)-*an*, q.v. 'Wegwärts'?? Götze, Kulturg. 141.

tarmă(e)- 'fasten, fix; blockade'. Götze, Madd. 84 and fn. 12; Sturtevant, Lang. 5.10 f., HG 90, 226, Chrest. 110.18.

tarmiske/a- 'fasten, fix; blockade'. KUB 17.28.1.13. See *tarma(e)-*.

tarnă- (*tarnăi*, pl. *tarnanzi*, pret. *tarnas*, infin. *tarnumanzi*) 'put in, down, on; let in, down, on; emit (urine); pitch (a tent), set (a stone figure); put into someone's power; let out, forgive'; with infin. 'let, permit'. Götze, Madd. 126 f., NBr. 64–76; Sturtevant, Lang. 7.167 f., 12, No. 3, HG 106, 245, 286 f.; Benveniste, BSL 33.142.

appan t. 'pardon'. Götze, KlF 1.229 f. 'Make tax-free'??? Götze, NBr. 72. 'Consecrate'? Chrest. 98.

kattanta t. 'admit'. Sommer, AU 427 s.v. tarnisk-.

parā t. 'let loose, let out; surrender (a person to good or ill)'. Götze, NBr. 73; Chrest. 218.24, 226. 'Surrender to slavery, enslave'??? Götze, NBr. 73 f. Rather 'release'? Chrest. 226.

parā parā t., midd., 'be scattered'. Götze, Lang. 11.188.

pariyan t. 'let go across; sacrifice (to a god)'. Götze, NBr. 72.

piran t. 'confess'. Götze, KlF 1.229, NBr. 65; Sommer, AU 175.

piran appa t. 'let (someone) go in and out'. Götze, NBr. 71.

piran arha t. 'retreat before (someone)'. Götze, AM 313.

piran katta t. 'sacrifice (to a god), surrender (to an enemy)'. Götze, NBr. 71.

tarnas (gen.), a dry measure, less than half a handful. Hrozný, SH 41 fn. 2; KBo. 5.2.1.27 (G).

tarnes- (pret. tarnesta, imper. 2 pl. tarnistin) 'put in, down, on, etc.'. See tarna-.

tarneske/a- (tarniskizzi, pret. pl. tarneskir) 'put in, down, on, etc.'. See tarna-.

tarnu- (dat. tarnuwi, tarnwi, abl. tarnuwaz, pl. tarnuwēs); É tarnu- 'retiring house, bath house'? Cf. Ehelolf, KlF 1.154 and fn. 2; Ranoszek, IF 52.167. Cf. tarna-.

tarnummar, verb. n. from tarna-.

tarnummen, pret. 1 pl. from tarna-.

tarpallis (acc. [tarpal]lin, nom. pl. tarpallis, acc. tarpallius) 'picture, representation', a substitute for a person in ritual. Sommer, BoSt. 10.17; Friedrich, Vert. 2.39.

⁎tarpanallassata (pret. 3 sg.?) 'incited to revolt'?? Friedrich, Vert. 1.174; Sommer, AU 108.

tarra- (taratta, pret. tarraddat) 'tremble(?), worry, concern oneself'. Friedrich, Vert. 1.153. Cf. Forrer, RHA 1.152 fn. 27.

tarranu- 'cause to tremble'? Chrest. 182.7, 17, 184.27, 195.

tarrawwa; see tarru.

tar(r)i(y)ashas = MĀNAḪTU 'weariness, pain'? See dariya- (G). Cf. Holma, JSFO 33.63 ('repos'); Weidner, Stud. 123 ('Not, Bedrängnis'); Ehelolf, Berl. Mus. Ber. 49.34 ('Fürsprache').

tarrū (also tarrawwa?) 'on the belly, face down'?? Götze, AOr. 5.6. 'On the wood, on the floor'?? Cf. taru.

tarruhh-; read tarhh-.

tarsike/a-; read *tarske/a-* or *tarskke/a-*.
tarsikke/a-; read *tarskke/a-*.
ᴸᵁ*tarsipālas* (gen. *tarsipāliyas*!), an official at court. Friedrich, Altorient. Stud. 1.53.
tarske/a- 'put in, down, on, etc.'. Götze, NBr. 66 f. See *tarna-*.
tarsk(k)e/a- (*taraskizzi, tarsikizzi, tarsikkisi*, pl. *tarsikanzi, tarsikkanzi, taraskanzi*) 'explain, announce'. Götze, Madd. 113 f. See *dara-*.
ᴸᵁ*TARTEN(N)U* 'commander-in-chief'. Sommer, AU 36–8; Koschaker, ZA NF 7.35 f.
ᴸᵁ*TARTEN(N)UTU* 'position of commander-in-chief'.
taru (GIŠ-*ru*, dat. *taruwi*) 'wood'. Ehelolf, OLZ 36.7.
taruhzi; see *tarhh-*.
taruiske/a-; read *tarwiske/a-*.
tarupp- (pret. 1 sg. *taruppun*, pl. *taruppir*, imper. 2 sg. *tarup*, midd. *taruptari*, pret. *taruptat*) 'twist, twine (wool, a rope, etc.); fasten together; assemble, herd together; make harmonious'. Götze, ZA 34.186, KlF 1.189, 222 f.; HG 83 f.
  anda t., equivalent to the simplex.
  arha t. 'untwist; unloose, remove'.
tarup(p)a(e)- (*taruppaizzi, darupaizzi*) 'twist, twine; fasten together; assemble; harmonize'. See *tarupp-*.
taruppeske/a- 'twist, twine, etc.'. See *tarupp-*.
taruppessar (dat. *daruppisni*) 'entirety'; dat. as adv. 'all together'. Hrozný, SH 71; Friedrich, Vert. 2.28; HG 152. Cf. *tarupp-*.
taruppiya/a- 'twist, twine, etc.'. See *tarupp-*.
ᴷᵁˢ*tarusha*, a part of a harness or a kind of harness. Hrozný, CH 64.4, 114.9; Walther, HC 260.78, 265.125.
tarwawwanzi (infin.) 'to roar'? Götze, Kulturg. 149 and fn. 4.
tarwiske/a- 'roar'?? KUB 25.37.1.5–7. Cf. *tarwawwanzi*.
TÁŠ; read ZÍZ.
-tas 'tui', gen. of *-tes*.
tas = ta + as 'et is'. Ungnad, ZA NF 2.104 fn. 1. Friedrich, ZA NF 2.293 f.; Sturtevant, JAOS 47.174–7, HG 199 f.; Hrozný, ZA NF 4.174.
dǎske/a- (*daskizzi*, pl. *daskanzi*, pret. *daskit*, 2 sg. *daskes*, imper. 2 pl. *dāsqaten, taskatten*) 'take, get, etc.'. See *da-*. HG 110.
taskupǎ(e)- (*taskupǎizzi*) 'howl, yell, shout'. Friedrich, ZA NF 5.53 f., Vert. 2.165; Ehelolf, KlF 1.400 and fn. 2.
taskupiske/a- 'howl, yell, shout'. See *taskupa(e)-*.

tasnu-; see *dassanu-*.
TAŠPUR = *hatraes* 'you sent, you wrote'.
TAŠPUR-ANNI 'you sent to me, you wrote me'.
tassan = *ta* + *san*.
dassanu- (part. *dassanuwan*, *tas*<*sa*>*nuwan*) 'make strong'. KUB 24.1.1.20; 24.2.1.16 (G). Cf. *dassus*.
dassanuske/a- 'make strong'. KUB 21.42.2.7.
dassawes- 'become strong'. Götze, KlF 1.185. See *dassus*.
dassesta (pret.) 'was valid'?? Forrer, Forsch. 1.32.40. 'Failed'?? Götze, KlF 1.128.
dassiyatar 'strength'. Friedrich, ZA NF 5.47 fn. 1. Cf. *dassus*.
dassus (also *tassus*) 'strong, heavy'. Hrozný, SH 8 and fn. 1; Friedrich, ZA NF 3.184; Sturtevant, RHA 1.86.
dassuwanza 'strong, heavy'. Friedrich, Vert. 1.80, ZA NF 3.184. See *dassus*.
tasta = *ta* + (*a*)*sta*.
tastaseske/a- (supine *tastaseskiwwan*, *tastasiskiwwan*) 'whisper, conspire'. See *tastasiya/e-*.
tastasiya/e- 'whisper, conspire'. Friedrich, Vert. 1.81; Götze, AM 245 f.; HG 215.
dasuwahh-; see *daswahh-*.
dasuwanza; see *daswanza*.
daswahh- (also *dasuwahh-*, *tasuwahh-*) 'make blind'. Ehelolf, KlF 1.394–8; HG 105. Cf. *daswanza*.
daswanza (also *dasuwanza*, *taswanza*) 'blind'. See *daswahh-*.
tatrahh- (pret. *tatrahhas*, *tatrahta*) 'instigate'? Forrer, Forsch. 2.10.23; Ranoszek, IF 52.167.
tattaluske/a- 'unbind, liberate'? Hrozný, SH 79; Holma, JSOF 33.1.32 f.
tattaránzi (3 pl.) 'they wipe' or the like. Ehelolf, KlF 1.147 and fn. 7.
taugas; read *tayugas*.
tăwal (also *tāwwal*, gen. *tāwwales*, inst. *tawalit*, *tawallit*, *tāwwalit*), a sacrificial drink. Ehelolf, KlF 1.138 and fn. 6.
[LÚ]*tăwalalas* (*dāwalalas*, dat. *tawalali*), one who prepares *tawal* or one who uses it. Cf. Tenner, HAT 24.
tāwana 'a second time'??? Sayce, RHA 1.7.24. 'Truly'? Friedrich ap. Ranoszek, IF 52.167.
[SAL]*Tawan*(*n*)*annas*, title of the Hittite queen. Götze, Kulturg. 87 f.
tawwal; see *tawal*.

taya/e- (*tăyizzi, tăyēzzi, dāyizzi, tăyyazi, dāyyazi, dāyyēzzi*) 'steal (an object), rob (a house)'. Hrozný, SH 54; Götze, Madd. 96; Sturtevant, Lang. 5.145; HG 88; Kurylowicz, EI 75.

tayaz(z)il (gen. *dayazilas, dayyazilas, tayazilas, tayizzilas*) 'theft'. Friedrich, Vert. 1.158; Sturtevant, Lang. 4.229, HG 126, 156.

tā(y)ugas (also *dāyugas, dāy<u>gas*) 'two years old'. Hrozný, SH 93; Sturtevant, Lang. 6.215, HG 144; Götze-Pedersen, MS 68; Hahn, Lang. 12.114 f. and fn. 43. Cf. *yugas*.

tayya/e-; see *taya/e-*.

TE 'cheek'.

TE is often written for KUŠ in omen texts.

-te (*-ti*) 'tuo', dat. of *-tes*.

tĕ- (*tezzi*, 2 sg. *tĕsi*, pret. *tēt, tīt*) 'speak, say'. Hrozný, MDOG 56.29, SH 2 and fn. 3, 241; Marstrander, Car. 147; HG 100; Götze-Pedersen, MS 68.

tehhi, tehhun; see *dai-*.

tĕkan (gen. *taknăs*, dat. *taknī, taknā, taknai*, abl. *taknăz*) 'earth'. Sommer, BoSt. 10.67; Friedrich, AOF 2.122 fn. 2; Pedersen, Group. 41; Kretschmer, Gl. 20.65-7; HG 118.

tekkusnu-; see *tekkussanu-*.

tekkusnuske/a- 'show, prove'. KUB 13.2.2.18. See *tekkussanu-*.

??*tekkussa-*; for forms that might belong to such a stem, see *tekkussanu-, tekkusse/a-, tekkusses-, tekkussiya/e-*.

tekkus(sa)nu- (also *tikkusnu-*) 'show, prove'. Hrozný, BoSt. 3.183 fn. 8; Sommer, BoSt. 10.30 fn. 1; Götze, Hatt. 54, AM 215; Friedrich, Vert. 2.138; Sturtevant, Lang. 8.120.

?*tekkusse/a-* (1 sg. *tekkussami* or *tekkussa<nu>mi*?, pret. *tekkussēt* or *tekkussiēt*?) 'show'? Friedrich, Vert. 2.138; Götze, AM 215 fn. 1; HG 100, 120 f. Cf. *tekkussanu-, tekkuses- tekkussiya/e-*.

tekkusses- (pret. *tekkussesta*) 'show' or 'appear'. Götze, Hatt. 106, AM 215 and fn. 1; HG 230.

?*tekkussiya/e-* (pret. *tekkussiēt* or *tekkussēt*?) 'show' or 'appear'. See *tekkusse/a-, tekkusses-*.

tekri 'very much'? Götze, AOr. 5.9.

TEL; read DU_6.

telipuri (neut. pl.?), governmental units in provincial towns? Götze, RHA 1.28 f.

ṬĒMU (often written TĒMU) 'message'.

LÚ ṬĒMI, LÚ ṬĒMU = *halugatallas* 'messenger'.

-ten (*-tin*) 'tuum', acc. of *-tes*.
tenzi; read *tienzi* and see *tiya/e-* 'take one's stand'.
tepanu-; see *tepnu-*.
?*tepawahh-* (pret. *tepawahta*?) 'make small, make light of'. Friedrich, IF 49.225; Sommer, AU 55.
tepawaz, abl. of *tepus*.
tĕpawĕss- (*tepawēszi*, pret. *tĕpawēsta*, part. *tĕpawĕssanza*) 'become small'. Götze, Hatt. 69; HG 232. See *tepus*.
tepawa, neut. pl. of *tepus*.
tepnu- (pret. *tepnutta*, part. neut. *tepanuwan*) 'make small; make light of'. Hrozný, BoSt. 3.170.24 and fn. 4; Friedrich, ZA NF 1.16; HG 128, 131 and fn. 95, 235. Cf. *tepus*.
tēpnumar 'humiliation'. Friedrich, KlF 1.291. See *tepnu-*.
tepnuske/a- 'make small, make light of'. Madd. 60. See *tepnu-*.
tepsanu- 'make sterile, make powerless'. KUB 24.3.2.53 (G). Cf. *tepsus*.
*tepsawwatar (dat. *tepsawwanni*) 'sterility'? KBo. 3.34.2.12. Cf. *tepsus*.
tepsus 'sterile'. Götze, Madd. 72 fn. 1.
tĕpus 'small'; *tēpu* 'a little'; *tepawaz* 'in small numbers'. Hrozný, SH 7; Götze, Hatt. 131; Carruthers, Lang. 6.163; HG 96, 128; Götze-Pedersen, MS 69.
TERĀNU 'convolution of the intestines'. See ŠA(G).TIR.
teripp- [t῾rep῾-] (*teripzi*, part. *terippan*) 'plough'. Götze, NBr. 62; HG 89.
*terippis [t῾rep῾is] (gen. *terippiyas*, *terippias*, abl. *terippiyaz*, neut. pl. *terippi-*ḪI.A) 'ploughed (of a field)'. See *teripp-*.
terippiske/a- 'plough'. KUB 13.1.4.25. See *teripp-*.
teriyalla; read *triyalla*.
teriyanna; read *triyanna*.
-tes (also *-tis*) 'tuus'. Hrozný, SH 128 f.; HG 194, 197.
teshaniske/a- 'appear in dreams'. Friedrich, ZA NF 2.288 and fn. 2; Götze-Pedersen, MS 69. Cf. *teshas* 'sleep, dream'.
teshas 'sleep, dream'. Friedrich, IF 43.258 fn. 4; Götze, KlF 1.232 and fn. 3; HG 160; Götze-Pedersen, MS 69. Cf. *zashais*.
teshas῾ (pret.) 'refrained'??? Götze-Pedersen, MS 41, 69. Rather 'slept'? *IŠTU SAL-TI t.* 'slept apart from a woman'? But cf. Friedrich, OLZ 39.306.
tesi, a time of year when thunder is heard. Sommer, BoSt. 4.23, 7.26; Friedrich, ZA NF 3.196 and fn. 4, Vert. 2.33 fn. 5.
tesi, 2 sg. of *te-* 'say'.

teske/a- (also *tiske/a-*) 'place, put'. Sommer, AU 64 fn. 1. See *dai-*.
teske/a- (also *tiske/a-*) 'take one's stand, stand'. Hrozný, BoSt. 3.150 fn. 4. See *tiya/e-* 'take one's stand'.
-tet, neut. and inst. of *-tes*.
*tĕtanas (acc. *tēdanan*, inst. *tēdanit*, pl. *tĕtanus*) 'hair'. Friedrich, Vert. 1.35 fn. 1; Sturtevant, Lang. 4.122, HG 145.
tethai (3 sg.) 'thunders'. Friedrich, Vert. 2.33 fn. 5; Götze, KlF 1.186 and fn. 10; Götze-Pedersen, MS 69. Cf. *tethit*.
tethessar (gen. *tethesnas*) 'thunder'. Friedrich, ZA NF 3.196 f., Vert. 2.33 fn. 5; Götze, Madd. 62. See *tethai*.
tethimas 'thunder'. Götze, KlF 1.186 and fn. 9; HG 156. See *tethai*.
tethiske/a- 'thunder'. See *tethai*.
tethit (pret.) 'thundered'? KUB 19.14.11. See *tethai*.
tettiya/e-; see *tittiya/e-*.
tezzi, 3 sg. of *te-* 'say'.
DI = DĪNU = *hanessar* 'justice, court, law-suit'.
DI; read SILIM 'health; kindness, favor'.
TI = *hwes-* 'live'.
TI = *hwesnu-* 'cause to live'.
TI = *hweswa(e)-* 'be alive'.
TI = *hweswatar* 'life'.
-ti; read *-te*.
tikkusnu-; see *tekkussanu-*.
DI.KUD 'justice, judgment'.
TIL 'end, complete; ended, complete'.
    NU.TIL 'not complete'.
TIL; read BE 'if'.
TIL; read BE 'master'.
TIL; read UG$_6$ 'die, death'.
TÍL; read DU$_6$.
^{GIŠ}DILIM; read ^{GIŠ}LIŠ.
^{GIŠ}DILIM.GAL, ^{DUG}DILIM.GAL; read LIŠ.GAL.
DIM (Forrer) = DÌM (Hrozný) = DIM$_4$ (Thureau-Dangin); read BULÙG.
-TIM is used by the Hittite scribes as an ideographic plural sign, equivalent to MEŠ. Sommer, AU 343.
DĪN, construct state of DĪNU.
-tin; read *-ten*.
DINGIR = ILU = *siunas, siunis, sius, karimn-* 'god, goddess'; also a determinative (transcribed ^{D}) before names of gods. Unless it is a determinative, DINGIR is usually followed by an

Akkadian phonetic complement (*-LIM*, *-LUM*) or by a plural sign.
DINGIR-*LIM-is kis*- 'become a god, die' (of Hittite kings).
Hrozný, SH 17 f.; Götze, Kulturg. 83 and fn. 4.
DINGIR-*LIM-nili* 'in the manner of a god'.
ᴸᵁDINGIR-*LIM-niyanza* = ᴸᵁ*siuniyanza* 'man of the god' or the like.
DINGIR-*LIM-niyatar*, DINGIR.MEŠ-*tar* = *siuniyatar* 'divinity'.
DINGIR.MAḪ 'giant'?? Forrer, RHA 1.145.
DINGIR.MEŠ, usually 'gods', but sometimes 'god'. Eheolf, ZA NF 9.177 fn. 1, 179 fn. 3.
ᴸᵁTIN.NA, ˢᴬᴸTIN.NA 'vintner, tavern-keeper'.
tin(n)u- 'paralyze, destroy'?? Götze, KlF 1.403 and fn. 3.
DĪNU = *hanessar* 'justice, court, law-suit'.
DIB = *epp-* 'take'.
DIBBA.GAG; read PÍŠ.
DIR; read SA₅.
ᴳᴵˢTIR or GIŠ TIR 'grove, wood, forest'.
ᴰTIR.AN.NA 'rainbow'.
DIRIG; read SA₅.
DIŠ; read 1 (see p. 190).
-tis; read *-tes*.
tishantes (pl.); *anda t.* w. dat. 'careful of'?? Friedrich, AOr. 6.361 and fn. 8.
tiske/a-; read *teske/a-*.
tissallin (acc.) 'capable of procreation'?? Friedrich, AOr. 6.366 and fn. 3.
tissatwa (neut. pl.) 'tongues'. KUB 12.34.1.6–10 (G).
DI.TAR; read DI.KUD.
ᵁᶻᵁ*tittitan* (acc.) 'nose'. Friedrich, IF 41.374 fn. 1; HG 146.
titnu-; see *tittanu-*.
titnuske/a-; see *tittanuske/a-*.
titta- (1 sg. *tittami*, pret. 1 sg. *tittanun*) 'cause to stand, place, assign'. KBo. 4.8.2.6; KUB 1. p. 8 = Bo. 2026 b; KUB 14.16.4.17. HG 216. Cf. *tittiya-*, *tittanu-*, *tiya/e-* 'stand'.
tit(ta)nu- 'cause to stand, place, appoint, arrange'. Hrozný, SH 76 fn. 3; Sturtevant, Lang. 6.156, HG 98, 141; Götze, AOr. 5.5. Cf. Götze-Pedersen, MS 70. See *titta-*.
anda t. 'reconcile, appease'.
paranda t. 'seduce, make rebellious'. Friedrich, Vert. 2.154.
sarā t. 'cause to stand up'. Sommer, BoSt. 10.51; KUB 25.1.6.20.

'Set up (food or drink before the gods)'. Götze, KlF 1.244.26. 'Accomplish'?? Hrozný, AOr. 3.442.42, 456.46. Cf. *sara dai-*.

tit(ta)nuske/a- 'cause to stand, place, appoint, arrange'. Götze, KlF 1.244.26, Madd. 26.33.

tittiya/e- (part. *tittiyanza, tettiyanza*) 'cause to stand, place, assign; add to'. Friedrich, ZA NF 2.51, AO 24.3.7.12; HG 216, Chrest. 148.33, 169, 182.12, 220.37, 43. Cf. *titta-*.

tiya/e- (*tiyazi, tiizzi*, SUM-*zi*, pl. *tianzi, tīyanzi*, 1 pl. *tīyaweni*, pret. *tiyat*, pl. *tiyēr, tiēr, tiyir*, 1 pl. *tiyawen*, part. *tiyănza*) 'place, put'. Marstrander, Car. 147; Sturtevant, OLZ 35.470, HG 153 fn. 31, 223; Götze-Pedersen, MS 21, 70. Cf. Sommer, AU 60. See *dai-*.

tiya/e- (*tiyazi, tiyēzzi, tiyazzi, tiizzi, tiyizzi*, 1 sg. *tiyami*, 2 sg. *tiyasi*, pl. *tianzi, tīyanzi, tienzi*) 'take one's stand; approach (also sexually); come, be (noon, evening, etc.), (of the sun) be (in the sky); mount (a horse, a chariot); take one's stand for (a person)'. Hrozný, SH 241 f.; Weidner, AOF 1.65 f.; Götze, AOr. 5.35, AM 313 f.; Götze-Pedersen, MS 69 f. Cf. *titta-, tittiya/e-*.

anda t. 'go in; combine, conspire'.

appa t. (w. dat.) 'stand aside for, give way to'. Sommer, AU 186 fn. 1.

appan t. (w. dat.) 'stand back of, help'.

arha t. (w. dat.) 'revolt from, desert'. Friedrich, Vert. 1.145.17.

hanti t. (w. acc.) 'stand before, resist'?? Götze, NBr. 6 and fn. 3. 'Bring before (a court), give information about'?? Sommer, AU 186 f.

IŠTU ŠA (w. Akkadian gen.) *t.* 'stand with, side with'. Friedrich, Vert. 1.144.17; Chrest. 94.

kattan t. (w. dat.) 'stand with, side with'. Chrest. 72.66, 94.

parā t. 'go forth'.

sarā t. 'stand up, start'. Friedrich, Vert. 2.210; Sommer, AU 154.

ser t. 'stand aloof'; w. dat. 'overlook, neglect'. Cf. Götze, Hatt. 74; Chrest. 66.52.

tiyamar 'a placing; things placed'? KUB 17.28.4.50. See *tiya/e-* 'place, put'.

tiyaneske/a- 'destroy'?? KUB 7.53.2.10, 12, 17.

*tiyatallas. See *tiya/e-* 'take one's stand'.

hanti t. 'opponent'?? Friedrich, IF 49.230 fn. 1. 'Informer'?? Sommer, AU 186 f.

hanti tiyatalles- 'become a *hanti tiyatallas*'. Cf. Götze, Madd. 136.

TIYĀTU 'asafoetida'.

tri- (nom. 3-*ēs* = *triēs or *trēs) 'three'. Marstrander, Car. 125; Ehelolf, OLZ 32.322–8.

triyahh- (pl. 3-*iyahhanzi*) 'make triple'. KUB 9.4.2.33; cf. 9.34.3.16.

triyal(l)a (*teriyalla*, *tariyala*, 3-*yalla*), designation of a drink offering; perhaps neut. pl. of the word for 'triple'. Sommer, BoSt. 10.77; Ehelolf, OLZ 32.322–8; Delaporte, Voc. 77.

triyan (3-*an*) 'for the third time, third'? Cf. Sommer, AU 272 fn. 1. See *tri-*. Cf. *tan*.

triyanna (3-*anna*, [*teri*]*yanna*) 'for the third time'. Sommer, AU 272 fn. 1.

DU = *arai-* 'rise'.

DU = *ya-* 'go'. Sommer, AU 384.

DU; read GUB 'stand, standing'.

DÙ = *kis-* 'become'.

DÙ = *ya/e-* 'make'.

DU₆ 'mound, ruined city'.

DU₈ = *la-* 'loose, unharness'.

DU₈-*si* = *karsi*?? 'without hesitation'?? Sommer, AU 108 f., 109 fn. 1.

-*du-* (after vowels usually -*ddu-*), substitute for -*ta* in the phrase -*du-za*, 'tibi, te'. Hrozný, SH 128; HG 194 and fn. 8, 197.

ᴰᵁᴳDU₁₀ × A, ᵁᴿᵁᴰDU₁₀ × A 'wash-basin'. Götze-Pedersen, MS 44 f.

tua, tuaz; read *twa, twaz*.

tuekkas; read *twekkas*.

tuel; read *twel*.

tuetaz; read *twetaz*.

tuhalzi, probably an animal name. Sommer, BoSt. 10.41. Cf. Götze-Pedersen, MS 42 f.

tuhhs- (midd. *túḫ-uḫ-ša*) 'purify or consecrate oneself (with the *tuhhwessar*)'. Cf. Kretschmer, KlF 1.299; KBo. 4.9.2.22, 31. Cf. *tuhhwessar*.

tuhhss- (*tuhhuszi*, *tuhsanzi*, *tuhhuissa*[*nzi*], midd. *tuhhusta*, pl. *tuhsanta*, part. *tuhhussantes*, infin. *tuhsuwanzi*, *tuhsuwwanzi*, *tuhhuswanzi*) 'take off, take away; bring to an end'; midd. 'take away; come to an end'. Friedrich, ZA NF 3.200; Sturtevant, Lang. 6.30.

tuhhuss-; read *tuhhss-*.

tuhhwessar (also *tuhhuwessar*, *tuhhwissar*, inst. *tuhhuwīsnit*), an implement for ritual purification or consecration. 'Censer'? Götze, NBr. 69 fn. 2. 'Flederwisch'?? Kretschmer, KlF 1.299. Cf. *tuhhs-*, *tuhhwis*.

tuhhwis 'smoke, vapor'? Götze, NBr. 69 and fn. 1.
ᴸᵁ*tuhkantis*, title of a certain important official. Sommer, AU 36-8.
tuhuhs-; read *tuhhs*-.
tŭhus(s)iya/e- (1 pl. *tūhusiyaweni*, pret. *tūhusiyait, tuhusiyait, duhusiyait*) 'stand one's ground, await an attack'. Hrozný, BoSt. 3.226.2; Friedrich, KlF 1.290; Götze, Madd. 126.
tuikkanza; read *twekkanza*.
tuikkas; read *twekkas*.
DUG 'vessel, cup'; also a determinative before words denoting a kind of vessel.
    DUG ḪI.ÚS.SA 'wash jug'.
TUG; read TUKU and see TUKU.TUKU.
TÚG 'piece of cloth, garment'; also a determinative.
    LÚ TÚG 'tailor'.
tuk (before an enclitic w. initial vowel, *tug*-, *tuqq*-) 'tibi, te'; dat. and acc. of *zik*.
DÙG.GA = *assus* 'good'.
tukkă- (*duqqări, tuqqări*, pret. *tuqqāt*) 'be assigned, fall to one's lot; be important'. Friedrich, Vert. 2.150; Mudge, Lang. 7.253; HG 230. Cf. *dukkis*-.
DUG.GAL; read ᴰᵁᴳGAL.
DUG.KAM; read ᴰᵁᴳUTÚL.
ᴸᵁDUG.QA.BUR 'potter'.
TÚG.GAR.NE; read ᵀᵁᴳNÍG.LÁM.
tuggaz; see *twekkas*.
dukkis- (*dukkiszi*) 'assign, appoint'? Sommer, AU 284. Cf. Sturtevant, Lang. 8.123 f., HG 230. Cf. *tukka*-.
TÚG.GÚ.È.A 'shirt'. Sommer, BoSt. 10.38.
    TÚG.GÚ.È.A SIG 'thin shirt'. Cf. Hrozný, CH 138.52.
TÚG.GÚ.UD.DU.A; read TÚG.GÚ.È.A.
TÚG.NÍG.LÁM; read ᵀᵁᴳNÍG.LÁM.
TÚG.DA; read ZÍD.DA.
TUG.TUG; read TUKU.TUKU.
TUKU; see TUKU.TUKU.
ᴳᴵˢTUKUL 'weapon'.
    LÚ ᴳᴵˢTUKUL 'weapon man, soldier'. Götze, NBr. 57. Cf. Sommer, OLZ 38.280.
    LÚ ᴳᴵˢTUKUL GÍD.DA 'man of the long spear'; designation of a member of some crack regiment or of a high official? Friedrich, Vert. 1.84.

DUGUD = *nakkis* 'heavy; important, revered; burdensome, difficult'.
LÚ DUGUD = LÚ *nakkis* 'vir gravis', a dignitary.
TUKU(.TUKU) = *kartimmiya/e-* 'be angry, quarrel'.
TUKU(.TUKU) = *kartimmiyawwanza* 'angry'.
TUKU(.TUKU) = *kartimmes-* 'become angry'.
TUKU(.TUKU) = *kartimmiyaz* 'anger'.
TUKU(.TUKU) = *kartimnu-* 'make angry, vex'.
TUG.ZAB.BI; read ḪUP-PÍ.
DUL (Forrer); read GIR₄.
TÚL = *luli-*? 'spring, well'.
tuliya/e- (acc. *tuliyan*, gen. *tuliyas*, dat. *tuliya*) 'council, assembly'. Sommer, BoSt. 7.14 fn. 2.
tummeni 1 pl. of *da-*.
DUMU = $M\bar{A}RU$ = *uwas*? 'son'.
DUMU-*las* (dat. DUMU-*li*) 'son, child'.
    DUMU É.GAL 'palace servant'.
    DUMU ᵁᴿᵁḪATTI 'a Hittite'.
    DUMU LUGAL 'prince'.
    DUMU ŠIPRI = MĀR ŠIPRI 'messenger'.
    DUMU-*atar*, DUMU.MEŠ-*latar* 'childhood'.
DUMU.LÚ.GÀL.LU = *antuhsas* 'human being, man'.
DUMU.NAM.LÚ.GÀL.LU = DUMU AMĒLŪTI = *antuhsatar, antuhsananza*? 'humanity, mankind, people'.
DUMU.NITA; DUMU.NITÁ; read IBILA.
DUMU.SAL = MĀRTU 'daughter, girl'.
DUMU.DUMU 'grandson'.
DUMU.UŠ; read IBILA.
TÙN; read GÍN.
ᴱ*tunnak(k)essar* (gen. *tunnakkesnas, dunnakkesnas, tunnakkissanas*, dat. *tunnakesna, tunnakisna*), a holy place in a temple. Ehelolf, ZA NF 9.186–90.
DUB = ṬUPPU = *tuppi* 'clay tablet'.
DUB; for ZÁ DUB read ZÁ KIŠIB.
duppali-, duppaleske/a-; read *appali-, appaleske/a-*.
tuppi 'clay tablet'. Friedrich, Vert. 2.139 and fn. 2.
DUBBIN 'finger nail, toe nail'.
ᴳᴵˢDUBBIN 'wheel'. See s.v. *lamniya/e-*.
*tuppuzzi (gen. *tuppuzziyas*) 'tablet'?? Götze, KlF 1.201.
tupran (part. neut.) 'bound'?? Götze, KlF 1.185 f., 186 fn. 3.
ᴸᵁDUB.SAR, ᴸᵁDUB.SAR GIŠ 'scribe'.

DUB.SAR-*ŪTU* (written -*UT-TU*) 'position of scribe, office of scribe'.
DÙR = *es*- 'sit; seat oneself'. Sommer, AU 32, 384; KUB 18.12.1.18 f.
TUR = *kappis*, *tepus*? 'small'.
TUR; read DUMU 'son, child'.
TÙR 'yard for cattle'.
dūr 'urine'. Friedrich, AOr. 6.359 and fn. 3.
turammit 'my team'? Hrozný, AOr. 1.284.
?*tūre/a*- or *tūriya/e*- (*tūrizzi* or *turiizzi*? pret. *tūrit* or *tūriit*?) 'harness'. See *turiya/e*-.
tūreske/a- (also *tūriske/a*-) 'harness'. Hrozný, CH 60.65, AOr. 3.456.41.
tŭriya/e- (*tŭriyazi*, pl. *tŭriyanzi*) 'harness'. Sommer, BoSt. 7.34 and fn. 3.
ᴸᵁ*TURTĀNU* variant for ᴸᵁ*TARTĒNNU*.
ᴳᴵˢTUR.TÚG; read GIŠ.TUR.TÚG.
TUR.UŠ; read IBILA.
tus = *ta* + *us*; see *tas*.
dusk- (pl. *duskanzi*, pret. 1 sg. *duskun*, verb. n. *duskummar*) 'play, enjoy oneself'. Hrozný, SH 42, 78; Ehelolf, OLZ 29.768 fn. 2; Friedrich, ZA NF 5.48, OLZ 39.308; Götze, Kulturg. 152 and fn. 5.
*tusgaratar (dat. *tusgaranna*) 'enjoyment'. KBo. 3.21.3.25. See *dusk*-.
*dusgarawanza (neut. pl.? *dusgarawanda*) 'joyful'. Cf. Forrer, RHA 1.152 fn. 28; HG 161.
dusgaraz (acc. *dusgarattan*, *dusgaradan*, gen. *tuskarattas*, dat. *dusqarati*, abl. *duskarattaz*) 'play, joy'. Götze, Madd. 79 and fn. 3; HG 149. See *dusk*-.
duskiske/a- (also *tuskiske/a*-) 'play, enjoy oneself'. See *dusk*-.
DUDIṬṬU (also *TUDITTU*, *TUTITTU*, *DUTITTU*) 'breast ornament'.
duddumeli (also *duddumili*) 'inaudibly, silently, secretly'. See *duddummiyanza*.
duddumiyahh- (imper. pl. *duddumiyahhandu*) 'deafen'. See *duddummiyanza*.
duddummes- (imper. *duddummisdu*) 'become deaf'. See *duddummiyanza*.
dud(d)um(m)iyanza (also *duddudmiyanza*) 'deaf'. Ehelolf, KlF 1.393–400.
duddunumas (gen. of *duddunumar) 'animadvertendus'. KUB 26.58.1.16 (G). For the morphology see HG 153. Cf. *dudduske/a*-, *dudduwanza*. See *duddunu*- p. 192.
dudduske/a- 'observe, keep watch over, administer, manage'. Ehelolf, Berl. Mus. Ber. 49.34; KUB 1.16.3.59; 24.3.1.36 (G). See p. 192.

duddudmiyanza; see *duddummiyanza.*
dudduwanza 'watching over, managing'? See p. 192.
dudduwares- (pret. *dudduwaresta*) 'break' (intransitive)? Götze, AM 214 f. Cf. *duwarna-.*
tuwa; see *twa.*
tuwalas; see *twalas.*
duwăn (also *duwwān, tuwan*) 'apart'. Hrozný, BoSt. 3.50 fn. 2; Götze, Madd. 136; Friedrich, Vert. 2.87 fn. 1, 168; Sturtevant, AJP 48.249. Cf. *twa, twaz.*
    duwan ... duwan 'in one direction ... in the other'. Hrozný, CH 80.12; Götze, Madd. 136.
duwanta 'apart'. Cf. Hrozný, BoSt. 3.50.26.
duwarnă- (*duwarnāi,* imper. *duwarnāu,* midd. *duwarnattari, duwarnaddāri*) 'break' (transitive); midd. 'be broken'. Hrozný, MDOG 56.38 and fn. 3; HG 128 f., 219 and fn. 16. Cf. *duwarne/a-.*
duwarne/a- (*duwarnizzi, tuwarnizzi, tuwarnazi,* pret. *duwarnit,* pl. *tuwarnir*) 'break'. See *duwarna-.*
duwarneske/a- 'break'. Hrozný, BoSt. 3.78 fn. 2.
tuwaz; see *twaz.*
tuwekkas, tuwekkanza; see *twekkas, twekkanza.*
tuwwa; see *twa.*
tuwwalas; see *twalas.*
duwwān; see *duwan.*
*tuzzis (nom. *tuzzias,* acc. *tuzzin,* gen. *tuzziyas,* dat. *tuzziya, tuzzi,* pl. acc. *tuzzius, tuzius*) 'army'. Sommer, BoSt. 10.11; Eheloff, SBPA 1925.268 fn. 6; Sturtevant, Lang. 4.229, HG 155.
tuzziya/e- 'encamp'. Tenner, HAT 21; Götze, Madd. 98 and fn. 3.
tuzziyanza 'army'. Friedrich, ZA NF 2.282.
tuzziyas, heteroclitic nom. of *tuzzis.*
twa (*twa, tuwa, tuwwa*) 'to a distance, afar'. Friedrich, Vert. 2.87; Benveniste, BSL 33.142 f.; Götze-Pedersen, MS 71. Cf. *duwan, twaz.*
twalas (*tuwwalas*) 'far, distant'. Friedrich, Vert. 2.86 f.; HG 159. Cf. *twa.*
twaz (*twaz, tuwwaz*) 'from afar'. See *twa.*
twekkanza (*twikkanza*) 'body, guild'. Hrozný, CH 44.45. See *twekkas.*
twĕkkas (NÍ.TE-*as,* dat. *twĕkki, twikki,* abl. *tuggaz,* pl. *twēggas,* acc. *twēkkus, twīkkus, tuwīggas*) sg. 'body, self'; pl. 'members, body; self'. Götze, Madd. 132 f., 133 fn. 2; Sommer, AU 418.

twĕl 'tui', gen. of *zik*.
twetaz (also *twedaz*) 'a te', abl. of *zik*.

U 'ten'; see p. 19.
ᴅU, a storm god; there were several. See ᴅIŠKUR.
U; read BÙRU 'hole'.
Ù 'grass, plant'; also a determinative with names of plants.
Ù = ŠUTTU = *teshas* 'sleep, dream'.
Ù (pret. Ù-*at*) 'appear in a dream'.
U₄; read UD.
U (written Ù = -*a* 'and'.
u- 'hither'. Hrozný, SH 70 fn. 1; Marstrander, Car. 118–21; Friedrich, Vert. 2.146; Sturtevant, Lang. 7.1–5, HG 101.
U- *anki*; read 10-*anki*. See p. 19.
ue-; for words beginning thus, see *we-*.
UḪ₄ = *alwanzahh-* 'bewitch, conjure'. Götze, NBr. 14 f.; Eheloff, OLZ 36.6 fn. 3.
UḪ₄ = *alwanzatar* 'witchcraft'.
uhhun; see *au-*.
Ù.ḪUB = *duddummiyanza* 'deaf'.
ūhzi; read *wehzi*. HG 58–61.
ui-; for words beginning thus, see *wi-* or *we-*.
ÙG; read UKÙ.
UG₆ = *akk-* 'die'.
UG₆ = *henkan* 'fate, death'.
UG₆; read BE 'master'.
UG₆; read BE 'if'.
UG₆; read TIL 'complete'.
ūk (before enclitics beginning with a vowel usually *ug-*, *ūgg-*) 'I'; in later texts *ammuk* is the usual nom.; *uk* as acc. or dat. is rare at all times. Hrozný, MDOG 56.33, SH 97 f.; Friedrich, Vert. 1.89; Petersen, Lang. 6.168, 11.204; Sommer, AU 33; HG 192.
U.GAG; U + KAK; read UḪ₄.
ᴸᵁÙ.KAB; read LÚ Ù.ḪUB. Friedrich, ZA NF 1.166 fn. 9.
ukel, *ukela* 'ego ipse'. See -*el*, -*ela*.
ukila; read *ukela*.
UG.TUR = *parsanas* 'leopard', q.v.
uktūrēs- (pret. *uktūrēsta*) 'become fixed, become endemic'. Friedrich, ZA NF 3.203; HG 232.

uktūris 'fixed, firm, strong; continuous, eternal'. Friedrich, ZA NF 3.195; Götze, Kulturg. 137 and fn. 11.
UGU = *sarā* 'up'.
UGU = *sarazzis* 'upper, highest; superior, best'.
UGU = *ser* 'above, over, upon; for; besides'.
ᴸᵁUKU; read ᴸᵁNIMGIR.
UKÙ = *antuhsas* 'human being, man'.
UKÙ = *antuhsatar, antuhsannanza* 'humanity, mankind, people'.
UGULA 'foreman'.
  UGULA LÚ.MEŠ *LIMTU* 'captain of a thousand men'.
UKUŠ; LÚ.MEŠ UKUŠ, ERÍN.MEŠ UKUŠ, a kind of troops; 'heavy armed troops'? Götze, AM 229 f.
UKU.UŠ; read UKUŠ.
ukus = *uk* + *us* 'ego eos'.
UL (usually written Ú-UL) = *natta* 'not'.
?*ules-* (pret. *ulesta*); *kattan sarā u.* 'conspire with'?? Friedrich, AO 24.3.7.32; Chrest. 184.33, 196. Perhaps one should read *kal-li-eš-ta*.
uliliyas (gen.?) 'field'. Sommer, AF 85.
ulis- (pret. *ulista*); *andan u.* 'join in'?? KUB 17.10.1.12 f. (W).
ulkessarahh-; see *walkessarahh-*.
UMMA 'as follows'; employed only in Akkadian introductory formulae. Sommer, BoSt. 10.1; Chrest. 84 f. Cf. Hrozný, SH 14; Götze, Hatt. 77 f., who believe that *U.* represents a Hittite noun for 'words' or the like.
ᴸᵁ*UMMEĀNU* = ᴸᵁ*ummiyann-* 'master workman; artisan'.
  DUMU *UM.MI.A.AN* 'artisan' or 'artisan's apprentice'. Hrozný, CH 134.23.
ᴸᚒ·ᴹᴱˢ*ummiyannes* (pl.) 'artisans'? KUB 10.1.1.5.
ummiyandus (acc. pl.) 'young'?? Hrozný, CH 110.9. 'Found'?? Walther, HC 264.120; cf. *wemiya/e-*.
UMMU = *annas* 'mother'.
U.MU; read UDUN.
ŪMU = *siwaz* 'day'.
UN; read UKÙ.
*unattallas (acc. *unattallan*) 'merchant'. Friedrich, ZA NF 2.46; HG 157, 292.
uni (often indeclinable; acc. *unin*) 'that, the aforementioned'. Friedrich, Vert. 1.155 f.; HG 201, 207.
ūnna-, unne/a- (*ūnnai*, pl. *ūnnanzi*, pret. 1 pl. *ūnnummen, ūnnummin*, imper. 2 sg. *unni*) 'lead hither, drive hither, bring; drive, ride,

march hither'. Sommer, BoSt. 10.75 fn. 1; Friedrich, ZA NF 2.52 f.; Sturtevant, Lang. 7.2 f., HG 214; Götze, AOr. 5.22 fn. 3. Cf. *unnes-, unniya/e-*.

ūnnes- (pret. *ūnnesta, ūnnista*) 'lead hither, drive hither, bring; drive, ride, march hither'. See *ūnna-*.

ŭn(n)iya/e- (pl. *ūnniyanzi, ūnnianzi, uniyanzi*) 'lead hither, drive hither, bring; drive, ride, march hither'. See *unna-*; cf. *neya/e-*.

unnummen; see *unna-*.

?*unu-* (midd. pret. *unuttat*) 'cause to be seen, show'; midd. 'show oneself'? KUB 17.5.1.5. Cf. *au-, aus-, u-*; but *unuttat* may be a variant form from *unuwa(e)-*.

unuanda; see *unuwa(e)-*.

UNŪTU (pl. *UNŪTE*) 'utensil, set of utensils'.

unuwa(e)- (*unuwwaizzi*, pl. *unuwanzi*, midd. *unuwatari*, 1 sg. *unuwahhari*, part. *unuwanza*, neut. pl. *unuanda*) 'adorn'. Sommer, BoSt. 10.74 f.; Götze-Pedersen, MS 72. Cf. *unu-*.

*unuwashas (pl. acc. *unuwashus*) 'adornment'. Götze, KlF 1.179 and fn. 3; HG 160; Götze-Pedersen, MS 72.

unuwwaizzi; see *unuwa(e)-*.

ŭp- (*ŭpzi*, pret. *ūpta*) 'rise' (of the sun). Hrozný, SH 3; Sommer, BoSt. 7.27; HG 102.

ᴸᵁ*UBĀRU* (pl. ᴸᵁ·ᴹᴱˢ*UBĀRŪTIM*) 'citizen'.

ᴸᵁ*Ū-BA-AŠ*; read ᴸᵁ*Ū-BA-RUM*.

↑*upati-* (gen. *upatiyas*, dat. *upati*) 'the east'? Forrer, Forsch. 1.8.30; Sturtevant, JAOS 54.368.44, 399. Cf. *up-*.

UPNU = hazzilas? 'handful'.

uppă- (*uppāi*, 1 sg. *uppahhi*, pl. *uppanzi*) 'send hither, send'. Hrozný, SH 122 fn. 2; Götze, NBr. 20 f., AOr. 5.22 fn. 3; HG 214. Cf. *uppe/a-, uppes-*.

uppe/a- (pret. pl. *uppir, upir*, imper. 2 sg. *uppi*) 'send hither'. See *uppa-*.

uppes- (pret. *uppesta*) 'send hither'. See *uppa-*.

uppessar (pl. *uppessar*-ḪI.A, *upessarri*-ḪI.A) 'gift'. Hrozný, SH 80 fn. 3; Götze, Hatt. 102; HG 152.

uppiske/a- 'send hither'. Hrozný, SH 122 fn. 2.

ᴳᴵˢ*UBRI*; read ᴳᴵˢ*ŠUKUR*.

UR 'wild dog, wild animal'.

ÛR = *happessar*? 'part of the body'. The ideogram means particularly 'leg, thigh; lap, loins, sexual parts'.

4.ÛR-*kis* 'quadruped'?? KUB 18.10.1.3 (Walther, by letter).

GIŠÛR 'beam'.
ura-; see *wara-*.
uritenan; see *weritenas*.
uriwaran; see *wariwaran*.
*ūrkis (acc. *ūrkin*) 'trace'. Ehelolf ap. Götze, KlF 1.196 fn. 2.
ūrkiya/e- (*ūrkiyaizzi*) 'trace, track, find'. Hrozný, CH 120.30. See *urkis*.
UR.KU; read UR.TÚG.
UR.MAḪ 'lion'.
UR.BAR.RA 'wolf'.
UR.BAR.RA = *Luwis* 'Luwian'. Cf. Ungnad, ZA NF 1.1–8.
URPU = *alpas* 'cloud'.
URRAM ŠĒRAM 'today and tomorrow, forever'? Friedrich, ZA NF 2.282.
ūrrir (pret. pl.) 'they burnt'. KBo 3.60.2.7. See *wara-*.
UR.SAG = *tarhwilannas* (gen. of *tarhwilatar*) 'mighty; hero'.
ursan (KASKAL-*an*, dat. *ursi*, pl. KASKAL-*sa*) 'road, journey, campaign'. Götze-Pedersen, MS 22, 54; Sommer, AU 410, s.v. KAS.
  ursan epp- 'undertake a journey'.
  ursi dai-, tittanu- 'put on the way'.
UR.TÚG 'dog'.
UR.TUR 'small dog, young dog'.
URU = *ĀLU* = *happiris* 'town, city; subdivision of a city'; also a determinative before names of towns and of countries.
  URU.AŠ.AŠ.ḪI.A 'towns, cities'.
  URU.AŠ.AŠ.ḪI.A BÀD 'fortified towns'.
  URU.BÀD 'fortified town'.
URU-*riyasessar* 'population'. Götze, Madd. 143 fn. 1, AM 134.6.
URU.ḪAL; read URU.AŠ.AŠ and see s.v. URU.
LÚURU₄.LAL; read LÚAPIN.LAL.
URUD.LID × A; read URUDDU₁₀ × A.
URUD(U) 'copper'; also a determinative.
  LÚ.MEŠ URUD.DA 'coppersmiths, metal workers'.
LÚURUD(U).NAGAR 'coppersmith, metal worker'.
GIŠURU.URUD; read GIŠBANŠUR.
UŠ; read NITA.
-*us* 'eos', acc. pl. of -*as*.
✢*usāiha* (pret. 1 sg.) 'I hindered, prevented' or the like. Friedrich, IF 49.229; Sommer, AU 161, 163.
Ú.SAL = *wellu* 'meadow'.

usantaris (also *usandaris*) 'bearing young'? KUB 12.58.1.28, 4.8-13.
   u. halis 'calf pen'?
uske/a- 'see, observe'. Hrozný, SH 56; Götze, Madd. 108 f.; HG 96, 117. See *au-, aus-.*
   menahhanda 'look for, wait for'. Sturtevant, JAOS 54.405.
UŠKĒN = *aruwaizzi* = 'he bows before, he worships'. Ehelolf, OLZ 27.580 f.; Götze-Pedersen, MS 37.
UŠKĒN = *henkzi, henga, hengari, henkatta* 'shows reverence'. *UŠKĒNU* = *henkanta* 'they show reverence'. Götze-Pedersen, MS 33-8. Cf. Sommer, BoSt. 10.27.
^{LÚ}*uskiskat(t)allas* (*uskisgatallas*, pl. acc. *uskiskattallus*) 'observer, watchman'. Götze, Madd. 106-10; HG 157.
**uskisgat(t)allatar* (dat. *uskisgattal[lanni]*, variant *uskiskitallanni*) 'watchmanship'. Götze, Madd. 108 and fn. 3; HG 151.
uskiske/a- 'see, observe'. Götze, Madd. 108.
uskiskitallanni; see *uskisgattallatar*.
^{LÚ}UŠ.KU; read ^{LÚ}GALA.
^{LÚ}UŠMAŠ; read ^{LÚ}AZU.
usneske/a-; read *ussneske/a-*.
usniya/e-; read *ussniya/e-*.
^{LÚ}UŠBAR; read ^{LÚ}AZU.
^{LÚ}UŠ.BAR 'weaver'.
ussaniske/a-; read *ussneske/a-*.
ussaniya/e-; read *ussniya/e-*.
ussiya/e- 'draw in, draw on', or the like. Götze, AOr. 5.22 fn. 3; but see HG 225.
ussneske/a- (pret. *ussaniskit*, midd. *usneskitta*) 'offer for sale, sell'. Walther, HC 266.146, 147; KUB 21.27.4.40 (G).
ussniya/e- (*ussaniyazi, usniyazi*, 2 pl. *usniyatteni*, pret. *ussaniyat*) 'offer for sale, sell'. Götze, Madd. 99 and fnn. 1, 2; HG 113.
UŠTAḪIZZU, causative pret. pl. of *AḪĀZU*, = *weriyer* 'they commissioned'. Sommer, AU 386.
^{GIŠ}Ú.ŠUM.GA; read ^{GIŠ}Ú.TAG.GA.
UD; read BABBAR 'white'.
UD = *ŪMU* = *siwaz* 'day'. Cf. UD.KAM.
UD-*tili*; see *siwatili*.
^{D}UD; read ^{D}UTU.
uda- (*udai*, 1 sg. *udahhi*, pl. *udanzi*, 1 pl. *utummēni*, pret. *udas*, 1 pl. *utumen*) 'bring'. Sommer, ZA 33.87 f.; Götze, Hatt. 110, AOr. 5.22 fn. 3; Sturtevant, Lang. 7.1-5, HG 101, 214. Cf. Götze-Pedersen, MS 17; but see Sturtevant, Lang. 11.38. Cf. *ute/a-*.

arha u. 'bring away'.
katta u. 'bring down'.
menahhanda u. 'bring to meet, bring to'.
ᴳᴵŨ.TAG.GA 'arrow'. Götze, Hatt. 104.
U + DAR.RA; see s.v. NINDA.
uda(s) 'such'??? Götze, Madd. 145 and fn. 2.
utĕ/a- (pret. pl. *utĕr, utir*) 'bring'. See *uda-*.
uteske/a- (1 sg. *utiskimi*, pl. *utinzi*, pret. pl. *uteskir*) 'bring'. See *uda-*.
UD.KAM = ŨMU = *siwaz* 'day'. An ordinal numeral, if one is used, stands after UD and is accompanied by KAM. Cf. UD.
UD.KAM-*tili*; see *siwatili*.
UD.KA.BAR; read ZABAR.
ᴸᵁUD.KA.BAR.DIB; read ᴸᵁZABAR.DIB.
udnalliske/a- 'bewitch, conjure'. KBo. 5.2.3.38, 53. Cf. *uddanalliya/e-*.
udnĕ (*udnē, udni*, one may as well transcribe *utne, utni*) 'country'. Hrozný, BoSt. 3.96 fn. 11; HG 97, 182; Götze-Pedersen, MS 79 f.; Bonfante, IF 52.223.
udnĕyanza (*udneyanza, udnēanza, udniyanza*, KUR-*eyanza*, acc. *udniandan*) 'country, population'. Friedrich, Vert. 1.85 f.; HG 159.
udniya, dat. of *udne*.
ᴳᴵˢUD.SAL.KAB, an implement with which a man is struck on the head. Deimel, No. 381.460.
UD.SAR (abl. UD.SAR-*za*) 'new moon, crescent'.
uddanalliya/e- (also *uttanalliya/e-*) 'bewitch, conjure'. Hrozný, BoSt. 5.33 and fn. 10; Götze, Madd. 97 and fnn. 5, 6. Cf. *udnalliske/a-*.
uddaniya/e- 'conjure'. Götze, Madd. 99.
uttăr (*uttar, uddār*, gen. *uddanas*) 'word; magic spell, magic formula; thing, affair; cause, law-case'. Hrozný, SH 65–8; Marstrander, Car. 141 f.; Sturtevant, Lang. 6.157, HG 84, 113, 164 f.; Kurylowicz, EI 75 fn. 1.
UD.DU.A; read Ê.A.
UDU 'sheep'.
ᴰUTU = ŠAMŠU (nom. ᴰUTU-*us*, acc. ᴰUTU-*un*, gen. ᴰUTU-*was*) = ᴰ*Istanus* 'sun'.
ᴰUTU-ŠI = ŠAMŠI (nom. ᴰUTU-ŠI-*mes*?, dat. ᴰUTU-*mi*) 'my sungod, my majesty', a standing designation of the reigning Hittite king. Hrozný, SH 4, etc.; Friedrich, Vert. 2.139; Chrest. 86.
UDU.A.LUM, a very valuable kind of sheep. Deimel, No. 538.153.
UDU.ÁŠ.SAL.GÀR 'lamb'. Hrozný, CH 54.36.
UDU.KUR.RA 'mountain sheep'.

UTÚL 'stew, pottage'.
ᴅᵁᴳUTÚL 'pot'.
utummeni, utumen, 1 pl. of *uda-*.
UDUN 'stove'.
UDU.NITA, UDU.NITÁ 'male sheep'.
UDU.ŠE 'fat sheep'.
UDU.SÍG + SAL 'female wool-bearing sheep'.
UDU.ŠIR 'ram'.
uwa- (pret. pl. *uwantat,* imper. 1 sg. *uwahharu*) 'appear, be seen'. Friedrich, ZA NF 3.203. Cf. *au-, aus-, u-*.
uwa-; see *we/a-* 'come'.
uwa(e)- (*uwaitta, uwaittari*) 'be pitied'. Sommer ap. Chrest. 171.
uwahnuw(w)ar, uwahnuwaw(w)ar; read *wahnu(w)ar*.
uwai (acc.) 'invidiam; iniuriam'. Chrest. 89. Cf. Götze, NBr. 2.6. Possibly the original meaning was 'pity'; cf. *uwa(e)-, uwainu-*.
uwāinu- (imper. 2 sg. *uwāinut, uwayanut*) 'cause to be pitied' (w. dat. of the person who feels the pity). KUB 6.45.3.35; 21.27.4.38. Cf. *uwa(e)-, uwai*.
uwakke/a-; read *wewakke/a-*. HG 58-60.
uwallu; imper. 1 sg. of *au-, aus-, u-* 'see'. Friedrich, IF 43.258 fn. 5; ZA NF 3.186 fn. 1.
uwantat; see *uwa-*.
uwanun; see *we/a-*.
uwanzi; see *au-, aus-, u-*.
uwarkantan; see *warkanza*.
uwas 'son'. Götze, ZA NF 2.81 f.
uwastai; see *wasta-*.
*uwatallas; ᴸᵁ̇·ᴹᴱˢ*parā uwatallus* (pl.) 'those who overlook, neglect'. Götze, Madd. 107 and fn. 1. Cf. *au-, aus-, u-* w. preverb *para*.
uwatar 'sight; review, parade'. Friedrich, AOF 10.295; Sturtevant, JAOS 56. 284-7. Cf. Götze, KlF 1.197 and fnn. 4-7.
uwate/a- (probably to be read *wate-*, but always written *uwatezzi,* pl. *uwadanzi, uwatanzi,* etc.) 'bring'. Hrozný, BoSt. 3.114 fn. 4; Sommer, BoSt. 4.10 fn. 2; Sturtevant, Lang. 7.3-5, HG 275 f.; Götze, AOr. 5.22 fn. 3.
   arha u. 'bring away'.
   katta u. 'bring down'.
   kattan u. 'secum adferre'.
   piran sarā u. 'bring up before'.
uwayanu-; see *uwainu-*.

uwellut; variant for *uwallu*?? Friedrich, ZA NF 5.47 fn. 2.
uwitar, uwitenas, etc.; see *watar*.
uyanun; read *weyanun* and see *weya-* 'drive, send'.
ÙZ 'goat'. Hrozný, CH 136.36 f., distinguishes between ÙZ and MÁŠ; but perhaps one should read MÁŠ in both places.
UZNU = *istamanas* 'ear'.
    UZNĀ (dual) 'ears'.
UZU (abl. UZU-*naz*) 'flesh, flesh and blood'; also a determinative before names of fleshy parts of the body. Cf. Götze, AM 247.
ᴸᵛUZÙ; read ᴸᵛAZU.
uzuhris; read ᵛ*zuhris*.
UZU.NI; read ᵘᶻᵘYĀ.
UZU.NI 'flesh and blood'? Götze, AM 247.
UZU.SA; read ᵘᶻᵘSA.
UZU.YĀ; read ᵘᶻᵘYĀ.
WA; read GEŠTU(G).
-*wa* (-*war* before forms of the pronoun-*as*), a particle normally appended to the first full word of each sentence in a direct quotation. Hrozný, SH 143 f., 185; Ungnad, ZDMG 74.417–22; Friedrich, Vert. 1.174 f., 175 fn. 1, ZA NF 5.43 f.; Sommer, AU 134. Cf. Sturtevant, Lang. 6.227, HG 121 and fn. 79.
wa-; see *we/a-*.
wā- (*wāi*) 'coo' (of a dove)? Götze, Madd. 142 and fn. 5.
?*waelis*; see *selis*.
wah-; see *weh-*.
wahannas; see *wehannas*.
*wahessar (gen. *wahesnas*); *wahesnas watar* 'water for rinsing'? KUB 7.1.1.28–34. Cf. *weh-*.
wahnu- 'cause to turn, turn, wind'. Sommer, BoSt. 4.4–8, 7.40 fn. 1, 10.72; Kurylowicz, Symb. Gramm. 102; Sturtevant, Lang. 6.152, HG 234. Cf. *weh-*.
  anda w. 'wind in, surround'.
  appa w. 'turn back'.
  arha w. 'turn (something) away, swing away'.
  parā w. 'bring (a litter) before the door'. KUB 11.32.3.8.
  piran w. 'praeverti, get ahead'; *w.* acc. 'get ahead of'. Götze, KlF 1.224 f.
  ser w. 'overthrow' or 'brandish over'? Chrest. 90.
  KARAŠ *w.* 'pitch a camp'. Götze, AM 318.

wahnu- = *warnu-* 'burn'. Götze-Pedersen, MS 28–32. Cf. Friedrich, OLZ 39.305 f.
wahnumar 'a turning'. Cf. *wahnuwwar*.
  appa w. 'a pardon'. Sturtevant, JAOS 54.401.
  arahzanta w. 'circuit, encirclement'. Sommer, BoSt. 4.6.
wahnuske- 'cause to turn, turn, wind'. See *wahnu-*.
wahnuw(w)ar (*uwahnuwwar, uwahnuwar, wahnuwwar; uwahnuwawar* and *uwahnuwawwar* are probably unintentional dittographies) 'circuit of a race track, lap'. Forrer, ZDMG 76.256; HG 57, 58, 116. Cf. Sommer, BoSt. 4.8 f. Cf. *wahnumar*.
wāin (acc.), something unpleasant. Sommer, Hirt Festschrift 2.294 fn. 2.
wăk- (*wāki*, pret. 1 pl. *wākwēn*, infin. *waganna, waqanna, wakanna*) 'bite'. Götze, Madd. 142; Friedrich, AOr. 6.373–6. 'Eat breakfast'? KUB 25.51.4.11 f. (G).
wagessar (also *wakkisar*); NINDA *w.* 'a bite of bread, breakfast bread', or the like. Cf. Friedrich, AOr. 6.376.
wagganza, variant for *warkanza* 'fat'. Friedrich, ZA NF 3.186, AOr. 6.375.
wakkăr- (*waqqāri, waggāri*, pret. *waqqares*) 'be lacking'; *mausswanzi wakkares* 'he almost fell'. Friedrich, Vert. 2.171 and fn. 1; HG 117.
wakkariya/e- (*waggariyazi, waqqariyazi, waggariyaizzi, waggariizzi*) 'revolt, rebel'. Sommer, BoSt. 7.47; Weidner, AOF 1.60 f.; Friedrich, ZA NF 1.11 and fn. 1; HG 117. Cf. Friedrich, Vert. 2.171. Cf. *wakkar-*.
wakkariyanu- (pret. 1 sg. BAL-*nunun*) 'cause to revolt'. Sommer, AU 218 fn. 1.
wakkariyawwar (*waqqariyawwar*) 'revolt, insurrection'. KUB 23.11.3.6. See *wakkariya/e-*.
waggasnu- (pl. *waggasnuanzi*) 'omit' or 'rear'?? Chrest. 119, 169.
wakkisar; see *wagessar*.
waksiya/e- 'be lacking'? Götze ap. Chrest. 169.
waksiyanu- 'cause to fall short of'? See *waksiya/e-*.
waksur, a vessel for relatively valuable foods. (G).
walahh-, walh-; read *walhh-*.
walhanna- (*walhannai*) 'strike, attack'. Götze, Madd. 130; HG 245. See *walhh-*.
walhanneske/a- (pl. *walhanniskanzi*, GUL-*anneskanzi*) 'strike, attack'. HG 238. See *walhh-*.

walhanniya/e- 'strike, attack'. HG 225. See *walhh-*.

walhh- (*walahzi*, GUL-*ahzi*, pl. *walhanzi*, *walahhanzi*, pret. *walahta*, GUL-*ahta*, 1 sg. *walahhun*, GUL-*ahhun*, *walhūn*, imper. 2 sg. *walah*) 'strike, attack'. Hrozný, BoSt. 3.206 fn. 5; Sommer, BoSt. 10.76 f.; Benveniste, BSL 33.137; Couvreur, Hett. *h* 19. Cf. HG 121.

walhheske/a- (*walahheskizzi*) 'strike, attack'. Sommer, AU 76. See *walhh-*.

walhhi (*walhi*, gen. *walhiyas*, *walahhiyas*, inst. *walhit*), a sacrificial drink. Tenner, HAT 24.

ᴸᵁ́*walhhiyalas* (*walahhiyalas*), one who prepares or one who uses *walhhi*. HG 159. See *walhhi*.

waliya/e- 'praise'. Forrer, Forsch. 1.260.52; Sommer, AU 230. Cf. *wallahhi*, *walleske/a-*.

walkessarahh- (*walkissarahhi*, pret. pl. *ulkessarahhir*) 'make expert, make skillful'. HG 59. See *walkessaras*.

walkessaras (*walkissaras*) 'expert, skillful'. Hrozný, SH 40; Friedrich, ZA NF 1.184, Vert. 2.170 and fn. 2; HG 144 and fn. 3.

wallahhi (1 sg.) 'I praise'? Götze, AM 262; see *walleske/a-*. Cf. *waliya/e-*.

ᵁᶻᵁ*wallas* 'leg'?? Sayce, RA 24.125; KUB 20.1.3.7.

wallas 'leg, support' (of the ᴳᴵˢ*istanan-*)?? KBo. 4.1.1.47–2.4.

walleske/a- 'praise'; w. -*za* 'boast'. Sommer, BoSt. 7.59 and fn. 1. See *waliya/e-*, *wallahhi*.

walli 'clipped' (of hides)'?? Hrozný, CH 140.13; Walther, HC 271.185.

walliyatar 'glorification, praise'. Götze, KlF 1.227, Kulturg. 156 and fn. 6. Cf. *waliya/e-*, *wallahhi*.

walluske/a- 'be strong'?? Forrer, Forsch. 2.30.12.

wantai- (pret. *wantais*) 'be warm, glow; be angry'. Götze, KlF 1.187 and fn. 3; Sturtevant, RHA 1.85; Carruthers, Lang. 9.158 f.

wantemas 'heat, lightning'. Götze, KlF 1.187 and fnn. 1, 2; Carruthers, Lang. 9.158 f.; Götze-Pedersen, MS 16 fn. 2.

wantes- 'become warm'. Ehelolf ap. Götze, KlF 187 fn. 3.

wantewantemas 'heat; lightning'. See *wantemas*.

wappiya/e- 'bark' (of a dog or like a dog). Götze, Madd. 145.

*wappus (gen. *wappuwas*, *wappuwwas*, *wappuas*, dat. *wappui*, *wappuwi*, pl. *wappus*) 'grave' or 'trench'?? Friedrich, ZA NF 3.192. 'Cave'??? Forrer, RHA 1.146. 'Earth, ground'? (G).

ᵁᶻᵁ*wappuzzi*, a variant for *appuzzi*. Ehelolf, ZA NF 9.173 fn. 1.

-*war-*; see -*wa*.

WORD LIST 177

wară- (midd. *warāni, waranni, urāni*, pl. *warandari*, imper. *warānu, urānu*, part. *warănza*) 'burn' (intransitive). Sommer, KlF 1.120–4, 346 and fn. 1; HG 58, 264; Benveniste, BSL 33.136 f.; Petersen, Lang. 9.20 f.; Götze-Pedersen, MS 74. Cf. HG 123.

warap-; read *warp-*.

warass-; read *warss-*.

waressa-; see *warressa-*.

waressis-; see *warresses-*.

warhuis; read *warhwis*.

warhunu- 'make rough; make inaccessible'. Götze, AM 238 f. Cf. *warhwis*.

warhwis (gen. *warhuwayas*) 'shaggy, with the wool unshorn; rough; inaccessible'? Götze, AM 238; Sturtevant, Lang. 10.268.

*wariwaranza (neut. *wariwaran, uriwaran*) 'burning'. Sommer, KlF 1.346 and fn. 1; HG 58 f.

warkanza (acc. *uwark[antan]*, neut. *warkan*, pl. *warkantes, wargantes, waggantes*). 'fat'. Friedrich, ZA NF 3.186.

warkan 'fat meat, animal fat'. KBo. 3.46.1.13.

⸸*warkus*, an unfavorable quality that is taken away from a god by ritual means. KUB 17.10.3.12.

warnu- (sometimes written *wahnu-*) 'cause to burn, burn'. Sommer, BoSt. 10.10; Friedrich, ZA NF 2.48 f.; Götze-Pedersen, 28–32, 74. *arha w.* 'burn up, burn down, burn completely'.

warnuske/a- 'cause to burn, burn'. See *warnu-*.

warp- (*warapzi*, pl. *warpanzi*) 'wash, bathe', especially with soap; often reflexive. Ehelolf, KlF 1.144–60; HG 91.

warpa, warpi (dat.); *w. dai-, tiya/e-* 'place in an enclosure, fence in; surround, besiege'. Götze, AM 237–9, 239 fn. 1.

warpallis 'strong'? Ehelolf, KlF 1.160; Hrozný, AOr. 4.115; Sturtevant, Lang. 10.267.

warpannalan '(ritually) washed'?? Ehelolf, KlF 1.160.

warpiske/a- 'wash, bathe', especially with soap. See *warpa-*.

warpuzi, a bronze implement used in washing. Ehelolf, KlF 1.156; HG 155.

warră(e)- (*warrāizzi*, pret. *warrait*, imper. 2 sg. *warrāi*); *anda w.* 'come to the rescue, bring as help'. Götze, ZA NF 2.15, AM 122.17. Cf. *warressa-, warris*.

warres(s)a- (2 sg. *warressatti, warrissatti, warrisatti*, pl. *warrissanzi*, part. pl. *warrissantes, war<r>essantes*) 'come to the rescue'.

Hrozný, BoSt. 3.174 fn. 6; Götze, Madd. 105, AM 210; Sturtevant, Lang. 7.171, HG 246.

anda w. is equivalent to *w.* alone.

warresses- (pret. *warressesta, warrissista*) 'come to the rescue'. Sturtevant, Lang. 8.127, HG 230. See *warressa-*.

warris (neut. *warri*, gen. *warras*) 'helpful'; neut. 'help'. Hrozný, BoSt. 3.174 fn. 6; Ungnad, OLZ 26, 572 fn. 3; Friedrich, Vert. 1.39 f., 2.92 f.

warrissa-; read *warressa-*.

⁑*warruwalanas*; see ⁑ *warwalani*.

ᴳᴵˢ*warsammas* or GIŠ *warsammas*, something that is burned. Götze, NBr. 60 f.

wars(a)nu- (*warsanuzzi*, pl. *warsanuanzi*, imper. pl. *warsnuandu, warasnuwandu, warsanuwandu*) 'cause to be well disposed, propitiate'. See *warss-*.

warsas 'rain'? Friedrich, Vert. 2.35 and fn. 5; Benveniste, BLS 33.138.

warse/a- (*warsezzi*) 'mulcere, mulceri'. See *warss-*.

warsiya/e- 'mulcere, mulceri'. See *warss-*.

warsiyanu- 'cause to be well disposed, propitiate'. Götze, KlF 1.192 fn. 4, NBr. 61 fn. 1. Cf. *warsanu-, warsiya/e-*.

warsiyaz (gen. *warsiyattas*) 'appeasement, propitiation'. Götze, Madd. 79 and fn. 10; HG 149. Cf. *warsiya/e-*.

warss- (*warsi, waraszi*, pl. *warassanzi*, pret. *warsta*) act. 'mulcere, stroke, rub, soothe, make propitious; reap (a field), clear (a mountain, a road)'; act. and midd. 'be well disposed, be propitious; be calm, be at rest'. Friedrich, ZA NF 3.202; Götze, KlF 1.192–7; Benveniste, BSL 33.137. Cf. *warsiya/e-*.

*warsŭl (gen *warsulas*, dat. *warsŭli*) 'appeasement, propitiation'. HG 148. See *warss-*.

?*wartanzi* (pl.) 'they tie or braid (horses' tails)'?? Forrer, ZDMG 76.258 f. Perhaps an error for *warsanzi*.

⁑*warwalani*, ⁑*warwalantes*, ⁑*warruwalanas* 'seed, descendants'. Sommer, BoSt. 7.58 and fn. 1, OLZ 33.757.

wăs- (*wăsi*, 2 sg. *wasti*) 'buy'. Sommer, BoSt. 10.74; Friedrich, Vert. 1.92 fn. 4, HG 113.

was-; see *wess-*.

wasiya/e- 'buy'. Sturtevant, JAOS 54.376.49. Cf. *was-*.

*waskus (pl. *waskwēs*, acc. *waskus*, gen.-dat. *waskuwas*) 'sin'? Friedrich, ZA NF 3.199; Götze, KlF 1.191; Sommer, AF 85.

wass-; see *wess-*.

*wassă- (pl. *wassanti*, midd. *wassāri*, imper. *wassāru*) 'put on (clothes), clothe'. Hrozný, BoSt. 5.38; Sommer, AU 108. Cf. *wess-, wass-*.
wasse/a- (*wassezzi*, 2 sg. *wassāsi*, pl. *wassanzi*, part. *wassanza*) 'put on (clothes), clothe, cover'. HG 223. Cf. *wess-, wass-*.
wasseske/a- (2 sg. *wasseskisi*) 'put on (clothes), clothe'. KUB 24.7.2.9. Cf. *wess-, wass-*.
wassi (also *wassi*-ḪI.A) 'clothes'??? Witzel, HKU 114.25, 116.40, 41.
wassiya/e- (*wassiyazi*, *wassiyazzi*, *wassiezzi*) 'put on (clothes), clothe, cover'. Ehelolf, KlF 1.153. Cf. *wess-, wass-*.
wassuttal 'garment'? KUB 11.13.5.12. Cf. *wess-*.
wast- (*wasti*, pret. pl. *waster*) 'sin, harm'. See *wasta-*.
wastă- (*wastăi*, *uwastai*, 2 sg. *wastăsi*, *wastati*, *wastatti*, pret. *wastas*, 2 sg. *wastas*, *wastais*, verb. n. *wasdumar*) 'be at fault, sin; harm'. Hrozný, CH 4.7, 8, 142.20, 23, 148.16; Sommer, BoSt. 10.2 fn. 1, 74; Friedrich, Vert. 1.178; Götze, Madd. 59 fn. 6.
katta w. 'sin with, violate (sexually)'.
wastais 'sin, injury'. Sommer, BoSt. 10.2 fn. 1; HG 147.
wastanu- 'cause to sin'; of a god 'make (something) a sin, interpret as a sin'. Götze, KlF 1.184. Cf. *wasta-*.
wasteske/a- 'be at fault, sin, harm'. Götze, KlF 1.214.1.
?*wasti* (2 sg.) 'you cause (an ox) to graze'? Ehelolf ap. Sommer, AU 391. Cf. *wesis, wesiya/e-*.
wastul (dat. *wasduli*, *wastulli*) 'injury, sin'. Hrozný, CH 148.6; Sommer, BoSt. 10.2, AF 85; Friedrich, Vert. 1.158; HG 148. Cf. *wast-, wasta-*.
wasdumar 'injury, sin'. Sommer, BoSt. 7.47. See *wasta-*.
wātar, wetăr (*watar, uwātar*, gen. *witenas, wetenas, wētnas*, dat. *witěni, weteni*, inst. *wetenit, wedanda*, pl.? *widār, uwitar*, dat. *uwitenas*) 'water'. Hrozný, MDOG 56.33, SH 61–5; Sommer, BoSt. 7.2 and fn. 3, AU 94 fn. 1; Sturtevant, HG 94, 113, 165, 169, Lang. 11.184.
wătarnahh- (*wătarnahhi*, pret. *wătarnahta, watarnahhis*) w. dat. 'communicate'; w. acc. 'command, challenge'. Götze, Hatt. 96; Friedrich, Vert. 2.22; Sommer, AU 223; Sturtevant, Lang. 6.157, HG 84, 113.
anda w. 'commend'.
watarnahhaz 'communication, command'. Götze, Madd. 79 fn. 11.
watarnahheske/a- 'communicate, command, challenge'. Zimmern, Streitberg Festgabe 434.47; KBo. 3.7.3.9.
watk- (midd. imper. 2 sg. *watqahhut*, verb. n. *watkuwwar*) 'leap'. Friedrich, Vert. 1.27, 2.156. See *watku-*.

watku- (*watkuzi, watkuzzi*, pret. *watkut*) 'leap, flee; set (of a star)'. Hrozný, BoSt. 3.14 fn. 1, CH 150.19, 22; Sommer, BoSt. 10.8 and fn. 1; Friedrich, ZA NF 2.54; Sturtevant, Lang. 6.220, 226 f., HG 235 and fn. 42. Cf. *watk-*.

watkunu- 'cause to flee, drive away'. See *watku-*.

    arha w. 'drive away'.

*wattais (acc. MUŠEN-*in*, pl. *wattaēs*) 'bird'? Friedrich, ZA NF 3.190 fn. 1; Götze-Pedersen, MS 61.

we/a- (*wizzi*, pl. *uwanzi, wenzi*, pret. *wet*, 1 sg. *uwanun*, pl. *wēr*) 'come'; sometimes a mere introduction to the following verb, in which case there is no sentence connective between them, and the subject follows *we/a-*. Hrozný, SH 75, 243 f.; Sommer, BoSt. 10.92; Friedrich, Vert. 1.162 f., 162 fn. 2; Meillet, MSL 23.258; Benveniste, BSL 33.137; Götze, AOr. 5.16 fn. 1; Götze-Pedersen, MS 73. Cf. Götze, Hatt. 84, Madd. 60 fn. 3. Cf. Sturtevant, Lang. 6.221, 7.9–13, HG 121 and fn. 79, 122.

    anda w. 'come in'.

    andan w. 'come in, take quarters in'. Götze, AOr. 5.19 f.

    appa w. 'come back'.

    arha w. 'come away, go away'. Sommer, AU 81 f.

    katta w. 'come down'.

    menahhanda w. 'come to meet, come against'.

    parā w. 'come forth'.

    piran appa w. 'go back and forth, versari' (especially in a temple). (G).

    piran sarā w. 'come up before'.

    sarā w. 'come up'.

wĕh-, wah- (*wĕhzi, wahzi*, pl. *wahanzi*, pret. 1 sg. *wehun*, part. *wahanza*, midd. *wēhtari, wehatta, wehattari*, pl. *wehantari, wehandari*), act. and midd., 'turn, fall; versari'. Hrozný, BoSt. 3.145 fn. 5; Sommer, BoSt. 7.40 and fn. 1; Sturtevant, Lang. 4.161, 12, No. 3, HG 220; Götze, NBr. 61; Götze-Pedersen, MS 74.

wehannas, wahannas; ANŠU.KUR.RA.MEŠ *w.* 'Zug-Pferde'?? Götze, NBr. 50.24, 55 and fn. 1, 61.

weheske/a- 'turn, versari; patrol'. Friedrich, ZA NF 5.38; Sturtevant, JAOS 54.402. Cf. *weh-, wah-*.

LÚ.MEŠ*wehesgattallas* (pl.) 'patrolmen'. See *weheske/a-*.

wĕk- (*wēkzi*, pl. *wekanzi*, pret. *wekta*, 1 sg. *wekun*, pl. *wekir*, part. *wekantan*) 'demand, ask, beg'. Sommer, BoSt. 7.55 and fn. 2; Friedrich,

IF 41.369 f.; Sturtevant, Lang. 6.214, HG 89. Cf. *wewakk-*, *wekiske/a-, weske/a-*.
   anku w., w. dat., 'invite to'?? Cf. Götze, KlF 1.210.4.
wekiske/a- 'demand, ask, beg'. Friedrich, Vert. 2.160. Cf. *wek-, weske/a-*.
wekuwar 'an asking'. See *wek-*.
wĕlku, welkuwan, a plant. Friedrich, ZA NF 1.182, 5.74; Benveniste, BSL 33.138.
wĕllu, wĕllus 'meadow'. Friedrich, ZA NF 1.181 f., AOF 4.94.
wemiske/a- 'come upon, find'. See *wemiya/e-*.
wemiya/e- (wemiyazi, wemiyazzi, wemiazzi, wemiizi, wemiēzi, wemiēzzi) 'come upon, find'. Sommer, BoSt. 7.47 fn. 3; Götze, Hatt. 90, AM 320; Friedrich, ZA NF 2.51; Benveniste, BSL 33.137; Sturtevant, Lang. 11.39.
   anda w. 'meet'.
   appan w. 'overtake, surprise'? Friedrich, ZA NF 2.278.
wen- (wenzi) 'sleep with (a woman)'??? Hrozný, CH 144.33; Zimmern-Friedrich, AO 23.2.30.77; de Groot, RHA 2.221–4. Rather 'attack, violate (a woman)'? Cf. HG 123; Götze-Pedersen, MS 65.
wer; see *we/a-*.
weriske/a- 'invite, summon, name'. See *weriya/e-*.
**werite-* 'be anxious, fear'. Götze, KlF 1.187 and fnn. 4, 5; Benveniste, BSL 33.138. See *weritenu-, weritiske/a-*.
weritemas (acc. *uriteman*) 'anxiety, fear'. HG 156. See *werite-*.
weritenu- 'make anxious, cause to fear'. See *werite-*.
weritiske/a- (werites<k>izzi, pl. *weritesk[anzi])* 'be anxious, fear'. KUB 4.4.2.11; 4.8.2.4. See *werite-*.
weriya/e- (weriyazi, weriyēzzi, weriizzi) 'invite, summon, name, commission'. Götze, Hatt. 97 f.; Friedrich, Vert. 1.173; Benveniste, BSL 33.138; Götze-Pedersen, MS 10.20, 45, 74.
   anda w., act. or midd. after dat., 'conspire with'.
weriyanniske/a- (2 sg. *werianniskisi*).
   piran w., after dat., 'conspire with'. Götze, Madd. 108.
wĕs 'we'. Hrozný, CH 157; Friedrich, Vert. 1.89 f., ZA NF 5.75; HG 114, 191, 196.
wes-; see *wess-* 'clothe'.
weseske/a- 'graze upon, eat up'. KUB 7.60.3.26; 24.7.2.57. Cf. *wasti, wesis, wesiya/e-*.
wesis (acc. *wesin, wesen*) 'pasture'. Sommer, BoSt. 7.60–2; Hrozný, CH 126 fn. 4; HG 92. Cf. *wasti*.

wesiya['price'. Ehelolf, ZA NF 9.182 fn. 4.
wesiya/e- (midd. *wesiyattari*, verbal n. gen. *wesiyawwas*) midd. 'graze upon, eat up'; verbal n. 'pasturing; government'. Friedrich, ZA NF 5.41; Götze, AM 222 f.; HG 226. Cf. *wasti*.
weskattallas (written *wiskattal*[*las*]) 'grunter, squealer'??? See *weske/a-* 'grunt'.
wēske/a- (also *wīske/a-*; written with *u*) 'drive, send'. Friedrich, Vert. 2.87 f. See *weya/e-*.
wēske/a- (also *wīske/a-*; written with *ú*) 'come'. Friedrich, Vert. 2.87 f.; HG 237. See *we/a-*.
wēske/a- (also *wīske/a-*; written with *ú*) 'demand, ask, beg'. Friedrich, Vert. 2.160; Götze, Madd. 113 and fn. 1. See *wek-*.
wēske/a- (also *wīske/a-*; written with *ú*) 'grunt' or 'squeal' (of a pig). Götze, Madd. 145 and fn. 1. Cf. *wiya/e-* 'grunt' or 'squeal'; but possibly associated with the preceding word.
wēss-, wass- (2 pl. *wistin*, midd. pl. *wēssanta*, infin. *wassuwanzi, wassuwwanzi*, sup. *wassuwan*, verb. n. *wassuwwar*) 'put on (clothes), clothe, cover'. Hrozný, BoSt. 5.38; Sommer, AU 217 fn. 1. Cf. *wassa-, wasse/a-, wassiya/e-, wessiya/e-*.
wēssiya/e-, variant for *wassiya/e-* 'put on (clothes), clothe, cover'. KBo. 2.9.1.29.
^{LÚ}*wēstaras* 'shepherd'. See *wesis*.
wesuriskattallas (also *wisuriskattallas, wesurisgatallas*) 'oppressor'? Cf. Hrozný, SH 56. See *wesuriya/e-*.
wesŭriya/e- (more often *wisūriya/e-*) 'press, oppress'. Götze, KlF 1.129; Ehelolf, KlF 1.139 fn. 4.
weda- (1 sg. *wedahhi*, pret. *wedas*, 1 pl. *wetummen, wedumen*) 'build'. See *wete-* 'build'.
wedă(e)- (*widaizzi*, 1 sg. *wedāmi*, pret. *widāit*) 'carry, bring'. Götze, Hatt. 81 f.; Friedrich, Vert. 1.42 f., 180; Sommer, AU 26 fn. 1; Benveniste, BSL 33.138; Sturtevant, Lang. 7.1–4, HG 214 and fn. 4.
*wetassas (dat. *witassi*); EZEN × ŠE *witassi* 'at the festival of the year'? Götze, NBr. 30 and fn. 2. See *wetti*.
wete/a- (*wetezzi*, pl. *wedanzi*, pret. *wetet*, 1 sg. *wetenun*, pret. *weter*) 'build'. Sommer, BoSt. 4.16 fn. 3, 10.4 fn. 1; AU 26 fn. 1; Götze, NBr. 26 f., AM 320; HG 92, 222. See *weda-*.
  appa w. 'restore'.
  ser w. 'build above'.
wete/a- (pret. *wetet*, pl. *weter*) 'carry, bring'. See *weda(e)-*.
wetenas, weteni; see *watar*.

weteske/a- 'build'. See *wete/a-* 'build'.
weteske/a- 'carry, bring'. See *weda(e)-*.
wetin 'building, edifice'? Sommer, BoSt. 4.16 fn. 3. Cf. Ranoszek, IF 52.168. Cf. *wete/a-*.
**wet(t)antatar* (dat. *wett[andanne]*, *widandanne*, MU-*anni*) 'period of a year'. Hrozný, AOr. 1.284; Friedrich, AOF 7.121; Götze, AM 210. Cf. *wetti*.
wettanza (MU.KAM-*za*) 'year'. Götze, AM 301. See *wettantatar*, *wetti*.
wetti (dat.; written *witti*) 'in a year'. Hrozný, AOr. 1.281 f.; Götze, NBr. 30 fn. 2, Lang. 11.190 fn. 12; HG 90; Götze-Pedersen, MS 61; Ehelolf ap. Boissier, Mantique 22 f., ZA NF 9.182. Cf. *wetassas*, *wettantatar*, *sawitesza*.
wetummar (verb. n.) 'a building, constructing'. Götze, AOr. 5.28.
  wedumas 'of building'. Friedrich, ZA NF 1.11.
wewakk- (*wewakki*, pl. *wewagganzi*, pret. *wewakta*?) 'demand, ask, beg'. Hrozný, BoSt. 3.180 fn. 6; Sommer, BoSt. 7.56 fn., AU 338.88; Götze, Madd. 38.88, 140; HG 215, 217. Cf. *wek-*.
wewakke/a- (*uwakkizzi*, pret. 1 sg. *wewakkinun*) 'demand, ask, beg'. See *wewakk-*.
wĕya/e- (written with *u*; *wiyazi*, *wiyazzi*, *wiēzzi*, *weizzi*, pl. *wiyanzi*, pret. *wiyat*, *wiēt*, 1 sg. *wiyanun*, *wienun*, pl. *wiēr*, imper. 2 pl. *wĕyattin*) 'drive, send'. Götze, Hatt. 57, KlF 1.176.48, AM 315; Friedrich, Vert. 2.146; Benveniste, BSL 33.138; HG 112. Cf. *weske/a-* 'send'.
  appanda w. 'send behind'.
  kattan arha w. 'drive out'.
  menahhanda w. 'send to meet, send against'.
  sarā w. 'drive up'.
wezza- (*wizzai*) 'bring'? HG 246. Cf. *weda(e)-*.
*wĕzzapănza (neut. *wizzapān*, neut. pl. *wēzzapānta*, *wizzapanta*) 'old'. Sommer, BoSt. 10.71; Friedrich, ZA NF 3.199.
WI; read GEŠTIN.
↟*winat* 'stakes'? Friedrich, ZA NF 5.55 f.
wis-; see *wess-* 'clothe'.
wisiya/e-; read *wesiya/e-*.
wiskattallas; read *weskattallas*.
wiske/a-; read *weske/a-*.
wisuriya/e-; read *wesuriya/e-*.
wida(e)-; read *weda(e)-*.
?*witai*; see *wiwidai*.

184   WORD LIST

widandanne; see *wettantatar*.
widar; see *watar*.
witassi; see *wetassas*.
witti; read *wetti*.
wiwǎi (3 sg.) 'grunts' or 'squeals' (of a pig). Götze, Madd. 144 f.
⁎*wiwidai*, ⁎*wiwitai* (3 sg.) 'brings'? Friedrich, Vert. 2. 216. (Possibly to be read *witai*).
wiya/e- (written with *u*); read *weya/e-* 'drive, send'.
wiya/e- (written with *ú*) 'invite'? Chrest. 122.
wiya/e- (written with *ú*) 'grunt' or 'squeal' (of a pig). Götze, Madd. 145 and fn. 1.
wiyeske/a- (1 sg. *wiyaiskimi*) 'invite'. Chrest. 114.14, 122.
wizza-; read *wezza-*.
wizzapan, wizzapanta; see *wezzapanza*.

YÀ 'oil'.
    YÀ ᴳᴵˢ*ŞIRTU* 'olive oil'.
    YÀ DUG.GA 'fine oil'.
ᵁᶻᵁYÀ = *warkan* 'fat meat, fat'.
YÀ = *iske/a-, iskiya/e-* 'anoint'.
-*ẎA* = -*mes* 'my'. Cf. -*I*.
-*ya*; see -*a*.
ya- (*iyatta, iyatari, iyattǎri*, pl. *iyanta, iyantari*) 'go, march'. Hrozný, SH 39 fn. 2, 152–9, Congr. 1.156–63; Götze, Hatt. 73 f.; HG 55, 88.
yǎ/ě- (*iyazi, iyazzi, yēzzi, yezi, yizi*, 1 sg. *iyami*, pl. *iyanzi, yěnzi*, pret. *iyǎt, yēt*, pl. *yēη*) 'make, do; bear, beget; celebrate (a festival); worship (a god)'; with two accusatives, 'do (something) to (a person)'. Hrozný, MDOG 56.37, SH 152–9; Götze, Hatt. 89, KlF 1.231; Pedersen, Group. 41; HG 111, 219, 280 f.; Götze-Pedersen, MS 51.
    eshar y. 'shed blood, commit murder'. Sommer, AU 98.
    istanzanas y. 'do what one pleases'. Sommer, AU 31.
    sakwet y. 'signal by eye, wink'. KUB 10.3.2.19.
    ser y. 'exalt, celebrate'.
YÀ.GIŠ 'tree oil'.
    YÀ.GIŠ *ŞIRTU*; read YÀ ᴳᴵˢ*ŞIRTU* 'olive oil'.
yanna- (*iyannai*, pret. *iyannis, iyannes*) 'go, march'. Sommer, BoSt. 10.22; Götze, Madd. 129 f.; Sturtevant, Lang. 7.169, HG 55 fn. 44, 245.
yanne/a- (*iyannizi*, imper. *iyanni*, supine *iyanniwan*) 'go, march'. KUB 14.1.1.74; 17.10.2.30; VBoT 111.3.4. Cf. *yanna-*.

yanniya/e- 'go, march'. Hrozný, BoSt. 3.180 fn. 5; HG 225. Cf. *yanna-*.
YÀ.NUN 'thick milk, butter'.
yanza (*iyanza*, DÙ-*anza*) 'complete, unblemished'? Götze ap. Chrest. 123. Otherwise Ehelolf, ZA NF 9.179 fn. 1. Cf. *ya/e-*, *iyada*.
^{UZU}YÀ.UDU = ^{UZU}*appuzzi* 'tallow'.
yēssar 'deed'. Sayce, RA 27.166.24. Cf. *ya/e-*.
yezzi; see *ya/e-*.
yukan (also *yugan*, dat. *yuki*) 'yoke'. Götze, IF 42.327 f.; Sommer, AU 164; Sturtevant, HG 96, JAOS 54.400.
yugas 'one year old'. Hrozný, SH 93 and fn. 3; Marstrander, Car. 116. Cf. *tayugas*.
yugassas 'yearling'? Sommer, BoSt. 10.46; HG 161. Cf. *yugas*.

-z; see *-za*.
ZÁ (the sign may also be read NA₄) = *ABNU* 'stone'; the underlying Hittite word is plurale tantum. The sign is also used as a determinative.
-za, *-z* (after final *-z* written *-asza*; after final *-n* usually *-zan*), enclitic reflexive of any person or either number; usually with the force of an 'ethical dative'. Frequently an English translation is impossible. Ungnad, ZDMG 74.417–28; Sommer, BoSt. 7.18 fn. 2, 39 fn. 2; Götze, AOr. 5.3–16; Götze-Pedersen, MS 38–40, 75, 80–3; Chrest. 87; Friedrich, OLZ 39.306-10. The particle is sometimes without reflexive force, merely marking the verb as perfective.
ZAḪ = *hark-* 'be destroyed'.
zāh- (*zāhi*) 'cross'? Forrer, Caucasica 9.22.14. Cf. *zahh-*, *zai-*.
zah(h)- (*zahzi*, pl. *zahanzi*, 1 pl. *zahhuweni*, midd. *zahtari*, pl. *zahhanda*, imper. pl. *zahandaru*) 'injure, fight'. Hrozný, CH 132.16; Götze, Madd. 118 and fn. 5; Sommer, AU 278 fn. 4. Cf. *zah-*.
zahhais (acc. *zahhain*, *zahhin*, dat. *zahhiya*) 'fight, battle'. Hrozný, SH 15; Sommer, AU 356; HG 147. See *zahh-*.
^{Ú}*zahheli*, *zahli* (also ZAG-*ahli*) = *SAḪLÛ* = ZAG.ḪI.LI, a weed that is sown over a destroyed building or city. Friedrich, ZA NF 1.187 f., Vert. 2.20.
zahhiske/a- 'injure, fight'. See *zahh-*, *zahhiya/e-*.
zahhiya/e- (act. and midd.) 'injure, fight'. Hrozný, BoSt. 3.174 fn. 8; Friedrich, ZA NF 2.164; HG 235. Cf. *zahh-*, *zahhais*.
zahhiyanu- (pret. 1 sg. MÈ-*yanunun*) 'cause to fight, give battle to' (w. acc. of the person). Götze, AM 62.60.
zahli; see *zahheli*.

zāi- (*zāi*, 2 sg. *zātti*, *zāsi*, pret. *zāis*, verb. n. *zāwar*) 'cross, pass, transgress'. Sommer, BoSt. 10.8 fn. 1; Götze, Hatt. 78; Friedrich, ZA NF 5.58. Cf. *zah-*.
  pariyan z. 'cross to the other side'.
zāinu- (also *zenu-*, written *zinu-*) 'cause to cross, cause to pass'. Friedrich, ZA NF 1.16; Sommer, BoSt. 10.8 fn. 1; HG 234 fn. 40. Cf. *zai-*.
zāiske/a- 'cross, pass, transgress'. See *zai-*.
$^{LU}ZĀIDU$; read $^{LU}ṢĀIDU$.
ZAG = *irhas* 'boundary, district'.
ZAG = *kunnas* 'dexter, favorable, good'.
ZAG = *kunnahh-* 'make right, bring to success; succeed'.
ZAG = *kunnatar* 'rightness, being right, favorableness'.
ZAG-*ahli*, a half-ideographic writing of *zahheli*, q.v.
zakilatar; read *zankilatar*.
ZA.GÍN 'lapislazuli; blue'.
^{GIŠ}ZAG.GAR, ^{GIŠ}ZAG.GAR.RA = ^{GIŠ}*istananas*, q.v.
zakkar 'excrement'. Weidner, Stud. 130; Holma, JSFO 33.44-7; Friedrich, AOr. 6.359 and fn. 3. Cf. *sakkar*.
zakkis (acc. ^{GIŠ}*zakkin*, ^{URUD}*zakkin*, pl. *zakkēs*) 'bolt (of a door)'? Cf. Götze, AOr. 5.22 fn. 3.
^{UZU}ZAG(.DIB) 'thigh, haunch'.
ZA.GUL; read GUG.
ZA.KUR; read ZA.GÍN.
^{GIŠ}ZA.LAM.GAR 'tent'.
zaluganu- 'hold back, cause to delay'? Götze ap. Friedrich, Vert. 2.170 and fn. 3; Friedrich, AOr. 6.370 and fn. 7.
zalukes- pret. *zalukesta*, *zalukista*) 'tarry, delay'? See *zaluganu-*.
ZA.LUM = *assuzeri* 'can'. Ehelolf, KUB 27, preface V.
✭*zam(m)urā(e)-* (*zammurāizzi*, pl. *zammurānzi*, pret. 1 sg. *zamuranun*) 'injure, attack', often with an acc. of the inner object (*memiyan*, *kwitki*, etc.). Friedrich, Vert. 1.71 f.; Sommer, AU 135. Cf. Sommer, AU 433.
-zan, variant for *-za*, q.v.
-zan = *-za* + *-an*. See *-as*.
zankilā- (pl. *zankilanzi*, imper. pl. *zankilāndu*) 'punish, fine'. Götze, KIF 1.190 fn. 2.
zankilatar (pl. *zankilatar-*ḪI.A, *zankilatarri-*ḪI.A) 'punishment'. See *zankila-*.
zanu- 'cook'. Sommer, BoSt. 10.15 fn. 1, 20. Cf. *zeya/e-*.

zanuske/a- 'cook'. Friedrich, ZA NF 1.178.
^{LÚ}ZAB; read ^{LÚ}ERÍN.
ZABAR 'bronze'.
^{LÚ}ZABAR.DIB 'cup-bearer'? Friedrich, Altorient. Stud. 52.
zappanu- 'cause to fall in drops, sprinkle'. Götze, Madd. 72 and fn. 8. Cf. *zappiya/e-.*
ZABBAR; read ZABAR.
zappiya/e- (*zappiyatta*) 'fall in drops, be sprinkled'? KBo. 3.23.1.11. Cf. *zappanu-*
zappiyaz (abl.) 'from dripping, from leaking'? KUB 9.15.3.13. Cf. *zappiya/e-.*
^{LÚ}*ZABTU* (also *ZABDU*); read ^{LÚ}*ṢABTU*.
^{ZA}*zapzagaiya* (also *zapzaqaya*), an ornament for the person. Sommer, BoSt. 10.36 and fn. 1.
✸*zarsiya* 'guest-friendship, freedom of the country'?? Forrer, Forsch. 1.146, 163 f. 'Guaranty of safety'? Sommer, AU 92 f., 131 f.
*zashais (acc. *zashain*, dat. *zashiya, zashī*, inst. *zashit*) 'dream'. Sommer, BoSt. 10.31; Götze, KlF 1.232; Götze-Pedersen, MS 23. Cf. *teshas* 'sleep, dream'.
zashimus (acc. pl.) 'dreams'? KUB 7.53.3.17. Cf. Götze, Madd. 120 fn. 4.
ZA.SIG₄; read ZA.LUM.
^{LÚ}ZADIM 'stone mason'. Deimel, No. 4.1. Others read ^{LÚ}AŠGAB.
zāwar; see *zai-.*
ze-, inseparable prefix, 'through, across'. HG 214, Milewski; L'Indo-Hittite et l'Indo-Européen 55 and fn. 1.
zea; read *zeya-.*
zēnanza 'autumn'. See *zenas.*
zĕnas 'autumn'. Ehelolf, SBPA 1925.267 fn. 2, KlF 1.149 f. (Hrozný, AOr. 3.441.3, understands the word as 'spring'.)
zennă- (*zinnai, zennai*, pret. 1 sg. *zennahhun, zinnahhun*, imper. *zinnāu*) 'put through, bring to an end, complete; destroy'; w. infin. 'finish'; midd. 'come to an end', (of the moon) 'finish waning'. Hrozný, SH 91; Weidner, AOF 1.64; Götze, Hatt. 75, 99; Sturtevant, Lang. 3.222, HG 214. Cf. *zenne/a-.*
zen(n)e/a- (*zinnizzi, zinizzi*, pret. *zinnit*, pl. *zinir*, imper. 2 sg. *zini*, part. *zennanza, zinnan*, verb. n. *zinnuwar*) 'put through, bring to an end, complete; destroy; finish'; midd. 'come to an end'. See *zenna-.*
zenu- (pret. pl. *zinuēr*) 'cause to cross, cause to pass'. HG 234. See *zai-.*

188   WORD LIST

zĕnuske/a- (also zĭnuske/a-) 'cause to cross, cause to pass'. Hrozný,
    CH 34.52, 35 fn. 17; HG 234. See zai-.
ᴳᴵˢzeriyalli (neut. pl.) 'masks; masked performers, mummers'? KBo.
    4.9.5.18; KUB 10.21.2.7; 11.23.5.12; 25.1.1.13.
ᴳᴵˢZERTU 'olive tree'.
    YA ᴳᴵˢZERTU 'olive oil'.
zēyă- (zēari, part. acc. zēandan, neut. zeyan, inst. zēyantet, zēāntet, neut.
    pl. zeyanta, zēanda) 'be cooked'. Sommer, BoSt. 10.20. Cf. zanu-.
ZI = istanza(n) 'breath, heart, soul; wish, desire; self'. Ehelolf, KlF
    1.144 fn. 2, 397 fn. 3; Götze, AM 321.
    ZI-as 'of the heart; wish, desire'. Friedrich, Vert. 2.142 f.
    ZI-as = hweswannas? 'of life'. Chrest. 174.
    ZI-TI = NAPIŠTI 'of life'. Chrest. 174.
ZI 'erhoben'. Götze, NBr. 77 and fn. 1.
ZI (nom. ZI-anza) 'thought suitable'. Götze, NBr. 30.
ZÍ 'gall-bladder; gall'.
zik [tsek] (usually written zĭg-, zigg-, or ziqq- before an enclitic beginning
    with a vowel) 'tu'. Hrozný, MDOG 56.25, SH 105–11; Marstran-
    der, Car. 8; Petersen, Lang. 6.174 and fn. 36; HG 190 f., 193, 195 f.
zikanzi; see zikke/a-.
zikila 'tu ipse'. See -el, -ela.
ᶻᴬZI.KIN = ᶻᴬhuwasi, q.v.
ᵁᴿᵁᴰZI.KIN.BAR = ᵁᴿᵁᴰsepikkustas 'brooch'? q.v.
zikiske/a- [tskˑeskˑe-] 'place, put, bury'. KUB 20.1.2.29. See
    zik(k)e/a-.
zik(k)e/a- [tskˑe-] (zikkizzi, pl. zikkanzi, zikanzi, pret. zikkit, 2 sg. zikkes,
    pl. zikkir) 'place, put; bury'. Friedrich, Vert. 1.81 f.; HG 71, 128,
    237; Sommer, AU 64 fn. 1. See dai-.
ᴵᴹZIKZIKU (for ZIQĪQU) 'stormwind'. Friedrich ZA NF 5.12.15.
zilan, zilayan 'toward this side' (of the flight of birds)? Götze, Kulturg.
    141. Cf. Sommer, OLZ 38.281.
zilati (dat. of an adjective?) 'future'? Forrer, Forsch. 1.101.8.
zilatiya, ⁺ziladuwa 'for the future'. Sommer, BoSt. 7.56–60, 64, AU
    51; Friedrich, ZA NF 5.47 fn. 1.
zilayan; see zilan.
ZIMITTU; see ṢIBITTU.
ZIMTU; read ṢIMDU.
zine/a-; read zenne/a-.
zinna-; read zenna-.
zinne/a-; read zenne/a-.

zinnuk 'completely'?? Hrozný, SH 180. 'Destruction'?? Cavaignac, RHA 1.104 and fn. 19.

zinu-, zinuške/a-; read *zenu-, zenuške/a-*.

zipittani, a liquid measure. Cf. Hrozný, CH 138.44, 139 fn. 2. 'Tub'?? Walther, HC 270.181.

ZĪBU 'jackal'.

ᴳᴵˢ*ZIRTU*; read ᴳᴵˢ*ZERTU*.

ZÍ.DA; read ZÍD.DA.

ZÍD.DA 'fine meal, flour'; something used as soap. Deimel, No. 536. 209; Ehelolf, KlF 1.154, 160.

ZITTU 'share'.

LÚ.MEŠ *ZITTI* 'sharers, members of one's retinue'.

ZÍZ, a kind of spelt.

-ZU (for *-ŠU* after dentals) 'his'.

ZU, ZŪZU 'half a shekel'. Sommer, BoSt. 10.35 f.

ᵁ*zuhriš* 'grass'. Hrozný, SH 203, CH 157; Sommer, BoSt. 10.63 fn. 2.

ᵁ*zuhritī* 'meadow, pasture'. Sommer, BoSt. 10.63; Hrozný, AOr. 3.440.3.

ZUN; read ḪI.A.

-ZUNU (for *-ŠUNU* after dentals) 'their'.

ᴸᵁ*zuppalaš*, a kind of servant in the royal kitchen. Friedrich, Altorient. Stud. 51.

ᴳᴵˢ*zupparu,* ᴳᴵˢ*zuppari* (inst. *zupparit*, pl. *zuppari*-ḪI.A) 'torch' or, less probably, 'lamp'. Sommer, BoSt. 10.54; Friedrich, AOF 6.114; HG 175.

ZUR; read AMAR.

ZÚR (Forrer); read SISKUR.

ZŪTU (*ZU-DU*) = *šišhau*?? 'sweat'.

⁕*zūwan* 'food, morsel, meat'? Sturtevant, JAOS 54.401.

ZŪZU; see *ZU*.

NUMERALS

A few Akkadian and Hittite words for numerals have been listed above in their alphabetic position. Far more frequent is the use of Sumerian ideograms for numerals. The ideogram for 'one half' is a vertical wedge cut at or below the middle by a diagonal wedge. For '1' to '9' the ideograms consist of the appropriate number of vertical (rarely horizontal) wedges. The ideogram for 'ten' is a single Winkelhaken (≺), which is repeated the appropriate number of times for '20', 30', '40', and '50'. '60' is written by the Akkadian word; but if it is combined with a ten it is denoted by a vertical wedge. In the following list we transcribe these ideograms with Arabic numerals, and the combinations are indicated with the help of the plus sign.

1/2 = *MEŠLU* = *taksan sarras* 'half'.
1 = *IŠTĒN* = *sanas* 'one, only, alone'. Also determ. before names of men.
1 = *saneta* 'altogether'.
1-*assa* 'singulus'? Ehelolf, OLZ 36.5 fn. 2.
1.KAM = *hantezzis* 'first'.
1-*ŠU* = 1-*anki* 'once'. See -*ŠU*, -*anki*.

2 (pl. 2-*us*, 2-*as*; 2-*elus*, 2-*ēla*) = *ŠINĀ(N)*, oblique *ŠINĒ(N)*, 'two, both'. Götze, Hatt. 80; Friedrich, ZA NF 5.57.
2 (pl. 2-*be*, 2-*usbe*, 2-*asbe*; 2-*elusbe*, 2-*ilabe*; 2-*etasbe*) 'both'. See 2 'two'.
2-*ĕl* 'both'. See 2 'two'.
2-*anna*, *tān* 'for the second time, second'. Sommer, AU 272 fn. 1. Cf. *tan*.
2(.KAM) = *ŠANŪ* = *tan* 'second'.
2-*ŠU* = 2-*anki* 'twice; twofold, double'. Sommer, AU 319 and fn. 1.

3 = *tri-* 'three'.
3 = *triyahh-* 'make triple'.
3 = *triyan* 'for the third time, third'. See 2-*anna*.
3 = *triyanna* 'for the third time, third'. See 2-*anna*.
3-*yalla* = *triyalla*, designation of a drink offering.
3.KAM 'third'.
3-*ŠU* = 3-*anki* 'thrice'. See 2-*ŠU*.

4 'four'.
4-*iyahh-* 'make quadruple'. See *triyahh-*.
4-*anna* 'for the fourth time, fourth'.
4.KAM 'fourth'.
4.ÙR-*kis* 'quadruped'?? See s.v. ÙR.

5 'five'.
5-*anna* 'for the fifth time, fifth'.
5.KAM 'fifth'.

6 'six'.
6-*anna* 'for the sixth time, sixth'.
6.KAM 'sixth'.

7 'seven'.
7-*anna* 'for the seventh time, seventh'.
7.KAM = *siptamas* 'seventh'.
7-ŠU 'seven times'.

8 'eight'.
8-*na* 'for the eighth time, eighth'.
8.KAM 'eighth'.

9 'nine'.
9-*na* 'for the ninth time, ninth'.
9-ŠU 'nine times'.

10 'ten'.
10-*na* 'for the tenth time, tenth'.
10.KAM 'tenth'.
10-ŠU = 10-*anki* 'ten times'.
10 + 2 'twelve'.
10 + 3.KAM 'thirteenth'.
10 + 4-ŠU 'fourteen times'.

20 'twenty'.
20.KAM 'twentieth'.
20-*anki* 'twenty times'.
20 + 1 'twenty one'.

30 'thirty'.
^{D}30 = ^{D}SIN = *armas*? 'moon'.

ŠUŠI 'sixty'.
ŠUŠI + 1 'sixty-one'.
60 + 10 'seventy'.

1 ME (also 1 ME-ḪI.A) 'one hundred'.
1 ME + 20 'one hundred twenty'.
8 ME 'eight hundred'.

1 LĪM 'one thousand'.

ADDITIONS AND CORRECTIONS

S.v. *arpasa-* add: The verb is sometimes used impersonally.
ᴰEN.ZU = ᴰ*SIN*, q.v.
After *halzai-*insert:
    frarranda h. 'revile in public'? Chrest. 148.32.
After *hantezzis* insert:
    hantezzi, hantezziyaz 'before, in front of, first'. Chrest. 108.38; KBo. 4.9.5.10.
hassanzipi (dat.) 'on the hearth-place'? KBo. 4.9.3.33, 5.40. Cf. *hassa, daganzipas.*
IṢABAT = *efizi* 'he takes'.
S.v. *kurur* add: Benveniste, Origines de la Formation des Noms 37f.
After *kwer-, kur-* insert:
    arha k. 'cut in two'. Cf. Chrest. 108.37.
After *kwetman* insert:
    k. ... nawi 'while ... not yet, before'.
*lenkuwatar (dat. *likuwanni*) 'a swearing'. KUB 9.31.1.42. Cf. *lenk-.*
LU ... Ū (LŪ) 'either ... or'.
BAR.GÚ.AM; read IDIGNA.
pittalwan (acc.) 'remainder, remaining', or the like. HT 1.1.48.
S.v. *fritlenu-* add: Friedrich, ZA NF 9.293.
S.v. *sanas* add: Nom. 1-*is.*
ŠU.LU; read ŠU.DIB.
ᴳᴵˢ*suruhhas* (gen.), a kind of wood. KBo. 4.9.4.30; KUB. 9.31.2.19.
TAR = *karss-* 'cut, cut off'.
TUPPU = *tuppi* 'clay tablet'.
duddu- (part. *dudduwanza*) 'observe, watch over, manage'. Ehelolf, Berl. Mus. Ber. 49.34; Friedrich, ZA NF 9.292, 295 fn. 1.
duddunu- 'put under observation; imprison'. Friedrich, ZA NF 9.292 and fn. 2.
widanda, dat. of *wettanza?* KBo. 3.22.64, etc.
S.v. ᴳᴵˢZERTU add: 'Olive(s)'.

www.ingramcontent.com/pod-product-compliance
Lightning Source LLC
Chambersburg PA
CBHW050802160426
43192CB00010B/1616